AF706268

How The Rich Stay Rich While You Struggle

Vishal Show

Published by VinTej Signatures, 2025.

HOW THE RICH STAY RICH WHILE YOU STRUGGLE

First edition. February 1, 2025.

ISBN: 979-8230342038

Written by Vishal Show.

Table of Contents

To my incredible wife,

Your unwavering love, support, and belief in me have been the foundation of my journey. Through every late night, every challenge, and every moment of doubt, you stood by my side, reminding me of my purpose.

This book is as much yours as it is mine. Your wisdom, patience, and encouragement have been my greatest strengths. Thank you for being my rock, my inspiration, and my greatest cheerleader.

Preface

Money is one of the most powerful forces shaping our lives, yet most people are never formally taught how to manage, grow, or protect it. Instead, we are left to navigate a financial system that often feels overwhelming, confusing, and rigged in favor of those who already understand how to use it to their advantage. The unfortunate reality is that while the wealthy leverage financial strategies, tax benefits, and investment opportunities to secure and expand their fortunes, the average person remains trapped in cycles of debt, paycheck dependency, and missed opportunities.

This book was created with a simple yet transformative mission: to give everyone access to the financial knowledge that the rich have used for generations to build and sustain wealth. It aims to break down complex financial concepts into actionable, easy-to-understand strategies that anyone can use to take control of their financial future. The idea that financial security is only for the elite is a myth—one that can be shattered with education, discipline, and the right mindset.

Throughout the chapters of this book, we will uncover the hidden tactics that the ultra-wealthy use to preserve and multiply their assets. You will learn how to avoid financial pitfalls that keep people stuck, how to maximize your earning potential, and how to create multiple streams of income that work for you. More than just a theoretical discussion, this book is designed as a practical guide to empower you with the tools, strategies, and mindset necessary to take control of your finances and start building real, lasting wealth.

We will cover everything from the tax-saving strategies that allow the wealthy to keep more of their earnings to investment techniques that provide financial security even in uncertain economic times. You will learn how to protect yourself from financial scams, how to shift your mindset from being a consumer to being an investor, and how to turn small financial wins into long-term prosperity.

No matter where you are on your financial journey—whether you are struggling to make ends meet, eager to start investing, or already on your way to financial independence—this book is for you. The information within these pages is not just theory; it is a roadmap to financial empowerment that has been used successfully by those who have achieved lasting wealth. The difference between those who stay trapped in financial struggles and those who break free is not luck; it is knowledge, action, and consistency.

Financial freedom is not reserved for a privileged few; it is available to anyone willing to learn, plan, and execute. The key to transforming your financial future lies in your ability to educate yourself, make informed decisions, and take consistent, strategic action.

This book is your invitation to take control of your financial destiny. It is your opportunity to step away from financial uncertainty and toward a future of security, independence, and abundance. The journey begins now. Are you ready to unlock the wealth-building strategies that the rich have known for decades? If so, let's begin.

Acknowledgments

Writing this book has been a journey filled with learning, challenges, and countless moments of reflection. It would not have been possible without the support, encouragement, and inspiration of so many incredible individuals.

First and foremost, I want to express my deepest gratitude to my wife, [Her Name]. Your unwavering belief in me, your patience during my long hours of writing, and your endless encouragement have been my greatest source of strength. This book would not exist without you.

To my family and close friends—thank you for your constant motivation and for always pushing me to chase my dreams. Your words of support have kept me going through every obstacle.

A heartfelt thank you to my mentors and the financial experts whose insights have shaped my understanding of wealth-building and financial freedom. Your knowledge and guidance have been invaluable in shaping the ideas in this book.

To my readers—thank you for your curiosity, your ambition, and your willingness to challenge conventional financial wisdom. This book is for you, and I hope it empowers you to take control of your financial future.

Finally, to everyone who played a role in this book's creation—editors, designers, and supporters—your contributions have been instrumental, and I appreciate every effort you've made to bring this project to life.

With gratitude,
Vishal Show

Acknowledgments

Writing this book has been a journey filled with learning, challenges, and countless moments of reflection. It would not have been possible without the support, encouragement, and inspiration of so many incredible individuals.

First and foremost, I want to express my deepest gratitude to my wife, [Her Name]. Your unwavering belief in me, your patience during my long hours of writing, and your endless encouragement have been my greatest source of strength. This book would not exist without you.

To my family and close friends—thank you for your constant motivation and for always pushing me to chase my dreams. Your words of support have kept me going through every obstacle.

A heartfelt thank you to my mentors and the financial experts whose insights have shaped my understanding of wealth-building and financial freedom. Your knowledge and guidance have been invaluable in shaping the ideas in this book.

To my readers—thank you for your curiosity, your ambition, and your willingness to challenge conventional financial wisdom. This book is for you, and I hope it empowers you to take control of your financial future.

Finally, to everyone who played a role in this book's creation—editors, designers, and supporters—your contributions have been instrumental, and I appreciate every effort you've made to bring this project to life.

With gratitude,
Vishal Show

The Premise of Hidden Financial Systems

Money is not just a tool for survival—it is a system of power. For the average person, financial success is about earning, saving, and investing wisely. But for the ultra-wealthy, money is not earned in the traditional sense; it is controlled, moved, and shielded through a hidden network of financial structures that most people don't even know exist. The key difference is access: while the majority follow mainstream financial advice, the elite exploit exclusive banking mechanisms, offshore entities, and sophisticated legal frameworks designed to keep their wealth growing indefinitely.

The world's richest individuals and corporations don't play by the same financial rules as the rest of society. They leverage complex tax codes, offshore havens, hidden banking systems, and legal loopholes to build and preserve wealth in ways that keep them permanently ahead. Meanwhile, the middle and lower classes struggle under a financial system designed to extract wealth from them rather than help them grow it. The traditional financial system, which is often presented as fair and accessible to all, is in reality a maze of hidden advantages for those with the resources to navigate it. From tax avoidance schemes to shell corporations shielding assets, the elite employ financial strategies that are out of reach for ordinary citizens.

This book, *How the Rich Stay Rich While You Struggle*, pulls back the curtain on the hidden financial world that the elite use to protect and multiply their fortunes. It will expose how wealth is accumulated, hidden, and passed down across generations, while the majority of people remain trapped in a cycle of financial struggle, stagnant wages, and rising debt. This is not just a story of inequality—it is a guide to understanding the financial mechanisms that separate the ultra-rich from the rest of society.

The Financial Game Is Rigged

Most people are taught a simple financial formula: work hard, earn money, save what you can, and invest in traditional assets like stocks and real estate. But the ultra-rich operate with a different playbook—one filled with shadow banking systems, offshore tax havens, exclusive investment vehicles, and legal strategies that allow them to build untouchable empires. They do not rely on conventional investment plans or retirement savings accounts. Instead, they utilize powerful wealth-preservation strategies, including trusts, hedge funds, and tax-efficient structures that keep them ahead of economic downturns and legislative changes.

This disparity is not an accident. It is the result of a system carefully designed to keep wealth concentrated at the top. While the average worker sees a significant portion of their income deducted in taxes, billionaires legally exploit tax loopholes, borrow against their assets to avoid taxation, and move money through shell companies to keep their fortunes growing tax-free. They do not rely on wages or salaries; they rely on the ability to manipulate financial systems in their favor. The use of complex financial instruments, from derivatives to private equity funds, enables them to multiply their wealth while minimizing risk. Even in times of financial crisis, the wealthiest individuals emerge unscathed, while the majority are left to bear the economic burden.

What This Book Will Uncover

In *How The Rich Stay Rich While You Struggle*, we will explore the hidden tactics the wealthy use to stay ahead, including:

- **The Wealth Illusion** – How the rich manipulate public perception to maintain control and create a false sense of economic fairness.

- **The Tax Code as a Tool for the Wealthy** – How billionaires legally pay lower tax rates than middle-class workers by leveraging loopholes, deductions, and offshore structures.

- **Offshore Accounts & Tax Havens** – Where and how the ultra-rich hide their money, from the Cayman Islands to Switzerland.

- **Insider Trading & Market Manipulation** – The ways financial elites influence markets, exploit regulations, and escape accountability.

- **Private Banking & Family Offices** – Exclusive banking systems not available to the public that offer tax avoidance and wealth growth strategies.

- **The Debt Trick: Why the Rich Never Sell Their Assets** – How the wealthy use debt to avoid taxes while maintaining luxurious lifestyles, using their assets as collateral to borrow money tax-free.

- **Real Estate & Shell Companies** – The billionaire strategy for asset protection, money laundering, and tax avoidance through real estate investments and corporate entities.

- **Psychological Warfare & Media Manipulation** – How the wealthy control public perception, finance politicians, and shape economic narratives.

- **The Debt Trap** – How the financial system keeps regular people trapped in credit and loans while making banks and financial institutions richer.

- **The Education Scam** – Why schools don't teach financial literacy, who benefits from keeping the public uninformed, and how elite institutions provide wealth-building secrets to the privileged.

- **The Future of Money** – How digital currencies, AI, and financial technology are shaping the next generation of wealth inequality, and why decentralized finance (DeFi) and blockchain are both opportunities and threats.

Knowledge is Power

Understanding the financial system is the first step toward breaking free from its constraints. This book is not just about exposing corruption and inequality—it is about arming you with the knowledge to navigate and challenge the system. The information contained within these pages is powerful. It will change how you view money, wealth, and financial independence. By understanding these hidden strategies, you can start thinking differently about your own financial future and make informed choices that protect you from the traps designed to keep you struggling.

By the end of *How The Rich Stay Rich While You Struggle*, you will have a deeper understanding of the financial world and practical strategies that can help you protect and grow your own wealth. Whether you are an employee looking for smarter ways to manage your earnings, an entrepreneur trying to build wealth without falling into common traps, or someone simply seeking financial freedom, this book will provide you with the insight needed to play the game differently.

The financial system is stacked against you—but only if you remain unaware. Once you see the game for what it is, you can start taking control of your financial destiny.

Are you ready to see how deep the rabbit hole goes?

PART 1:

THE FINANCIAL ILLUSION – UNDERSTANDING THE RIGGED SYSTEM

Chapter 1: The Wealth Illusion – Why the Rich Keep Getting Richer

The Money Game You're Not Invited To

Imagine two people living in the same city, but in entirely different financial realities. One earns $50,000 a year, working a steady job, paying nearly 25% of their income in taxes, struggling with bills, and barely saving anything for the future. They rely on a paycheck-to-paycheck cycle, where any unexpected expense—a medical bill, a car repair—can throw their finances into chaos. The stress of financial instability weighs on them daily, and despite working hard, they feel stuck in an endless loop with no clear way to build lasting wealth.

The other person makes $5 million annually but plays by an entirely different set of financial rules. Instead of losing a quarter of their income to taxes, they leverage legal loopholes, tax deductions, and strategic investments to reduce their tax burden to less than 5%. They don't worry about medical bills, car repairs, or monthly expenses. In fact, they don't even rely on their income to sustain their lifestyle. Instead, they use tax-efficient investment strategies, compounding assets, and financial structures that legally shield their wealth. While the first individual works tirelessly just to stay afloat, the millionaire is growing their wealth effortlessly, using compounding investments, tax-deferred accounts, and financial structures that legally shield their income.

The question is: How is this possible? And more importantly—how can you start thinking like the wealthy to shift your own financial trajectory?

The Hidden Rules of Wealth

The difference between these two individuals isn't just the amount of money they make—it's the way they understand and use the financial system. The truth is, the ultra-rich don't just have more money—they operate within an entirely different financial ecosystem, governed by rules that the average person isn't even aware exists. These individuals don't simply earn more; they navigate a system designed to multiply their wealth exponentially while minimizing risk, taxation, and financial exposure.

The financial system favors those who understand its intricacies and know how to manipulate it. While the middle class and working class are encouraged to follow conventional financial wisdom—saving diligently, investing in standard retirement plans, and avoiding debt—the wealthy embrace a vastly different strategy. They employ advanced wealth-building techniques such as leveraging strategic debt, maximizing tax-efficient investments, utilizing offshore accounts, and employing wealth preservation tactics that ensure their money continuously generates returns.

The key difference is access to knowledge and specialized financial tools that remain out of reach for the average person. The ultra-rich don't rely on simple savings accounts or conventional investments; they create complex financial structures, often using trusts, shell companies, and tax havens to shield their wealth from unnecessary taxation. They hire top-tier financial advisors, accountants, and legal experts to craft customized strategies that allow them to grow their fortunes without being burdened by the financial constraints placed on the general population.

This book will expose the hidden financial mechanisms that allow the wealthy to safeguard and expand their fortunes. You'll learn about the tax loopholes they exploit, the legal structures that protect their assets, and the investment strategies that ensure they stay ahead. By understanding these techniques, you'll gain insight into how wealth truly functions in today's world and, more importantly, how you can start applying similar strategies to improve your own financial standing.

Why You've Never Been Taught This

If these wealth-building strategies are so effective, why aren't they taught in schools? The answer is simple: The financial elite benefit from the majority remaining financially uninformed. Schools focus on teaching people how to become good employees, not how to build lasting wealth. Instead of educating students about real-world financial principles, the system prioritizes skills that maintain economic stability rather than promoting upward mobility.

Think about it—how much did you learn in school about real-world financial strategies like tax planning, wealth management, or leveraging assets for passive income? Probably very little. Instead, you were likely taught how to budget on a fixed income, manage personal debt responsibly, and save for retirement through employer-sponsored plans like a 401(k). While these are important, they are merely survival tactics, not wealth-building strategies.

The traditional path that society pushes—get a degree, find a stable job, work hard, save diligently, and retire comfortably—is a formula designed to keep people in a cycle of financial dependency. This model worked in past generations when wages grew alongside inflation and pensions provided security. However, in today's economy, this approach is outdated and ineffective for achieving true financial independence.

The system wasn't designed to make the average person wealthy—it was designed to keep wealth concentrated at the top. But once you understand the hidden mechanics of financial power, you can begin to break free from the limitations placed on the middle class and start making decisions that build long-term wealth.

The ultra-rich follow a different set of financial principles from an early age. They learn about strategic investing, tax loopholes, business structures, and asset protection—knowledge that allows them to multiply wealth rather than simply earn and spend. They understand that financial education is power, and by keeping this knowledge exclusive, they maintain their economic advantage over the masses.

What This Book Will Teach You

This book isn't just about exposing the system—it's about teaching you how to use it to your advantage. You'll learn:

- How the wealthy legally minimize their taxes (and why the middle class pays the highest rates)
- How to shift from earning through labor to earning through assets
- The power of leverage and using other people's money to build wealth
- Why debt can be a tool for financial growth instead of a burden
- How to protect your money from inflation and economic downturns

By the time you finish this book, you'll have the knowledge to start thinking and acting like the wealthy—breaking free from the financial traps that keep most people struggling and positioning yourself for true financial independence.

Welcome to How the Rich Stay Rich While You Struggle. Let's uncover the truth behind the financial system and learn how to play the game like the wealthy do.

Once you understand how this system truly functions, you can begin to shift your own approach—breaking free from traditional financial limitations and adopting strategies that align more closely with the methods of the elite.

The Money Flow of the Wealthy vs. The Middle Class

Money doesn't just come in and go out the same way for everyone. The way the wealthy handle money is fundamentally different from how the middle class and working class manage their finances. While most people rely on a fixed paycheck and spend their income on living expenses, the wealthy follow a strategic system designed to ensure that their money continuously works for them. Understanding these differences is key to transforming your own financial approach.

How the Middle Class Earns and Spends Money

For the majority of people, financial survival depends on **linear income**—trading time for money. A person works a job, receives a paycheck, and then uses that income to cover necessary expenses: rent or mortgage, bills, groceries, insurance, and perhaps some savings if there's anything left over. This cycle repeats every month, with little room for wealth accumulation.

One of the biggest challenges the middle class faces is that they are **taxed before they even see their money**. Income taxes are automatically deducted from their paychecks, reducing the amount they have to work with before they even begin budgeting. After paying for necessities, discretionary spending often takes up any remaining funds, leaving little for investments or long-term wealth building.

Additionally, middle-class wealth is often tied up in liabilities disguised as assets. For example, a home is typically considered an asset, but for many middle-class families, it functions more like a liability—requiring mortgage payments, maintenance costs, and property taxes. Without additional income streams, their financial growth is slow, and unexpected expenses can create serious financial strain.

How the Wealthy Handle Money Differently

In contrast, the wealthy **never rely on a single source of income**. They prioritize **multiple streams of revenue**, including business ownership, stock investments, real estate, intellectual property, and passive income sources. Rather than depending on a paycheck, they create **systems** where money continuously flows into their accounts, whether they work or not.

One of the most critical differences is **when they are taxed**. The wealthy don't earn income the way a salaried employee does; instead, they generate wealth through capital gains, business earnings, and investments—many of which are taxed at lower rates than traditional income. By structuring their wealth strategically, they reduce tax liability and retain more of their earnings.

Another major distinction is how they use debt. While the middle class views debt as something to avoid, the wealthy **leverage debt to create more wealth**. They use low-interest loans to acquire income-generating assets, allowing them to grow their net worth without depleting their own capital. They understand that smart borrowing—such as taking out loans to purchase appreciating assets like rental properties—can lead to long-term financial gain.

The Cycle of Wealth Creation

The wealthy operate on a **wealth cycle**, which continuously multiplies their money:

1. **Acquire income-generating assets** – Instead of spending money on liabilities, they invest in stocks, real estate, and businesses that generate revenue.
2. **Reinvest earnings** – Profits from investments are reinvested to expand their portfolio and increase passive income streams.
3. **Minimize taxes legally** – Through tax-advantaged accounts, offshore investments, and strategic deductions, they ensure they pay as little tax as possible.
4. **Leverage debt strategically** – Instead of avoiding debt, they use it to acquire more assets, ensuring that their money continues working for them.
5. **Protect and preserve wealth** – Using legal structures such as trusts and holding companies, they shield their wealth from unnecessary taxation and economic downturns.

Bridging the Gap

The middle class can begin shifting their financial approach by adopting the habits of the wealthy. This includes **building multiple income streams**, prioritizing **assets over liabilities**, and learning **tax-efficient investment strategies**. While the financial system is designed to keep wealth concentrated at the top, understanding these principles can help anyone break free from the paycheck-to-paycheck cycle and start creating long-term financial security.

◈ *Example: Warren Buffett openly admits that he pays a lower tax rate than his secretary due to how his income is structured.*

A crucial difference here is that the middle class primarily earns money through labor, while the rich earn money through **capital appreciation**—stocks, real estate, and business ownership. The system rewards ownership over labor, keeping the wealthy at the top.

Why Taxes Are Optional for the Ultra-Wealthy

One of the biggest reasons the rich stay rich? They minimize their taxes legally through sophisticated loopholes:

- **Offshore Accounts:** Moving money to tax havens like the Cayman Islands or Switzerland.
- **Capital Gains vs. Salary:** Instead of earning a salary (which is heavily taxed), the wealthy rely on **investment income**, taxed at lower rates.
- **The Step-Up in Basis Loophole:** Heirs inherit assets at their current value, avoiding capital gains taxes.
- **Trusts & Foundations:** Wealthy families set up trusts to pass down money without triggering estate taxes.

◈ *Example: Jeff Bezos paid zero income tax in multiple years despite being worth over $100 billion—because he structured his wealth in stocks and investments, not salary.*

For the ultra-rich, taxes are a game of avoidance, not obligation. They hire top-tier accountants and lawyers to ensure they never pay more than the bare minimum. Meanwhile, the middle class carries the tax burden, funding government programs the wealthy don't need to rely on.

The Myth of Hard Work: Why Effort Alone Won't Make You Rich

Most people are taught that working hard leads to wealth. But billionaires don't work 100x harder than the average person—*they use different financial strategies.*

- **Passive Income is Key:** The rich focus on acquiring income-generating assets (stocks, real estate, businesses) instead of relying solely on wages.
- **The Network Effect:** They leverage elite connections, gaining access to exclusive deals, insider knowledge, and private investments not available to the public.
- **Ownership Over Labor:** They own businesses, patents, and real estate, while others work for them.

◈ *Example: The Walton family (Walmart) earns billions annually—not from working, but from dividends on their company stock.*

Understanding this distinction is critical. If you are solely dependent on your labor for income, you are at a disadvantage in the financial system.

Interactive Element: Quiz – Are You Playing the Wealth Game?

Answer these questions to see how aligned you are with wealth-building strategies.

1. Do you primarily earn money through a salary, or do you have passive income sources?
2. Are you using tax-efficient investment strategies?

3. Have you explored leveraging assets instead of just saving cash?
4. Do you reinvest your money into appreciating assets?
5. Do you understand the tax code well enough to legally minimize your taxes?

◈ *If you answered 'no' to most of these, this book will show you how to start shifting your mindset and strategies.*

The System Is Rigged—But You Can Learn to Play

The financial system wasn't designed to make the average person wealthy. It was designed to **keep the rich on top**. But by understanding the hidden strategies and loopholes used by the elite, you can start applying similar principles to build and protect your own wealth.

In the next chapter, we'll dive deep into **how billionaires legally avoid taxes while the rest of society foots the bill.**

Action Step:

- **Start tracking where your money goes**: Are you spending like the middle class, or reinvesting like the wealthy?

- **Research tax-efficient investment strategies** that can help you keep more of your money.

- **Prepare to rethink what you know about taxes and wealth creation.**

By the end of this book, you will have the tools and knowledge to play the same financial game as the rich—turning wealth accumulation into a strategy rather than a dream.

Chapter 2: The Tax Code – A Tool for the Wealthy

How the System Was Designed

Taxes are often viewed as an unavoidable burden—something every working individual must pay to fund government programs, public infrastructure, and social services. But what if I told you that the tax system isn't designed to take from everyone equally? In reality, it has been carefully structured to favor those who understand its complexities. While the average worker sees a large portion of their paycheck disappear in deductions before they even touch it, the ultra-wealthy operate within an entirely different tax reality—one where loopholes, deductions, and sophisticated strategies allow them to legally minimize or even eliminate their tax burden.

This isn't by accident. The modern tax code was shaped by the wealthy, for the wealthy. Politicians and policymakers—many of whom are deeply connected to elite financial circles—have structured tax laws in ways that incentivize wealth accumulation for the rich while keeping the middle class stuck in a cycle of high taxation and limited financial mobility. Over decades, new tax policies have been introduced under the guise of economic growth, job creation, or business incentives, but these policies largely benefit those who already have substantial wealth.

The average worker is often unaware of these advantages because tax laws are intentionally complex, requiring specialized knowledge to navigate effectively. The wealthy employ teams of tax attorneys, accountants, and financial planners whose sole purpose is to find and exploit legal tax strategies. As a result, while the middle class diligently files their taxes each year, hoping for a refund, the ultra-wealthy strategically manipulate the tax code to ensure they pay as little as possible.

In this chapter, we'll break down how the tax system disproportionately affects different income levels, why the rich pay significantly less in taxes, and the specific tactics they use to shield their wealth from the government. Understanding this reality is the first step toward leveling the playing field and adopting smarter financial strategies that allow you to keep more of what you earn.

How the Tax System Favors the Rich and Burdens the Middle Class

The tax system is often presented as a fair and balanced structure, designed to ensure that everyone pays their fair share. However, when you dig deeper, it becomes clear that the way taxes are structured overwhelmingly benefits the wealthy while placing the heaviest financial burden on the middle class.

The Two Types of Income: Labor vs. Capital

At the heart of this imbalance is the stark difference in how labor income and capital income are taxed—a distinction that plays a crucial role in widening the wealth gap. Most middle-class workers rely on wages or salaries, classified as labor income. This income is subject to a progressive tax system, meaning the more one earns, the higher the tax rate applied. Additionally, payroll taxes, which fund Social Security and Medicare, are automatically deducted from each paycheck, reducing take-home pay and leaving limited room for meaningful wealth accumulation.

Conversely, the wealthy generate most of their income through investments—stocks, real estate, and business ownership—collectively known as capital income. Rather than being taxed at the high rates imposed on wages, capital gains and dividends are taxed at significantly lower rates, typically between 15-20%. This creates a situation where billionaires, who derive their wealth primarily from investments, often pay a lower effective tax rate than middle-class workers earning a steady paycheck.

To make matters more inequitable, labor income is taxed immediately, while capital income is often taxed only when an asset is sold, allowing the wealthy to defer taxation indefinitely. Additionally, the ultra-wealthy leverage financial strategies like tax-loss harvesting and reinvesting dividends into tax-sheltered accounts to further minimize or even eliminate their tax obligations. The result? A system where the middle class bears the brunt of tax burdens while the richest individuals legally sidestep much of it, preserving and growing their wealth virtually untaxed.

Why Billionaires Pay Less in Taxes Than Their Employees

A striking example of this disparity is the fact that some of the richest people in the world, including tech billionaires and hedge fund managers, pay a lower effective tax rate than the people working for them. This is because wealthy individuals have access to tax strategies that minimize their taxable income, while middle-class workers have their taxes deducted from their paychecks before they even see their money.

The Wealthy Avoid Traditional Income Taxes Through Various Methods

- **Stock-Based Compensation:** Instead of taking a salary, many executives are compensated with stock options. These are only taxed when sold and at much lower capital gains rates.

- **Offshore Accounts & Trusts:** By legally moving money into tax-friendly countries, they can delay or avoid taxation altogether while maintaining control over their assets.

- **Debt Loopholes:** Many billionaires borrow against their assets rather than selling them, allowing them to access cash without triggering a taxable event. This strategy, known as the "Buy, Borrow, Die" method, enables them to fund lavish lifestyles without paying capital gains taxes.

- **Pass-Through Entities:** Business owners can structure their income through pass-through entities such as LLCs and S-corporations to significantly reduce their tax liability by avoiding double taxation.

- **Depreciation Deductions:** Real estate investors, in particular, benefit from depreciation deductions, allowing them to claim paper losses while their properties continue to appreciate in value.

- **Carried Interest Loophole:** Hedge fund managers classify their income as investment earnings rather than wages, allowing them to pay much lower capital gains tax rates rather than standard income tax rates.

Meanwhile, the middle class has very few options for reducing their tax liability. Their taxes are taken out before they even receive their paycheck, leaving them with less flexibility and fewer opportunities to build wealth. Unlike the ultra-wealthy, they do not have access to complex tax strategies or teams of advisors to minimize their tax burden.

The Hidden Cost of Payroll Taxes

Another often-overlooked factor in the tax system is payroll taxes, which fund Social Security and Medicare. These taxes are applied to wage earners at a flat rate of around 15% (split between the employee and employer). However, for high earners, this tax is capped at a certain income level, meaning that billionaires pay a much smaller percentage of their total income in payroll taxes compared to the middle class.

For example, if someone earns $50,000 per year, they pay the full payroll tax on their entire income, which directly impacts their take-home pay. However, for someone earning $10 million per year, payroll taxes apply only to a small fraction of their total income—specifically, only up to the income cap set by the government (which changes yearly but remains a tiny portion of ultra-high earnings). This means that while a middle-class worker sees a noticeable deduction for payroll taxes, a billionaire contributes only a minuscule portion of their earnings to these programs.

Furthermore, many of the ultra-wealthy do not even earn their income through wages but rather through investments, which are not subject to payroll taxes at all. As a result, while middle-class workers are required to contribute a significant portion of their earnings to Social Security and Medicare, billionaires can often bypass these taxes entirely, further compounding the wealth disparity.

Who Really Funds the Government?

Despite the popular belief that the rich pay the majority of taxes, the reality is that middle-class workers shoulder a disproportionate share of the tax burden. While the wealthy find ways to shelter their income through trusts, offshore accounts, and creative accounting tactics, the average worker is left to fund government programs through automatic paycheck deductions, with little room for maneuvering.

Moreover, many large corporations, despite reporting billions in profits, often pay little to no federal income tax due to aggressive tax avoidance strategies. These companies utilize tax credits, deferments, and deductions that allow them to legally shrink their taxable income to near zero. Some even receive government subsidies or tax refunds despite their massive earnings, creating a scenario where taxpayers are essentially subsidizing the wealthiest institutions.

To make matters worse, tax laws often change in ways that benefit corporations and high-net-worth individuals while placing a heavier load on middle-class earners. Many industries have successfully lobbied for tax breaks, allowing them to shield significant portions of their earnings while leaving everyday citizens to cover the shortfall. The result? The financial responsibility of running the country falls increasingly on the shoulders of ordinary taxpayers, perpetuating an economic divide that becomes harder to bridge with each passing year.

What Can You Do?

The tax code is not designed to be fair—it is designed to reward those who understand its intricacies. The good news is that by learning the strategies used by the wealthy, middle-class individuals can start taking advantage of legal tax strategies to keep more of their earnings and build real financial security.

Next, we'll explore the specific tax loopholes and strategies that the wealthy use to legally minimize their tax burden—and how you can apply some of these techniques to your own finances.

Loopholes, Deductions, and Tax Havens Used by Billionaires

The Secret World of Tax Avoidance

For the ultra-wealthy, taxes are not a fixed burden but a strategic game—one where the right moves can eliminate or significantly reduce their obligations. Unlike the average taxpayer, billionaires operate within an entirely different financial ecosystem, one where tax laws are not a set of rigid rules but a flexible framework that can be maneuvered to their advantage. With access to elite financial advisors, tax attorneys, and political lobbyists, they employ an intricate web of legal loopholes, sophisticated deductions, and offshore tax havens to shield their immense wealth from government taxation.

This strategic tax avoidance is not the result of fraud or illegal activities; rather, it exists within the gray areas of financial law—an intentionally complex system designed to benefit those who understand how to exploit it. High-priced legal teams actively shape tax policy in favor of their wealthy clientele, ensuring that the laws provide multiple avenues to minimize their obligations while maximizing their assets.

To grasp how billionaires successfully avoid taxes, it is essential to examine three primary areas: strategic loopholes, powerful deductions, and offshore tax havens. These tools allow the ultra-rich to preserve their fortunes while the middle class bears the bulk of the tax burden. Here, we will explore the most common and effective tactics they employ, including offshore accounts, trust funds, shell companies, and real estate depreciation, all of which contribute to an ever-growing wealth divide.

Exploiting Tax Loopholes: The Hidden Path to Tax-Free Wealth

The Carried Interest Loophole

One of the most controversial and widely debated tax loopholes is the carried interest provision, which allows hedge fund managers and private equity executives to classify their earnings as investment income rather than wages. This distinction is crucial because investment income is taxed at a much lower capital gains rate (often 15-20%) compared to regular income tax rates that can reach up to 37%. By structuring their earnings in this way, billionaires in the finance sector pay significantly less tax than the employees working for them.

For example, a hedge fund manager who earns $100 million in carried interest may only pay around $15-20 million in taxes due to the lower capital gains tax rate, whereas a salaried worker earning $100,000 might pay $25,000 or more in federal income tax alone. This stark difference highlights how the tax system is designed in a way that disproportionately benefits the ultra-wealthy.

The reasoning behind the carried interest loophole is that it supposedly incentivizes long-term investment and economic growth. Proponents argue that taxing this income at lower rates encourages investment firms to take financial risks that ultimately benefit the broader economy. However, critics contend that it is nothing more than an unjustified giveaway to Wall Street and private equity firms, who use the provision to avoid paying their fair share of taxes.

Despite repeated calls for reform, efforts to close the carried interest loophole have been blocked by powerful lobbying groups. Wall Street firms and private equity executives spend millions of dollars annually lobbying Congress to ensure this provision remains untouched. While politicians from both major parties have occasionally expressed support for eliminating the loophole, little has been done to enact real change.

The justification for the carried interest loophole is that it incentivizes investment and economic growth, but critics argue that it is an unjustified giveaway to the financial elite. Despite repeated attempts by lawmakers to close this loophole, strong lobbying efforts by Wall Street have ensured its survival. As a result, billionaires continue to exploit this provision to avoid billions in taxes while everyday workers see their wages taxed at higher rates without access to such sophisticated financial maneuvers.

The "Buy, Borrow, Die" Strategy

Many billionaires avoid paying capital gains taxes altogether by leveraging their wealth in a cycle known as "Buy, Borrow, Die." Instead of selling assets and triggering taxable events, they use their holdings—such as stocks, real estate, or private equity—as collateral for massive loans from financial institutions. These loans provide them with tax-free liquidity while allowing their assets to continue appreciating in value.

Since loan proceeds are not considered income, they are not subject to taxation. This allows billionaires to fund their lavish lifestyles, invest in new ventures, and acquire even more assets, all without incurring a tax liability. They can further manipulate their financial position by refinancing their loans periodically, rolling over debt while continuing to grow their net worth tax-free. Financial institutions willingly provide these loans due to the high-value collateral, making it a risk-free transaction for both parties.

A classic example of this strategy in action is Elon Musk, who has publicly acknowledged using his Tesla shares as collateral for loans rather than selling them. By doing so, he avoids capital gains taxes while still gaining access to billions in cash. Similarly, other tech and finance billionaires follow this strategy to maintain liquidity without triggering taxable events.

The final stage of the "Buy, Borrow, Die" cycle occurs upon the billionaire's death. Under current tax laws, when assets are passed on to heirs, they receive a "stepped-up cost basis." This means that if a billionaire originally acquired stocks for $10 million and they appreciated to $100 million over time, the heirs would inherit them at the new $100 million value. This erases any unrealized capital gains that would have been taxable if the assets had been sold during the billionaire's lifetime. As a result, the cycle continues, allowing generational wealth to accumulate while legally avoiding taxes for decades, if not indefinitely.

Pass-Through Entities and Shell Companies

By setting up businesses as pass-through entities such as **Limited Liability Companies (LLCs)** and **S-Corporations**, wealthy individuals can avoid double taxation and significantly reduce their taxable income. Pass-through entities allow business income to be reported on an individual's tax return rather than being subject to corporate tax; thereby lowering overall tax rates.

Many billionaires also use shell companies—corporations with no actual business operations—to channel income, reduce liabilities, and move money into lower-tax jurisdictions. For instance, multinational corporations frequently establish shell companies in tax havens such as the **Cayman Islands** or **Bermuda** to legally hold intellectual property rights. By charging their U.S. or European subsidiaries hefty licensing fees for using these intellectual properties, they can shift profits overseas and avoid paying corporate taxes in higher-tax jurisdictions.

A notable example of this strategy is the case of Apple Inc., which set up subsidiaries in **Ireland** to take advantage of the country's low corporate tax rates. Through complex profit-shifting arrangements, Apple was able to minimize its global tax obligations, demonstrating how both individuals and corporations use such structures to maximize wealth retention.

Deductions That Work Only for the Wealthy

Real Estate Depreciation and Tax Write-Offs

Real estate investors, including some of the wealthiest individuals in the world, benefit from massive tax deductions through depreciation. Even though properties typically appreciate in value over time, the IRS allows owners to deduct depreciation as if their assets were losing value. This creates what is known as a "**paper loss**," which can be used to offset taxable income from other sources, effectively reducing or even eliminating tax liability. For example, an investor who purchases an apartment complex for $10 million can claim **annual depreciation deductions**, even if the property's market value increases to $15 million. This allows them to report lower taxable income while simultaneously growing their real estate portfolio.

The benefits of depreciation extend beyond just reducing taxes. Real estate investors can also use a technique called "**cost segregation**," which accelerates depreciation deductions by breaking a property down into individual components such as plumbing, electrical systems, and fixtures—each of which depreciates at a different rate. By front-loading these deductions, investors can claim larger tax benefits in the early years of ownership, freeing up more capital for reinvestment.

Furthermore, when investors eventually sell their properties, they can utilize a 1031 exchange to defer paying capital gains taxes by reinvesting the proceeds into another property. This cycle of tax deferral enables them to keep rolling their profits into new investments while delaying tax obligations indefinitely. This combination of depreciation, cost segregation, and tax deferral strategies helps the wealthy continue expanding their real estate empires while minimizing their tax burdens.

Philanthropy as a Tax Shield

Charitable giving is often seen as a noble act, but for billionaires, it doubles as an effective tax strategy that allows them to preserve wealth while shaping their own philanthropic legacies. By donating to private foundations or donor-advised funds (DAFs), they can claim significant tax deductions that lower their taxable income, sometimes down to zero, while still maintaining control over how the funds are distributed. Unlike direct donations to charities, these vehicles allow billionaires to set up long-term financial structures that give them decision-making power over how and when the money is spent.

For instance, a billionaire can donate millions to their own private foundation, take an immediate tax deduction, and then use those funds to pay family members high salaries as board members or executives of the foundation. Additionally, they can direct the money toward causes that align with their business interests, such as funding educational programs that create a future workforce tailored to their industry or lobbying groups that promote policies favorable to their enterprises.

A well-known example is the Bill & Melinda Gates Foundation, which, while making significant contributions to global health and education, also enables tax-efficient wealth distribution. Similarly, Facebook co-founder Mark Zuckerberg and his wife Priscilla Chan created the Chan Zuckerberg Initiative as an LLC instead of a traditional foundation, allowing for even greater flexibility in funding both charitable and profit-driven initiatives without the same regulatory oversight.

This strategic philanthropy ensures that billionaires can minimize their tax liability while still wielding significant influence over public policies, research agendas, and societal priorities, further reinforcing their power and control over the economic landscape.

Offshore Tax Havens: The Global Playground of the Ultra-Wealthy

Why Billionaires Love Tax Havens

Offshore tax havens, such as the **Cayman Islands**, **Switzerland**, and **Luxembourg**, provide secrecy and tax advantages that make them highly attractive to billionaires seeking to minimize their tax burdens. These jurisdictions offer low or zero corporate tax rates, strict privacy laws, and strong asset protection mechanisms, making it exceedingly difficult for governments to track and tax the wealth stored there. In many cases, billionaires use complex legal structures such as shell companies, trusts, and offshore bank accounts to obscure the true ownership of their assets, effectively shielding their wealth from taxation and regulatory oversight.

For example, the Cayman Islands, a well-known offshore financial hub, houses thousands of subsidiaries of multinational corporations and high-net-worth individuals who take advantage of its tax-neutral policies. Similarly, Switzerland, historically famous for its stringent banking secrecy laws, has long been a preferred destination for billionaires looking to store vast amounts of money without government interference. Luxembourg, on the other hand, serves as a strategic location for corporations and individuals looking to benefit from its favorable tax treaties and lenient financial regulations.

The impact of these offshore tax havens extends beyond mere tax avoidance. They also allow billionaires to conduct financial transactions in secrecy, fund political lobbying efforts without scrutiny, and move money globally without triggering regulatory red flags. Despite global efforts to crack down on tax evasion and increase financial transparency, the ultra-wealthy continue to exploit these tax havens through sophisticated legal maneuvers, ensuring their fortunes remain largely untouched by tax authorities.

How Offshore Accounts Work

Offshore accounts are financial accounts opened in foreign jurisdictions that provide tax advantages, privacy, and asset protection. While they are often associated with illicit activities, they are entirely legal when used properly. High-net-worth individuals and corporations leverage offshore accounts to minimize tax burdens, protect assets from lawsuits, and facilitate international business transactions.

Example: Using an Offshore Trust to Shield Assets

A billionaire who wants to shield their wealth from high taxes or legal claims might set up an offshore trust in a jurisdiction with strong asset protection laws, such as the **Cook Islands** or **Belize**. Here's how it works:

1. The billionaire transfers their assets (cash, stocks, or real estate) into a trust managed by a trustee in the offshore country.
2. Because the assets are now legally owned by the trust, they

are no longer in the billionaire's name, shielding them from creditors or legal judgments.

3. The trust is structured in a way that allows the billionaire to retain indirect control over the assets while benefiting from low or zero taxation.

Example: Profit Shifting with Intellectual Property

A multinational corporation might set up a subsidiary in a tax haven like Bermuda to hold its intellectual property rights. Here's how the scheme works:

1. The corporation registers its patents or trademarks in the Bermuda subsidiary.
2. The parent company in a high-tax country pays the Bermuda subsidiary expensive licensing fees to use the intellectual property.
3. These fees count as business expenses, reducing the parent company's taxable income in the high-tax country.
4. Meanwhile, the Bermuda subsidiary collects the fees but pays little to no corporate tax, allowing the corporation to shift profits offshore legally.

Example: Using Shell Companies for Anonymity

A wealthy individual may want to invest in real estate without revealing their identity. They might create a shell company in the British Virgin Islands (BVI) and use that company to purchase property in major cities like New York or London. Because BVI does not require disclosure of company ownership, the individual can own significant assets while remaining anonymous.

These strategies demonstrate how offshore accounts and financial structures help the wealthy minimize taxes and protect their wealth while operating within legal frameworks.

The Role of Baking Secrecy Laws

Countries like Switzerland have historically provided ironclad banking secrecy, allowing billionaires to store vast sums of money with little fear of government intervention. Swiss banks, renowned for their strict confidentiality policies, enabled the ultra-wealthy to conceal assets from tax authorities for decades. While international regulations such as the Common Reporting Standard (CRS) and the Foreign Account Tax Compliance Act (FATCA) have increased transparency, wealthy individuals still utilize sophisticated legal structures to shield their fortunes. These include offshore trusts, anonymous shell companies, and multi-layered corporate entities designed to obscure ownership. Jurisdictions like the Cayman Islands and Luxembourg offer additional avenues for tax avoidance, allowing billionaires to legally maneuver their wealth beyond the reach of tax authorities while maintaining financial secrecy.

The Unfair Advantage

The tax system is not broken—it is working exactly as designed, favoring those who have the resources to manipulate it. While middle-class workers see their wages taxed before they even receive their paychecks, billionaires play an entirely different game, using loopholes, deductions, and tax havens to minimize their obligations and maximize their wealth.

For those outside the billionaire class, understanding these strategies is essential. While you may not have access to the same elite financial tools, you can learn from them and implement smart tax strategies to protect and grow your own wealth. The more you understand the rules of the game, the better equipped you'll be to navigate the system in your favor.

Corporate Tax Avoidance Strategies & Wealth Preservation through Trusts and Foundations

The Corporate Tax Game

Billion-dollar corporations and ultra-wealthy individuals do not pay taxes in the same way as the average person. While small businesses and everyday workers are taxed directly on their income, major corporations and billionaires leverage a vast array of legal loopholes, corporate structures, and strategic maneuvers to minimize their tax obligations.

At the core of this system are corporate tax avoidance strategies that allow businesses to shift profits offshore, manipulate deductions, and exploit legal ambiguities to reduce taxable income. Simultaneously, wealth preservation mechanisms such as trusts and private foundations enable billionaires to shield their fortunes from taxes while maintaining control over their assets.

This section will explore these techniques, revealing how the world's wealthiest maintain and expand their financial empires with minimal tax burdens.

Corporate Tax Avoidance Strategies

Profit Shifting and Transfer Pricing

One of the most powerful tools in corporate tax avoidance is profit shifting, where multinational companies move their profits to low-tax or no-tax jurisdictions to reduce their tax liabilities. A key method for doing this is **transfer pricing**, which involves setting artificial prices for transactions between a company's subsidiaries across different countries. By overpricing or underpricing goods, services, or intellectual property within the company, profits can be shifted to subsidiaries in tax havens, minimizing overall tax payments.

Example: Apple's Irish Subsidiary Scheme

Apple, one of the most profitable corporations in the world, famously used a legal loophole in Irish tax law to route billions of dollars in profits through subsidiaries with almost no tax liability. By setting up companies in Ireland that held its intellectual property rights, Apple charged its U.S. operations high licensing fees, effectively shifting profits offshore. This allowed Apple to avoid paying billions in taxes while maintaining control over its cash reserves.

Despite international efforts to curb these practices, transfer pricing remains one of the most widely used tax avoidance techniques among multinational corporations.

The Double Irish with a Dutch Sandwich

A now-infamous tax strategy, the **Double Irish with a Dutch Sandwich**, allowed companies to shift profits through multiple offshore entities to avoid paying U.S. and European taxes.

- A company establishes two subsidiaries in Ireland (hence, the "Double Irish").

- One Irish entity holds intellectual property rights and collects royalties from international sales.

- These royalties are passed through a **Dutch** subsidiary to avoid withholding taxes.
- The funds are then transferred to another Irish subsidiary headquartered in a tax haven like Bermuda.
- This structure effectively eliminates tax obligations on billions in revenue.

Though this specific loophole was phased out in 2020, similar tax-avoidance structures still exist, highlighting the adaptability of corporate tax planning. Many firms have transitioned to newer hybrid tax schemes that achieve similar results while staying within the evolving legal framework.

Tax Inversions

Some corporations relocate their headquarters to low-tax countries through **corporate inversions**, where a U.S.-based company merges with a foreign company to shift its official tax domicile overseas while continuing to operate in the U.S. This maneuver is often executed to escape higher U.S. corporate tax rates while retaining access to U.S. markets and government contracts.

Example: Burger King Moves to Canada

When Burger King merged with Canadian chain Tim Hortons in 2014, the new parent company was headquartered in Canada, which has a lower corporate tax rate than the U.S. This allowed Burger King to significantly reduce its tax bill while maintaining its U.S. operations. Corporate inversions like this have saved companies billions, despite criticism that they undermine domestic tax revenues.

Inversions are a perfect example of how companies use legal technicalities to minimize their tax burden while continuing to enjoy the benefits of doing business in high-tax regions.

R&D Tax Credits and Other Incentives

Governments often provide tax incentives to encourage innovation, but large corporations frequently exploit these programs to further reduce their tax burdens. The **Research & Development (R&D) tax credit**, for example, allows companies to deduct a significant portion of R&D expenses. While intended to foster innovation, this credit is often used to offset massive corporate tax liabilities with expenses that companies would have incurred anyway. In some cases, corporations even categorize routine operational costs as R&D to maximize deductions, further reducing their taxable income.

Example: Amazon's Near-Zero Tax Rate

Amazon, despite earning billions in profits, has paid little to no federal income tax in certain years due to aggressive use of tax credits, deductions, and stock-based compensation write-offs. The company reinvests heavily in R&D, allowing it to claim substantial tax credits while also benefiting from accelerated depreciation on infrastructure investments. Additionally, Amazon has leveraged stock-based compensation to reduce taxable income, as employee stock options can be deducted as an expense, even though they don't represent an immediate cash outflow. This strategy ensures that despite dominating the e-commerce and cloud computing industries, Amazon effectively avoids significant tax obligations.

Beyond Amazon, other tech giants such as Google and Facebook also benefit from R&D tax incentives, often funneling billions into research projects that, while innovative, would have likely been pursued even without tax advantages. These tax credits, while legal, highlight how major corporations can leverage government programs to lower their tax burdens in ways that smaller businesses and individual taxpayers cannot.

Wealth Preservation through Trusts and Foundations

Trusts: The Ultimate Wealth Shield

For the ultra-rich, trusts provide an unparalleled way to preserve wealth across generations while minimizing tax exposure. Trusts are legal entities that hold assets on behalf of beneficiaries, often shielding them from estate taxes, creditors, lawsuits, and even government scrutiny. By leveraging these structures, billionaires can ensure that their wealth remains intact and protected from financial risks.

Billionaires establish trusts in offshore jurisdictions with favorable laws, ensuring they retain control over their assets while legally avoiding tax payments. These trust structures allow them to pass down their fortunes without triggering significant estate taxes. In some cases, complex layers of trusts are created, such as dynasty trusts, which can sustain wealth for multiple generations while sidestepping inheritance taxes. Additionally, irrevocable trusts can transfer assets outside of an individual's taxable estate, reducing their overall tax liability. Some ultra-wealthy individuals even use secretive discretionary trusts, where the beneficiaries are not predetermined, further complicating any attempts at taxation or legal claims.

Foundations: Philanthropy or Tax Strategy?

Private foundations, while often associated with charitable giving, serve as powerful tax and wealth management tools. Billionaires establish foundations to claim massive tax deductions while retaining control over how the money is spent. These foundations allow them to shelter significant portions of their wealth from taxation while projecting an image of generosity and philanthropy.

By leveraging tax-advantaged foundations, billionaires can maintain financial influence while benefiting from significant tax breaks. These structures allow them to preserve generational wealth under the guise of philanthropy, all while enjoying the flexibility to channel their fortunes into investments that align with their interests. In many cases, these foundations fund initiatives that ultimately serve the founder's business or personal agenda—such as lobbying efforts, political influence, or corporate sponsorships—rather than purely altruistic causes. Some of the largest private foundations hold billions of dollars in assets, enabling them to shape industries, economies, and policies, all while securing substantial tax savings.

The Unfair Playing Field

Corporate tax avoidance and wealth preservation mechanisms enable the ultra-rich to legally minimize their tax obligations while maintaining control over their vast financial empires. These strategies, though legal, contribute to a growing wealth gap by allowing the elite to accumulate wealth at an unprecedented rate while middle-class taxpayers bear the brunt of the tax burden.

Understanding these strategies is the first step toward leveling the financial playing field. While most people cannot exploit these systems to the same extent as billionaires, awareness can drive policy discussions, financial literacy, and smarter tax planning for individuals and small businesses alike.

The Cost of Tax Avoidance: Who Pays the Price?

The Hidden Consequences of Tax Avoidance

While billionaires and multinational corporations legally maneuver their way through tax loopholes, the financial burden does not simply disappear—it shifts onto the shoulders of the average taxpayer. Governments rely on tax revenue to fund essential services such as education, healthcare, infrastructure, and social security. When corporations and the ultra-wealthy successfully avoid paying their fair share, the responsibility of sustaining public services disproportionately falls on middle-class workers and small businesses.

This disparity creates a widening economic divide, where everyday citizens must compensate for the shortfall through higher personal income taxes, increased consumption taxes, and reduced access to critical government-funded programs. Meanwhile, corporations and the ultra-wealthy continue to amass fortunes, leveraging financial loopholes to ensure their wealth remains untouched. The effects are particularly severe in developing nations, where the lack of corporate tax contributions can mean the difference between building new schools and hospitals or leaving communities underserved.

In many cases, these tax avoidance strategies force governments to borrow heavily, increasing national debt levels. The burden of repaying these debts often falls on future generations, perpetuating a cycle where working-class families struggle to keep up with rising costs while the financial elite continue to thrive. Understanding how these systems work is crucial to advocating for fairer tax policies and ensuring that economic growth benefits all members of society, not just the privileged few.

Now, we will explore the real-world consequences of corporate tax avoidance, examining the scale of lost tax revenue, its impact on society, and the ongoing global efforts to curb these exploitative practices.

The Scale of Lost Tax Revenue

Global tax avoidance is not a minor issue—it represents one of the most significant drains on national economies. According to the Tax Justice Network, corporations and wealthy individuals use tax havens and loopholes to deprive governments of an estimated **$483 billion annually**. This revenue could otherwise be used to improve public infrastructure, fund social programs, and reduce national debt. These tax losses translate to billions in underfunded schools, hospitals, and social welfare programs that could drastically improve the quality of life for millions of people worldwide.

Case Study: The United States Tax Gap

The U.S. Internal Revenue Service (IRS) estimates that the annual **"tax gap"**—the difference between what is owed and what is actually collected—exceeds **$600 billion**. A significant portion of this gap is due to corporate tax avoidance strategies, leaving the government underfunded and forcing policymakers to compensate by increasing taxation on wage earners or reducing spending on essential services. This shift means fewer public investments in areas like healthcare, education, and infrastructure, which disproportionately affect low- and middle-income citizens.

One striking example is the way multinational tech companies shift profits to tax havens such as Ireland and the Cayman Islands. Despite generating billions in revenue from American consumers, companies like Apple, Google, and Amazon use complex tax structures to declare profits in countries with lower tax rates, reducing their effective tax burden. Meanwhile, small and medium-sized businesses that lack access to these financial loopholes end up shouldering a disproportionate tax burden, stifling economic competition.

Case Study: Developing Countries Suffer the Most

According to the United Nations, developing countries lose nearly **$200 billion** per year due to corporate tax avoidance. This loss represents more than the total foreign aid these countries receive, meaning that while multinational corporations extract profits from these regions, they contribute little to their development. For instance, companies operating in African and Latin American countries often use complex financial structures to shift profits to tax havens, avoiding local taxation.

One infamous example is how mining and oil companies register their profits in jurisdictions with lower tax rates rather than the countries where they extract natural resources. This practice deprives local governments of much-needed revenue, limiting their ability to invest in education, healthcare, and infrastructure. Instead of reinvesting in local economies, these funds remain untaxed and inaccessible to the very nations that need them most.

Countries in Africa, Latin America, and Southeast Asia struggle to provide essential public services like healthcare and education due to this massive financial drain. Without adequate tax revenues, governments are forced to rely on international loans, increasing their financial vulnerability and dependence on external aid.

The Impact on Public Services and Society

When corporations and billionaires avoid taxes, governments must compensate for the shortfall in other ways—often at the expense of working-class citizens.

Education

Underfunded schools, outdated textbooks, and overcrowded classrooms are direct consequences of lost tax revenue. Countries with weak tax enforcement often struggle to finance public education, widening the gap between rich and poor students. For example:

- In the U.S., states that receive less tax revenue often resort to cutting teacher salaries and eliminating extracurricular programs.

- In developing nations, tax avoidance by corporations operating within their borders means governments cannot afford to build new schools or hire qualified educators.

Healthcare

Many countries rely on corporate and income taxes to fund public healthcare systems. When major corporations shift profits offshore, governments must either increase the tax burden on individuals or cut healthcare spending. The consequences include:

- **Longer wait times** and **fewer medical professionals** in public hospitals.

- Increased **out-of-pocket healthcare costs** for citizens, disproportionately affecting low-income families.

- **Delayed medical research and vaccine distribution,** as seen during the COVID-19 pandemic when underfunded healthcare systems struggled to cope with demand.

Infrastructure and Public Safety

Roads, bridges, transportation networks, and emergency services all rely on tax revenue. Countries with significant corporate tax avoidance often experience deteriorating infrastructure. For example:

- The **Flint Water Crisis** in Michigan was partially due to insufficient public funding for water infrastructure maintenance.
- Developing countries often lack reliable electricity and sanitation due to tax losses from multinational corporations operating within their borders.

The Burden on Middle-Class Taxpayers

As corporations and billionaires sidestep taxes, middle-class workers and small businesses are left to make up the difference. This results in:

- **Higher income tax rates for individuals.** Governments must raise personal income tax rates to compensate for lost corporate tax revenue.
- **Higher costs of living.** To make up for lost revenue, governments introduce new consumption taxes (like VAT and sales tax), disproportionately impacting lower-income individuals.

- **Reduced government benefits.** Many social welfare programs, such as unemployment benefits and pensions, face budget cuts due to tax losses.

Case Study: The 2017 U.S. Tax Cuts and Jobs Act

When the U.S. government introduced the **Tax Cuts and Jobs Act** in 2017, it significantly reduced corporate tax rates from **35% to 21%**. While proponents argued this would boost economic growth, the reality was that:

- Corporations used the savings to **buy back stock** and increase shareholder wealth rather than reinvesting in worker wages.

- The U.S. national deficit grew, prompting discussions on cutting social programs such as **Medicare and Social Security**.

- The burden of taxation increasingly shifted to individuals and small businesses, who did not receive comparable tax breaks.

The Global Effort to Combat Tax Avoidance

Recognizing the dangers of large-scale tax avoidance, governments and international organizations are working to close loopholes and improve tax transparency.

The OECD's Global Minimum Tax

In 2021, the **Organisation for Economic Co-operation and Development (OECD)** proposed a **global minimum corporate tax rate of 15%** to prevent corporations from shifting profits to tax havens. Over **130 countries** signed onto the agreement, which aims to:

- Reduce corporate tax avoidance by ensuring multinational companies pay at least 15% in any country where they operate.
- Limit the effectiveness of offshore profit shifting.
- Increase government tax revenues to fund essential services.

Stronger Tax Enforcement in the U.S. and EU

- The **U.S. Inflation Reduction Act (2022)** allocated billions to the IRS to strengthen tax enforcement, particularly targeting corporations and high-net-worth individuals.
- The **European Union** has introduced laws requiring companies to publicly disclose profits and taxes paid in each country where they operate, increasing transparency.
- Several countries, including the **United Kingdom, France, and Australia**, have introduced digital service taxes targeting tech giants like Amazon, Google, and

Facebook, which historically paid minimal local taxes despite massive revenues.

A Broken System in Need of Reform

Corporate tax avoidance is not just a financial issue—it is a societal crisis. Billionaires and multinational corporations have successfully manipulated tax laws for decades, growing their wealth while public services remain underfunded and working-class taxpayers shoulder an increasing burden.

While international efforts are making progress in closing loopholes, the fight is far from over. For meaningful change, policymakers must continue tightening regulations, increasing enforcement, and ensuring that taxation is fair for all.

At the same time, everyday citizens must recognize the power of financial literacy and advocacy. By understanding these tax avoidance strategies and their consequences, we can push for reforms that create a fairer, more sustainable economic system for future generations.

Chapter 3: Offshore Accounts & Tax Havens – Hiding Wealth in Plain Sight

Offshore accounts and tax havens have long been the secret weapon of the world's wealthiest individuals and corporations. These financial hideouts serve as intricate networks that enable the elite to legally (and sometimes illegally) shield their wealth from taxation, scrutiny, and regulation. While the average taxpayer has little choice but to pay what they owe, the ultra-rich and multinational corporations strategically shift their assets across borders, capitalizing on the cracks and loopholes of a fragmented global financial system. This allows them to minimize tax obligations, obscure financial dealings, and, in some cases, evade legal consequences altogether. The offshore financial world is not merely a side effect of globalization—it is an intentional and well-oiled machine designed to preserve wealth at the highest levels of society.

In this chapter, we will explore what tax havens are, why they exist, and how they function as financial safe havens for the elite. We will also examine major financial scandals such as the **Panama Papers** and **Pandora Papers**, which exposed the hidden world of offshore wealth. Finally, we will break down the methods used by businesses to shift profits globally, ensuring they pay little to no tax.

Understanding offshore tax havens is crucial in exposing the inequalities of the financial system and the mechanisms that keep wealth concentrated at the top. Let's uncover how the wealthy hide their money in plain sight.

What Are Tax Havens, and Why Do They Exist?

Tax havens are jurisdictions with little or no tax liability, high levels of financial secrecy, and lax regulations that attract corporations and wealthy individuals looking to minimize their tax burdens. These locations often serve as legal loopholes, allowing money to flow in and out with minimal oversight from global authorities. With the rise of globalization and digital banking, the ease of transferring assets across borders has only strengthened the appeal of these financial safe havens, making them an indispensable tool for wealth accumulation and preservation.

Why Do Tax Havens Exist?

Tax havens serve multiple purposes, including:

- **Attracting foreign capital:** Many small economies position themselves as tax havens to bring in banking business and foreign investment. The influx of foreign funds often benefits local financial institutions, property markets, and service industries, even if it comes at the cost of global tax fairness.

- **Legal tax minimization:** Countries with higher tax rates drive corporations and wealthy individuals to seek alternative, low-tax environments. These jurisdictions promote themselves as business-friendly, offering incentives that allow corporations to shift profits and reduce tax burdens legally.

- **Financial privacy and asset protection:** Offshore banking allows individuals to hide their wealth from prying eyes, including government agencies, creditors, and sometimes even family members. These secrecy laws also make it difficult for law enforcement agencies to track illicit activities, leading to concerns over money laundering and financial crimes.

- **Regulatory arbitrage:** Different jurisdictions have varying levels of financial regulation. By choosing to bank in tax havens with minimal oversight, wealthy individuals and corporations can bypass stringent financial rules, ensuring fewer restrictions on their capital movements and investment strategies.

Countries that operate as tax havens often claim that their policies promote economic growth and create employment opportunities. However, in reality, they contribute to wealth inequality, global tax avoidance, and economic imbalances. By enabling the wealthiest individuals and largest corporations to minimize their tax contributions, these jurisdictions shift the financial burden onto the middle class and small businesses, exacerbating socio-economic disparities worldwide.

The World's Most Popular Tax Havens

Some of the most well-known tax havens include:

- **Cayman Islands** – A premier destination for hedge funds and multinational corporations due to its complete absence of corporate tax, income tax, or capital gains tax. This jurisdiction is often used to store wealth and facilitate complex investment structures that help shield earnings from tax authorities.

- **Switzerland** – Historically known for its stringent banking secrecy laws, Switzerland has long been a haven for hidden wealth. Although recent international pressure has led to some reforms, it still provides a stable, low-tax environment for wealthy individuals and corporations.

- **Panama** – A notorious tax haven offering easy incorporation of offshore entities with little financial disclosure. Its lax regulations have attracted individuals seeking secrecy, making it a focal point in financial scandals such as the Panama Papers.

- **Singapore** – A rising financial hub that attracts multinational corporations and high-net-worth individuals with its favorable tax policies, stable economy, and banking privacy protections. It serves as a major gateway for wealth moving throughout Asia.

- **British Virgin Islands** – A jurisdiction home to thousands of shell companies, many of which exist solely for tax avoidance purposes. The BVI offers minimal taxation and regulation, making it a top choice for those seeking to obscure ownership and shift profits offshore.

These jurisdictions are not just financial curiosities; they are integral to the way the wealthy and corporations manage their fortunes, often at the expense of taxpayers worldwide. Governments and regulatory bodies struggle to rein in these practices due to the complex, international nature of offshore finance.

The Panama Papers & Pandora Papers: What They Exposed

The **Panama Papers (2016)** and **Pandora Papers (2021)** were two of the largest financial leaks in history, exposing how the world's elite—including politicians, celebrities, and business moguls—use offshore accounts to hide wealth and evade taxes. These investigations uncovered a vast, interconnected network of offshore entities that facilitated everything from tax avoidance to money laundering, corruption, and even funding illicit activities. They painted a clear picture of how the financial system is often skewed in favor of the wealthiest individuals and corporations, leaving everyday taxpayers to bear the burden of lost revenues.

Key Revelations:

- The **Panama Papers** revealed how the law firm Mossack Fonseca, based in Panama, specialized in creating offshore shell companies that allowed clients to obscure their financial assets and avoid taxation. The leak contained 11.5 million documents exposing the secret dealings of over 214,000 offshore entities linked to world leaders, business tycoons, and criminals.

- The **Pandora Papers** built upon these revelations, exposing a new wave of offshore financial activities by global elites, including real estate acquisitions, shell companies, hidden bank accounts, and covert investment holdings in tax havens such as the British Virgin Islands, Switzerland, and the Cayman Islands. The leak included nearly 12 million files detailing how 35 world leaders and over 300 public officials shielded wealth offshore.

- Both leaks highlighted how financial secrecy enables large-scale tax evasion, corruption, and the siphoning of wealth away from public resources. They demonstrated how offshore finance is not limited to a handful of corrupt individuals but is a systemic issue affecting economies worldwide.

These investigations sparked global outrage and forced governments to address financial secrecy with increased regulation and international cooperation. However, despite heightened scrutiny, offshore banking remains an indispensable tool for the ultra-rich, who continuously adapt their strategies to stay ahead of evolving tax laws and enforcement efforts.

The Ethics and Consequences of Offshore Banking

While offshore banking is legal in many cases, it raises serious ethical concerns and has broad economic consequences:

- **Governments lose trillions in tax revenue**, leading to underfunded schools, hospitals, and public infrastructure. This loss of funding creates significant challenges for national economies, particularly in developing countries that rely on tax revenue for essential services and economic stability. The gap in revenue often forces governments to cut budgets for crucial sectors, directly impacting the quality of life for millions of citizens.

- **The tax burden shifts to the middle class**, as governments compensate for lost revenue by raising income and consumption taxes. With corporations and the ultra-wealthy avoiding taxation through offshore mechanisms, the responsibility of funding public services disproportionately falls on everyday workers. This leads to increased financial strain on households, reduced disposable income, and a widening gap between the rich and the poor.

- **Illicit activities flourish**, including money laundering, fraud, and corruption, due to the lack of transparency in tax havens. The secrecy offered by these jurisdictions allows organized crime syndicates, drug cartels, and corrupt officials to funnel illicit funds undetected. This not only erodes trust in the financial system but also fuels criminal enterprises and destabilizes economies by diverting resources away from productive and legitimate economic activities.

The presence of offshore banking networks creates a financial playing field that favors those with access to wealth and power while leaving average citizens and small businesses at a disadvantage. Regulators worldwide are working on policies to combat offshore tax avoidance, but the fight is far from over. As long as there are loopholes, the wealthy and corporations will continue to exploit them. Meaningful reform requires global cooperation, stronger enforcement mechanisms, and increased financial transparency to ensure fair taxation and economic justice.

The Global Fight Against Tax Havens

Offshore accounts and tax havens are a key component of how the world's wealthiest individuals and corporations maintain and grow their fortunes while avoiding taxation. The exposure of major financial leaks like the **Panama Papers** and **Pandora Papers** has sparked debates on financial transparency, but meaningful reforms are slow.

Understanding these hidden financial systems is essential in demanding accountability and advocating for fairer taxation policies. The more we uncover about how the wealthy shield their fortunes, the better equipped we are to push for economic fairness and transparency in global finance.

PART 2:

THE HIDDEN MONEY MACHINES

Chapter 4: The Power of Private Banking & Family Offices

The Exclusive Financial World of the Ultra-Rich

For the average person, banking is a straightforward affair—open an account, deposit money, take out loans, and perhaps invest in basic financial products. But for the ultra-wealthy, an entirely different banking system exists—one that offers unparalleled financial advantages, secrecy, and access to exclusive investment opportunities. This is the world of **private banking** and **family offices**, a hidden financial ecosystem designed to preserve and multiply wealth across generations while minimizing tax burdens and legal exposure.

Private banking and family offices operate in ways that most people can barely comprehend. These institutions serve as financial fortresses for the elite, offering personalized services that go far beyond what any traditional retail bank provides. From offshore banking structures and investment funds that ordinary investors cannot access to high-level asset protection strategies, private banking is a sophisticated mechanism that ensures the rich not only stay rich but continue to grow their fortunes exponentially.

While many see banks as places to store money and access loans, private banks function as **strategic wealth management hubs**, working behind the scenes to navigate tax loopholes, financial secrecy laws, and complex legal structures. Meanwhile, family offices act as **personal financial dynasties**, overseeing everything from investments and tax planning to philanthropy and succession strategies for billionaires and multimillionaires.

Understanding the role of private banking and family offices is crucial to grasping how wealth remains concentrated at the top. These entities are not simply about storing money but about leveraging financial power in ways that are largely inaccessible to the middle class. As we delve into this hidden financial world, we will uncover how these exclusive institutions operate, the strategies they employ, and how they ultimately shape the global economy in ways that benefit the few at the expense of the many.

What is Private Banking?

Private banking is a highly specialized financial service designed exclusively for high-net-worth individuals (HNWIs) and ultra-high-net-worth individuals (UHNWIs). Unlike traditional retail banking, which offers standardized financial products to the general public, private banking provides bespoke financial solutions tailored to the unique and often complex needs of the wealthy. These services go beyond basic banking and encompass a holistic approach to wealth management, including exclusive investment opportunities, tax optimization strategies, estate planning, philanthropic advisory, and legacy preservation. With a focus on confidentiality, elite clientele benefit from direct access to expert financial advisors, personalized service, and privileged investment vehicles unavailable to the average consumer.

Private banking is more than just a banking relationship—it is a gateway to a global financial network designed to protect, grow, and transfer wealth seamlessly across generations. The rich do not simply deposit money into bank accounts; they strategically leverage financial tools and global banking systems to ensure that their wealth not only remains intact but continues to grow with minimal tax exposure and maximum returns.

Definition and Purpose of Private Banking

Private banking is a distinct sector of the financial industry that provides exclusive, concierge-like wealth management services to affluent clients. It is built on the principles of discretion, exclusivity, and tailored financial solutions. Unlike standard banking, which offers generic financial products to the general population, private banking takes a bespoke approach to financial planning, ensuring that every client's portfolio aligns with their long-term goals, risk tolerance, and global investment ambitions.

The key purpose of private banking is to provide comprehensive financial solutions that allow the ultra-wealthy to manage their money efficiently, shield it from excessive taxation, and pass it on to future generations with minimal erosion. This includes asset diversification, risk management, strategic philanthropy, and navigating complex financial structures, often spanning multiple jurisdictions.

How Private Banks Differ from Retail Banks

While retail banks cater to the masses with savings accounts, loans, and credit cards, private banks operate on an entirely different level. Their exclusive clientele enjoy unparalleled financial benefits and services that go far beyond what is available to the general public:

- **Personalized Service:** Private banking clients receive dedicated relationship managers or personal bankers who act as financial concierges, curating bespoke investment strategies and wealth preservation plans. These professionals provide access to private equity, offshore banking structures, and investment vehicles that are not accessible to retail banking clients.

- **Exclusive Investment Opportunities:** Clients gain access to highly lucrative investment vehicles such as hedge funds, venture capital, direct private investments, and specialized portfolios tailored to market trends. Many private banks also offer custom-built investment portfolios that align with clients' specific interests, whether in sustainable investing, emerging markets, or alternative assets.

- **Tax Optimization Strategies:** The ultra-wealthy use private banks to implement sophisticated tax planning strategies, including the use of offshore trusts, shell companies, and other legal financial structures designed to minimize tax liabilities. Private banks employ teams of tax experts to ensure clients can legally navigate international tax laws while reducing their overall burden.

- **Secrecy and Confidentiality:** Privacy is a cornerstone of private banking. Many institutions operate in jurisdictions with strong banking secrecy laws, ensuring that clients' financial activities remain hidden from public scrutiny. This level of discretion is particularly attractive to business moguls, celebrities, and political figures who wish to protect their wealth from legal claims, government oversight, and unwanted attention.

- **Higher Entry Requirements:** Private banking is reserved for the financial elite. Unlike standard banking services, which are accessible to the general public, private banking requires clients to meet high asset thresholds—often starting at $1 million in investable wealth and reaching upwards of $50 million for ultra-exclusive financial institutions. Some of the most prestigious private banks cater only to billionaires and multi-generational dynasties.

The Role of Private Banks in Wealth Preservation

Private banks play a crucial role in ensuring that the wealth of the elite remains intact and continues to grow. By leveraging financial engineering, global investment strategies, and legal frameworks, these institutions help their clients legally reduce tax burdens, protect assets from lawsuits, and strategically allocate wealth for future generations.

One of the most significant aspects of private banking is the ability to shield assets from economic instability and legal claims. Through the use of offshore trusts, multi-jurisdictional banking strategies, and diplomatic financial structures, private banks ensure that their clients' wealth remains protected even in times of global financial turmoil. Additionally, these banks often facilitate intergenerational wealth transfer strategies, ensuring that dynastic wealth is maintained across multiple generations.

The Expanding Influence of Private Banking in the 21st Century

The role of private banks has expanded significantly in recent years, particularly as globalization has created new financial challenges and opportunities. With the rise of digital banking, cryptocurrency investments, and artificial intelligence-driven portfolio management, private banking institutions are evolving to cater to the modern wealthy elite. Many now offer specialized services in digital asset management, impact investing, and geopolitical risk analysis to help their clients navigate an increasingly complex financial landscape.

Furthermore, private banks are no longer just for individuals; they now play an integral role in multinational corporations, sovereign wealth funds, and even governments seeking strategic financial guidance. The lines between personal and institutional wealth management are increasingly blurred, with private banks acting as key financial advisors in major global economic decisions.

Understanding private banking is key to unraveling the hidden financial world of the ultra-rich. In the next section, we will explore the concept of family offices and how they serve as private financial dynasties for the wealthiest individuals and families worldwide.

The Global Network of Private Banks

Some of the most prestigious private banks operate globally, offering services that span multiple jurisdictions to optimize wealth management. Notable private banks include:

- **UBS & Credit Suisse (Switzerland):** Longstanding leaders in private banking, known for their discretion, wealth management expertise, and extensive experience handling ultra-high-net-worth clients. These banks offer bespoke financial solutions, including tailored investment strategies, estate planning, and asset protection mechanisms. Their Swiss banking secrecy laws, though weakened in recent years, have historically made them a preferred choice for individuals seeking financial privacy.

- **J.P. Morgan Private Bank (USA):** One of the most influential private banks in the world, J.P. Morgan specializes in high-level investment advisory services, estate planning, and risk management. With access to extensive global resources, the bank provides cutting-edge investment strategies, catering to billionaires, business moguls, and institutional clients. It also facilitates large-scale philanthropic endeavors through tailored charitable giving structures.

- **HSBC Private Bank (UK & Hong Kong):** A global powerhouse in wealth management, HSBC offers a broad range of services, including offshore banking, customized investment solutions, and multi-generational wealth planning. With strong ties to Asian and European markets, HSBC caters to international clients seeking access to diversified financial markets and tax-efficient investment vehicles.

- **Deutsche Bank Private Wealth Management (Germany):** Known for its sophisticated financial services, Deutsche Bank provides bespoke tax structuring strategies, estate planning solutions, and alternative investments such as private equity, venture capital, and fine art. The bank's extensive expertise in navigating European regulatory frameworks makes it an attractive option for high-net-worth individuals across the continent.

- **Bank of Singapore:** A rising force in Asia's wealth management sector, Bank of Singapore caters to affluent clients seeking premier financial services, including discretionary portfolio management, structured lending, and wealth transition strategies. Its strong presence in Singapore—a leading financial hub with investor-friendly regulations—makes it a key player in servicing ultra-wealthy families across Asia and beyond.

Each of these institutions provides tailored solutions to ensure their wealthy clientele maximize returns while minimizing exposure to risks and taxation. With an expansive network of financial experts, cutting-edge technology, and regulatory loopholes at their disposal, these banks continue to shape the financial strategies of the global elite.

Private Banking Strategies for Wealth Preservation

Private banks employ a variety of sophisticated financial strategies to help clients grow and protect their wealth:

1. **Offshore Banking & Tax Havens**

    ○ Many private banks facilitate offshore accounts in low-tax jurisdictions such as the Cayman Islands, Switzerland, and Singapore.

    ○ Offshore banking ensures financial privacy and shields assets from government oversight and potential legal claims.

2. **Custom Investment Portfolios**

    ○ Unlike standard investment accounts, private banking clients receive customized portfolios that align with their long-term financial goals.

    ○ These portfolios often include alternative assets like art, commodities, real estate, and private equity.

3. **Multi-Generational Wealth Planning**

○ Estate planning services ensure that wealth transitions seamlessly from one generation to the next with minimal taxation.

○ Private banks help set up family trusts, dynastic structures, and strategic charitable donations that align with wealth preservation objectives.

4. **Private Credit & Lending Solutions**

○ High-net-worth individuals often require unique lending solutions, such as securities-backed loans, art financing, and real estate funding.

○ Private banks offer low-interest loans against assets, enabling clients to leverage their wealth without liquidating holdings.

The Secrecy and Controversies of Private Banking

While private banking provides undeniable advantages, it also exists in a shadowy realm of finance that has been scrutinized for enabling tax evasion, money laundering, and financial secrecy. Major scandals have exposed how private banks have facilitated the concealment of illicit funds, allowing corrupt officials, criminals, and oligarchs to hide their wealth from authorities.

The Power and Privilege of Private Banking

Private banking continues to be a cornerstone of wealth management for the global elite. Through exclusive services, customized financial strategies, and a network of offshore solutions, private banks empower the wealthy to grow and shield their fortunes in ways unavailable to the average individual. As financial regulations evolve, private banking institutions adapt, finding new ways to ensure that their affluent clients maintain control over their assets while benefiting from a system designed to favor those with immense wealth.

Family Offices – The Secret Financial Teams of the Ultra-Rich

What is a Family Office?

A family office is a private wealth management firm dedicated to serving a single affluent family or a small group of ultra-wealthy individuals. Unlike traditional wealth management services offered by private banks, family offices provide a highly customized and comprehensive financial strategy tailored to the specific needs of the family they serve. These offices oversee everything from investment management and tax planning to estate structuring, philanthropy, and even personal lifestyle services such as security, travel planning, and private education for heirs.

The primary purpose of a family office is to preserve and grow multi-generational wealth while ensuring that the family's financial affairs remain confidential and efficient. Many of the world's billionaires and dynastic families rely on family offices to navigate complex financial landscapes, minimize tax burdens, and maintain control over their assets across generations. These entities not only function as financial hubs but also serve as strategic think tanks that help shape the family's future financial and personal legacy.

Types of Family Offices

There are two primary types of family offices: single-family offices (SFOs) and multi-family offices (MFOs). While both serve similar functions, they differ in structure and client base.

- **Single-Family Offices (SFOs):** These are exclusive financial entities created to serve only one family. They offer complete control over wealth management, tax structuring, and legacy planning while ensuring maximum privacy. SFOs are typically reserved for families with a net worth exceeding $100 million, as the operational costs can range from several hundred thousand to millions of dollars annually. Many of the world's most powerful families, such as the Rockefellers and Rothschilds, have operated SFOs for generations, using them to consolidate their wealth, influence, and economic power across continents.

- **Multi-Family Offices (MFOs):** These offices manage the financial affairs of multiple affluent families, pooling resources to offer economies of scale. MFOs provide many of the same services as SFOs but at a lower cost, making them accessible to families with net worth's starting at $30 million or more. Some MFOs function as elite investment clubs where wealthy families can collaborate on major financial ventures, gaining access to unique business opportunities and private investments unavailable to the general public.

Core Functions of a Family Office

Family offices function as sophisticated financial powerhouses, managing virtually every aspect of an ultra-wealthy family's wealth. Their core responsibilities include:

- **Investment Management:** Unlike traditional investment firms, family offices develop customized portfolios that align with the family's long-term vision. They invest in equities, bonds, private equity, hedge funds, venture capital, and alternative assets such as art, rare collectibles, real estate, and cryptocurrency. Some family offices have exclusive access to pre-IPO investments and high-level mergers and acquisitions, ensuring they maximize returns while mitigating risk.

- **Tax Optimization & Asset Protection:** Family offices specialize in global tax strategies, utilizing offshore accounts, trusts, and corporate structures to legally minimize tax exposure. They also implement asset protection strategies to shield wealth from lawsuits, creditors, and political instability. Through complex financial vehicles such as shell companies, anonymous trusts, and international tax havens, family offices ensure that fortunes remain protected from unnecessary government intervention and taxation.

- **Estate & Succession Planning:** One of the primary objectives of a family office is to ensure smooth generational wealth transfer. Estate planning structures such as family trusts and foundations help secure financial legacies while avoiding excessive estate taxes and probate processes. The ultra-wealthy use dynastic structures to perpetuate wealth for centuries, ensuring that their descendants maintain influence and financial power long after they are gone.

- **Philanthropy & Impact Investing:** Many ultra-wealthy families use their fortunes to support charitable causes. Family offices establish private foundations, donor-advised funds, and social impact investment portfolios to align wealth with philanthropic goals while also leveraging tax benefits. These philanthropic arms are often designed to influence global policies, fund political initiatives, and shape the world in ways that align with the family's values and long-term interests.

- **Risk & Crisis Management:** From market downturns to geopolitical risks, family offices develop financial contingency plans to protect wealth from unforeseen crises. They also handle reputation management, ensuring that family members remain shielded from negative publicity. Some family offices even employ crisis teams, PR strategists, and legal experts to manage high-profile scandals, business disputes, and other threats to the family's public image.

- **Lifestyle & Concierge Services:** Some family offices extend their services beyond finance, managing private jets, yachts, real estate portfolios, luxury travel arrangements, and even hiring personal security teams. They handle everything from acquiring rare art pieces to booking exclusive experiences, ensuring that family members enjoy a seamless, ultra-luxurious lifestyle without concerns about logistics or management.

How Family Offices Differ from Traditional Wealth Management Firms

Traditional wealth management firms serve a broad clientele, offering standardized financial services. Family offices, on the other hand, are entirely bespoke, catering to the highly specific needs of ultra-high-net-worth individuals. The key distinctions include:

- **Exclusivity & Customization:** Family offices provide tailor-made financial solutions, while traditional firms offer pre-packaged investment products.

- **Long-Term Perspective:** Unlike wealth management firms that focus on short-term returns, family offices prioritize multi-generational wealth sustainability, ensuring that financial dynasties remain intact for centuries.

- **Greater Control:** Wealthy families retain full control over investment decisions rather than relying on external fund managers, giving them more direct influence over their economic empire.

- **Confidentiality & Security:** Family offices ensure discretion, safeguarding financial and personal information from public scrutiny. Many of the world's most influential figures operate through these offices to maintain financial privacy and security.

The Rising Influence of Family Offices

The number of family offices has surged in recent years as ultra-wealthy individuals seek greater control over their financial affairs. The shift away from traditional banks and investment firms is driven by a desire for more personalized service, increased privacy, and the ability to invest in unique opportunities such as direct private equity deals and venture capital startups.

Many family offices now operate like mini financial institutions, employing teams of top-tier investment analysts, tax specialists, and legal experts. Some of the world's wealthiest individuals, including Jeff Bezos, Elon Musk, and Warren Buffett, utilize family office structures to oversee their financial empires discreetly. The ability to leverage cutting-edge financial technology, artificial intelligence, and geopolitical analysis has given family offices an unprecedented level of influence over global markets and economic policies.

The Global Expansion of Family Offices

As wealth continues to globalize, family offices are setting up operations in financial hubs worldwide, from New York and London to Singapore and Dubai. These jurisdictions offer favorable tax regimes, financial stability, and strategic access to emerging markets, making them ideal locations for family office headquarters. Some family offices also operate in regulatory gray areas, allowing them to leverage financial loopholes that provide unparalleled investment advantages.

The rise of family offices signifies a fundamental shift in how the ultra-rich manage their wealth. These financial powerhouses ensure that fortunes remain intact for generations, leveraging sophisticated investment strategies and legal structures that shield assets from taxation and regulatory scrutiny. In the next section, we will explore how private banks collaborate with family offices to create an even more impenetrable financial ecosystem for the world's elite.

The Services & Strategies of Private Banking

& Family Offices

Tax Optimization & Offshore Structures

Private banks and family offices specialize in crafting highly sophisticated tax strategies that help high-net-worth individuals (HNWIs) legally reduce their tax burdens while maintaining asset protection and financial privacy. Through a combination of **shell companies, trusts, and offshore entities**, the ultra-rich optimize tax efficiency and secure their wealth for future generations. These financial structures are designed not only to minimize taxes but also to provide strategic advantages in estate planning, wealth transfer, and regulatory compliance avoidance.

- **Offshore Entities & Tax Havens**: Many affluent individuals establish corporations in tax-friendly jurisdictions such as the Cayman Islands, Bermuda, or Luxembourg to benefit from low or zero corporate tax rates. These entities allow income and profits to be redirected, significantly reducing overall tax liabilities. Offshore structures are also used to defer taxes indefinitely, meaning profits can be reinvested without being taxed until repatriated.

- **Trusts & Foundations**: Wealthy individuals utilize trusts in tax-favorable locations to protect assets from inheritance and estate taxes. By placing assets in an irrevocable trust, they technically no longer own the assets, thereby avoiding hefty estate taxes. Many ultra-rich families use dynasty trusts, which allow assets to pass through multiple generations without incurring additional estate taxes, ensuring long-term wealth preservation.

- **Tax-Loss Harvesting**: Private banks advise clients on strategically selling assets at a loss to offset taxable gains elsewhere, a practice frequently employed by hedge funds and investment managers. By carefully selecting underperforming assets and liquidating them at the right time, wealthy investors can significantly reduce their tax burdens while maintaining a balanced portfolio. This strategy is often combined with repurchasing similar assets shortly after the sale, a tactic known as tax-loss harvesting optimization, allowing continued exposure to market gains while benefiting from immediate tax deductions.

- **Residency & Citizenship Strategies**: Some high-net-worth individuals obtain citizenship or residency in tax-friendly countries to benefit from favorable tax laws. Programs like Malta's Individual Investor Programme and Portugal's Golden Visa scheme provide attractive tax incentives for the wealthy. By obtaining residency or a second passport in jurisdictions with low tax rates, they can legally shift their tax residency and significantly reduce their overall tax liability. Additionally, some countries offer favorable tax regimes for new residents, such as non-domiciled tax status, which exempts foreign income from local taxation. This strategy allows the ultra-rich to protect their wealth while maintaining financial flexibility and international mobility.

Exclusive Investment Opportunities

The investment landscape available to the ultra-rich is fundamentally different from what the average investor can access. Private banks and family offices open doors to high-yield investment opportunities that provide significant financial advantages.

- **Hedge Funds & Private Equity**: Unlike traditional stock market investments, hedge funds and private equity firms offer bespoke investment strategies with higher potential returns. These funds often require multi-million-dollar minimum investments, limiting access to only the wealthiest individuals. They provide unique strategies such as distressed asset investing, leveraged buyouts, and complex derivatives trading, which are not available to the general public.

- **Venture Capital**: Family offices frequently participate in pre-IPO funding rounds and early-stage investments in high-growth startups, capturing wealth-building opportunities before they reach public markets. Many of the world's wealthiest investors have built their fortunes by backing unicorn startups before they became billion-dollar companies.

- **Art & Collectibles as Investments**: The ultra-wealthy allocate substantial portions of their portfolios to alternative assets such as fine art, rare collectibles, and vintage wines. These assets appreciate over time while also offering a level of wealth preservation not tied to traditional financial markets. High-value collectibles often serve as stores of value during economic downturns and can be transferred discreetly across borders without the same regulatory scrutiny as financial assets.

- **Real Estate Holdings**: Through the use of shell companies and special-purpose entities (SPEs), private banking clients acquire luxury real estate in prime locations while minimizing tax exposure and shielding ownership details from public records. High-end properties in global cities like London, New York, and Dubai often serve as wealth storage vehicles rather than primary residences.

Secrecy & Asset Protection

One of the most critical aspects of private banking is ensuring absolute financial privacy and asset security. Private banks and family offices deploy a variety of strategies to shield their clients from scrutiny, lawsuits, and regulatory oversight.

- **Banking Secrecy Laws**: Some countries, such as Switzerland and Liechtenstein, have long upheld stringent banking secrecy laws, ensuring that account holders' identities and transactions remain private. Even with increased global financial transparency regulations, loopholes still exist that allow discreet wealth management.

- **Anonymous Trusts & Foundations**: The ultra-wealthy often establish trusts and foundations with nominee directors, preventing their personal names from appearing in public records while still maintaining control over assets. These structures are frequently used to obscure ownership in high-profile transactions.

- **Numbered Accounts & Multi-Jurisdictional Banking**: High-net-worth individuals leverage numbered accounts and spread assets across multiple jurisdictions to avoid detection, ensuring greater protection against government scrutiny and legal challenges. This diversification of banking locations also protects against currency risk, expropriation, and geopolitical instability.

- **Asset Diversification for Risk Mitigation**: Private banking clients structure their assets across various classes and locations, ensuring protection against political instability, currency fluctuations, and financial crises. Some family offices even create bespoke insurance policies to protect against specific financial risks, further safeguarding their wealth.

Philanthropy as a Tax Strategy

Billionaires and ultra-high-net-worth individuals frequently engage in philanthropy, not just for altruistic reasons but as a strategic tool to minimize tax obligations while preserving wealth.

- **Charitable Foundations**: Many billionaires establish private foundations, such as the Bill & Melinda Gates Foundation, which allow them to direct philanthropic efforts while enjoying tax deductions and control over how funds are allocated. These foundations often invest in for-profit ventures that align with the founder's interests, ensuring influence even as they claim charitable status.

- **Donor-Advised Funds (DAFs)**: These financial vehicles enable the wealthy to make charitable contributions and receive immediate tax benefits while retaining influence over how and when the funds are distributed. DAFs have been criticized for allowing billionaires to park money in tax-advantaged accounts without a requirement to distribute those funds to actual charities in a timely manner.

- **Art Donations & Cultural Philanthropy**: Donating valuable artworks or historical artifacts to museums and cultural institutions provides substantial tax deductions while maintaining legacy and influence. Many ultra-rich families use art donations as a way to transfer wealth tax-free while keeping their prized collections within family-controlled institutions.

- **Impact Investing & ESG Strategies**: Many ultra-rich individuals use impact investing as a means to generate financial returns while also fulfilling philanthropic goals. Investments in environmental, social, and governance (ESG) funds allow for tax efficiency while aligning financial interests with social responsibility. Many large corporations and ultra-wealthy individuals market their philanthropic endeavors as a way to shape public perception while maintaining tax-advantaged financial strategies.

The Financial Playbook of the Ultra-Wealthy

Private banks and family offices provide unparalleled financial advantages to the world's wealthiest individuals, offering a combination of **tax efficiency, exclusive investments, secrecy, and strategic philanthropy**. These mechanisms ensure that the rich not only preserve their wealth but continue to expand it across generations. While regulatory agencies attempt to crack down on financial secrecy and aggressive tax strategies, the financial elite continuously adapt, leveraging legal frameworks and cutting-edge financial instruments to maintain their privileged status in the global economy.

How Private Banking Shields Assets from Legal Claims & Governments

Financial Layers & Asset Protection Strategies

Private banks are experts in constructing financial layers that create substantial barriers between wealth and legal claims. These layers are designed to make it incredibly difficult for authorities, creditors, or governments to seize assets. By leveraging multi-jurisdictional banking, intricate corporate structures, and legal loopholes, the wealthy can effectively shield their money from potential threats.

- **Layered Ownership Structures**: Private banking clients often utilize complex, multi-tiered ownership structures that obscure asset ownership. By holding assets through multiple entities—such as offshore trusts, shell companies, and nominee accounts—the true owner remains hidden from prying eyes.

- **Legal Firewalling**: Private banks assist their clients in legally distancing themselves from their own wealth by setting up independent trustees and directors. This prevents assets from being directly linked to the beneficial owner in the event of lawsuits or governmental asset freezes.

- **Banking in Secrecy Jurisdictions**: By maintaining accounts in countries with strong financial secrecy laws, individuals can reduce the risk of asset exposure. Even with increasing international regulations, certain jurisdictions still offer a high level of confidentiality, limiting the ability of external parties to trace ownership.

Cross-Border Banking & Offshore Structures

One of the most effective ways private banking shields wealth is through **cross-border banking and offshore entities**, which allow individuals to place their assets outside the reach of domestic legal systems.

- **Multi-Jurisdictional Accounts**: Private banks encourage clients to distribute their wealth across multiple countries, reducing the risk that a single government can seize their assets. If one jurisdiction attempts to freeze funds, the individual still has access to wealth in other regions.

- **Shell Corporations**: These entities, often registered in tax havens, have no real business operations but serve as holding companies for assets. By layering ownership through multiple shells, individuals can effectively separate themselves from direct asset ownership, making legal claims difficult to enforce.

- **Trusts & Foundations**: Offshore trusts are structured so that the settlor relinquishes direct ownership of assets while still maintaining control through carefully crafted agreements. Family foundations in places like Liechtenstein or Panama allow assets to be shielded while technically being held for philanthropic or legacy purposes.

- **Foreign Bank Secrecy**: Countries like Switzerland, the Cayman Islands, and Singapore have historically provided strong banking secrecy protections, preventing unauthorized access to financial records. Even as transparency regulations evolve, strategic banking in these jurisdictions still offers advantages.

Legal Loopholes That Protect Wealth from Seizure

Despite legal efforts to curb financial secrecy, many **loopholes** still allow the wealthy to safeguard their money from lawsuits, creditors, and even governments.

- **Bankruptcy-Proof Trusts**: Some jurisdictions allow the creation of self-settled asset protection trusts that make it extremely difficult for creditors to access funds, even in cases of bankruptcy.

- **Limited Liability Entities (LLCs)**: By holding assets under LLCs in specific states or countries, individuals limit their personal liability, ensuring that personal creditors cannot seize corporate-owned assets.

- **Homestead Exemptions & Asset Exempt Laws**: Certain countries and U.S. states, such as Florida and Texas, provide generous homestead exemptions that protect primary residences from legal claims, regardless of their value.

- **Pre-Litigation Planning**: Private banks advise clients on proactive asset protection measures long before legal troubles arise, ensuring that funds are structured in ways that limit exposure.

- **International Insurance Policies**: Wealthy individuals often take out high-value insurance policies, such as offshore life insurance or private placement insurance, which can serve as tax-advantaged shelters that are difficult for creditors or governments to penetrate.

The Invisible Fortress of Private Banking

Private banks offer the ultra-wealthy a **sophisticated fortress of financial protection**, ensuring their assets remain beyond the reach of legal claims, government intervention, and economic disruptions. Through **layered financial structures, cross-border banking, and legal loopholes**, the elite can secure their fortunes for generations while minimizing financial exposure.

Despite growing regulatory efforts to enhance transparency and accountability, the world's richest individuals continue to leverage these advanced strategies, adapting their financial defenses to an ever-changing legal landscape. As a result, true financial security remains an exclusive privilege of the ultra-rich, leaving the average individual with far fewer means to protect their wealth.

The Dark Side of Private Banking

The Scandals of Private Banking: A History of Corruption

Private banking has long been associated with prestige, exclusivity, and financial sophistication. However, beneath this polished surface lies a history riddled with scandals, financial crimes, and ethical violations. Some of the world's most prominent financial institutions have been implicated in money laundering, tax evasion, and fraud, revealing the darker aspects of this secretive industry. The unchecked power and secrecy of private banking have allowed the ultra-rich, corporations, and even criminal networks to manipulate the global financial system for their benefit, often at the expense of ordinary citizens.

Swiss Banking Leaks & Secrecy Controversies

Switzerland has historically been the epitome of banking secrecy, attracting wealth from across the globe due to its strong privacy laws. However, numerous leaks and investigations have shattered the illusion of absolute confidentiality, exposing how private banks have facilitated illicit financial activities.

- **HSBC Swiss Leaks (2015):** A massive data leak from HSBC's Swiss subsidiary revealed that the bank had assisted clients in evading taxes and hiding wealth offshore. The leak implicated politicians, celebrities, and business magnates who had secretly stashed billions beyond the reach of tax authorities. The scandal triggered international investigations, yet many of those exposed faced little to no legal consequences.

- **Credit Suisse Scandals:** Over the years, Credit Suisse has been embroiled in multiple financial scandals, including aiding tax evasion and handling money linked to criminal enterprises. In 2022, leaked account data from the bank exposed links to corrupt officials, drug lords, and human rights violators. The revelations reinforced the perception that private banks prioritize their wealthiest clients over ethical considerations.

- **UBS Tax Evasion Case:** UBS, another major Swiss bank, was forced to pay multibillion-dollar settlements after being caught helping American clients evade taxes. The scandal exposed how Swiss banks actively marketed secret accounts to wealthy individuals seeking to avoid taxation. Despite penalties, UBS and other banks continue to find ways to protect their clients from tax scrutiny through increasingly complex legal structures.

Private Banks & Money Laundering: The Unseen Criminal Network

Private banking has repeatedly been linked to money laundering, where illicit funds are disguised as legitimate assets. Many financial institutions have been caught facilitating transactions for criminals, corrupt politicians, and sanctioned entities. The lack of transparency and accountability in private banking allows vast sums of dirty money to move through the system without detection.

- **Deutsche Bank & Money Laundering Failures:** One of the most notorious cases involved Deutsche Bank, which was fined billions for failing to prevent money laundering. Investigations uncovered that the bank had processed billions of dollars in suspicious transactions, including funds linked to Russian oligarchs and organized crime. Despite regulatory fines, Deutsche Bank has remained a key player in global finance, illustrating how penalties often fail to create meaningful change.

- **Danske Bank Scandal:** The largest money-laundering scandal in history, Danske Bank's Estonian branch funneled over $230 billion in suspicious funds, much of it linked to criminal organizations and corrupt officials. Private banking services played a crucial role in disguising these transactions. The scale of the scandal demonstrated how deeply embedded financial corruption can be within the world's largest banking institutions.

- **HSBC & Drug Cartels:** HSBC was fined nearly $2 billion after it was revealed that the bank had laundered money for drug cartels in Mexico, allowing billions in illicit funds to move through its accounts with little oversight. While the bank paid a record fine, no high-ranking executives were held personally accountable, raising concerns about the effectiveness of financial regulations.

The Lack of Oversight & Accountability in Private Banking

Despite repeated scandals and increased regulatory scrutiny, private banking remains a largely unregulated sector with limited accountability. High-net-worth individuals and corporations continue to exploit legal loopholes, and enforcement actions often result in fines rather than meaningful reforms. The financial industry's influence on lawmakers has made it difficult to pass effective regulations, allowing misconduct to persist.

Weak Regulatory Frameworks

- Private banks operate in jurisdictions with **minimal regulatory oversight**, allowing them to offer secrecy and tax advantages to their clients. Many offshore financial centers, such as the Cayman Islands and Luxembourg, thrive due to their lax enforcement mechanisms.

- Many financial institutions engage in **"willful blindness,"** ignoring suspicious transactions and prioritizing profits over compliance. Compliance departments often lack the power or incentive to challenge high-net-worth clients engaging in unethical or illegal financial behavior.

- International regulatory bodies, such as the Financial Action Task Force (FATF), have struggled to enforce strict global standards due to differing national policies and lobbying from financial institutions. Efforts to impose stronger regulations are often met with fierce resistance from banking industry lobbyists.

Penalties That Barely Deter Wrongdoing

- When banks are caught in financial crimes, the consequences are often limited to **monetary fines**, which are a fraction of their annual profits. These penalties are seen as a cost of doing business rather than a deterrent.

- Rarely do individual bankers face **criminal charges**, allowing financial institutions to continue their questionable practices with minimal risk. Even in cases where wrongdoing is proven, executives often walk away with multimillion-dollar severance packages rather than jail sentences.

- Settlements and non-prosecution agreements allow banks to **avoid admitting guilt**, further weakening deterrence. Governments often fear destabilizing major financial institutions, leading them to impose fines rather than criminally prosecuting those responsible.

Can These Systems Ever Be Regulated?

Private banking's ability to operate in secrecy makes meaningful regulation incredibly difficult. Governments and financial regulators face significant challenges in cracking down on illicit financial activities due to:

- **Jurisdictional Challenges:** Many private banks operate in multiple countries, making it difficult for any single government to enforce regulations. Offshore banking hubs remain a major roadblock to transparency efforts.

- **Powerful Lobbying Efforts:** The financial industry exerts significant influence on policymakers, ensuring that reforms remain limited or ineffective. Banks donate millions to political campaigns, ensuring that financial oversight remains weak.

- **Evolving Financial Strategies:** As regulations tighten, banks and their wealthy clients develop new strategies to maintain secrecy and reduce transparency. Emerging technologies, such as cryptocurrency and decentralized finance, present new opportunities for financial secrecy.

What Regular People Can Learn from Private Banking

While the vast majority of individuals cannot access the elite financial services offered by private banks, there are legal strategies that can be applied to improve financial security and wealth management:

- **Legal Tax Planning:** Utilizing tax-efficient investments, retirement accounts, and legal deductions can help optimize taxation.

- **Investment Diversification:** Wealthy individuals invest in alternative assets like private equity, hedge funds, and real estate. Regular investors can benefit from diversifying their portfolios beyond traditional stocks and bonds.

- **Asset Protection Strategies:** Setting up trusts, estate planning, and insurance-based wealth preservation strategies can provide security against unforeseen financial risks.

Ultimately, while the world of private banking remains shrouded in secrecy and controversy, understanding its mechanisms can empower individuals to make better financial decisions and advocate for a fairer financial system. The influence of private banks on global finance is unlikely to wane, but increased awareness and policy reforms could lead to a more transparent and accountable financial landscape.

Chapter 5: The Debt Trick – Why the Rich Never Sell Their Assets:

How the Wealthy Live Off Their Wealth Without Paying Taxes

The ultra-wealthy have mastered a financial strategy that allows them to enjoy their wealth without selling off their most valuable assets—and without paying the hefty taxes that regular people face on their income. Instead of relying on salaries or liquidating their investments, they leverage a sophisticated yet legal method that keeps their fortunes intact while ensuring continuous financial growth. This method centers on the idea that **assets appreciate over time** and that as long as these assets remain unsold, they avoid capital gains taxes.

Tax Avoidance vs. Tax Evasion: The Legal Loophole

One crucial distinction that allows this system to function is the difference between **tax avoidance** and **tax evasion**. Tax evasion—illegally hiding income from tax authorities—can lead to serious legal consequences. However, tax avoidance—strategically using the tax code to minimize liabilities—is completely legal and widely practiced among the ultra-wealthy. This fine line allows billionaires to structure their financial lives in ways that keep tax burdens low while still being legally compliant.

The Power of Appreciating Assets

The key to the rich staying rich is simple: **never sell assets that increase in value**. Real estate, stocks, businesses, and even fine art tend to appreciate over time. When the value of an asset increases, it provides greater financial leverage without triggering a taxable event. As long as the asset remains unsold, the owner doesn't owe any taxes on its increased worth. The wealthiest individuals capitalize on this by using their assets as collateral for loans—giving them access to vast sums of money without technically realizing income, which would be taxable.

The "Buy, Borrow, Die" Strategy

One of the most effective wealth-preservation techniques used by billionaires is known as the **Buy, Borrow, Die** strategy. This approach allows them to grow their wealth indefinitely while avoiding taxes at every stage of the process. Here's how it works:

Step 1: Buy – Acquiring Appreciating Assets

The first step is to **purchase assets that will increase in value over time**. The ultra-wealthy strategically invest in:

- **Real estate**: High-value properties in desirable locations that appreciate and generate rental income.
- **Stocks & Equities**: Blue-chip stocks, private equity, and other high-growth investments.
- **Businesses**: Private companies, intellectual property, and other ventures that produce long-term gains.
- **Art & Collectibles**: Rare paintings, luxury watches, vintage cars, fine jewelry, rare wines, and other alternative assets that appreciate over time.

These assets serve a dual purpose: they **increase in value over time** and act as collateral for future borrowing. The key is not just acquiring any assets, but those with strong appreciation potential. Ultra-wealthy individuals often work with financial advisors, investment firms, and tax strategists to carefully curate a portfolio that minimizes risk while maximizing long-term gains.

Additionally, many of these assets provide **passive income streams**, further increasing their financial leverage. For example:

- **Real estate** investments often yield rental income while their market value appreciates.

- **Dividend-paying stocks** provide ongoing cash flow without requiring the sale of shares.

- **Intellectual property** such as patents, trademarks, and copyrights generate continuous revenue.

- **Collectibles and luxury goods** can be loaned out to museums, galleries, or exhibitions, bringing in additional earnings.

The combination of appreciation and income generation ensures that these assets continue compounding wealth while remaining untaxed until sold—which, in many cases, never happens.

Step 2: Borrow – Accessing Wealth Without Paying Taxes

Instead of selling these valuable assets (which would trigger capital gains taxes), the wealthy **borrow against their holdings**. Since **loans are not considered taxable income**, billionaires can fund their lavish lifestyles by:

- Taking out low-interest loans against their stock portfolios or real estate.

- Using their businesses as leverage to access cash while maintaining control.

- Pledging valuable art or other collectibles as collateral for financing.

Banks and private lenders offer special loan products tailored to the ultra-wealthy, allowing them to borrow vast sums of money at extremely low interest rates. These loans are then used to buy more assets, perpetuating the cycle of wealth accumulation.

Additionally, borrowing against assets instead of selling them allows billionaires to **maintain ownership and control** over their wealth while sidestepping capital gains taxes. Unlike the average person, who might take out loans for consumption (such as mortgages or car loans), the wealthy use borrowed money to further increase their assets and net worth. This continuous cycle of borrowing and reinvesting ensures that their financial power expands with minimal tax exposure.

Another advantage is that these loans often come with **flexible repayment terms**, and in some cases, the interest on the borrowed money is even deductible from taxable income, further reducing tax liabilities. Some billionaires even structure their finances so that their businesses or investments cover the loan interest payments, making it an almost cost-free strategy.

Step 3: Die – Passing on Wealth Tax-Free

The final step in this strategy ensures that wealth remains within the family **without triggering major tax consequences**. Upon death, the wealthy pass on their assets to their heirs using legal loopholes such as:

- **Step-up in basis**: When an heir inherits assets, their tax basis is reset to the asset's current market value, **eliminating capital gains taxes on past appreciation**.

- **Trusts & Estate Planning**: Special trust structures shield wealth from estate taxes and legal claims.

- **Life Insurance Strategies**: Large life insurance policies provide tax-free inheritances while covering potential estate tax liabilities.

By structuring their wealth in this way, billionaires ensure that their fortunes transfer to the next generation **without ever being significantly taxed**.

Moreover, estate planning techniques allow them to control how their wealth is distributed, often placing assets into **dynasty trusts** that last for generations, further shielding their fortune from taxation and external claims. Many billionaires also establish **philanthropic foundations**, which not only secure their legacy but also provide additional tax benefits by reducing taxable estate values.

This strategy ensures that their family wealth remains intact, allowing successive generations to benefit from compounding financial advantages. Through careful legal structuring, billionaires essentially create **a self-sustaining financial empire** that remains largely untouched by taxation.

Real-Life Examples of the "Buy, Borrow, Die" Strategy

Several high-profile billionaires and financial elites have successfully used this method to maintain and grow their fortunes:

- **Elon Musk**: Instead of selling Tesla stock, Musk has taken out massive loans against his shares to fund his lifestyle and investments. By leveraging billions in loans, he avoids triggering capital gains taxes while maintaining his equity in Tesla. This strategy allows him to access liquidity without diminishing his ownership stake or incurring tax liabilities.

- **Jeff Bezos**: The Amazon founder has repeatedly borrowed against his stock holdings instead of cashing out and paying taxes on the gains. By taking advantage of low-interest loans, Bezos ensures that his net worth continues to grow while avoiding capital gains taxes that would apply if he sold his shares.

- **Warren Buffett**: Despite being one of the world's richest individuals, Buffett pays very little in personal taxes because he avoids selling assets and instead borrows against them. He reinvests earnings through Berkshire Hathaway while keeping his personal taxable income minimal.

This strategy illustrates how the financial system disproportionately benefits those who already have immense wealth. While regular people rely on taxable income to survive, billionaires use their existing assets to **unlock cash, avoid taxes, and pass on their wealth tax-free**.

The **Buy, Borrow, Die** strategy highlights the vast differences in how wealth is accumulated and maintained between the ultra-rich and the average citizen. While most people earn wages that are heavily taxed, billionaires leverage their assets in ways that minimize tax burdens and maximize financial flexibility. Understanding these techniques provides insights into how wealth is truly built—and why the system is designed to favor those who already have it.

This cycle of wealth accumulation ensures that the financial elite not only remain at the top but also expand their influence, shaping economic policies and financial markets in their favor. The more assets they control, the greater their access to financial tools unavailable to the average person. While tax reforms and regulations have been proposed to curb these advantages, powerful lobbying efforts and political influence have largely maintained the status quo.

For everyday individuals, understanding these strategies can be both frustrating and enlightening. While replicating the exact tactics of billionaires may not be feasible, there are lessons to be learned. Using legal tax planning strategies, making smart investments, and protecting wealth through trusts and estate planning can help individuals optimize their own financial security. The key takeaway is that **owning appreciating assets and strategically leveraging them is one of the most powerful financial tools available—one that the wealthy have mastered to perfection.**

Using Debt as a Tax Shield

For the ultra-wealthy, debt is not a burden—it is a powerful financial tool that allows them to access cash without incurring taxes while keeping their assets intact and continually growing. Unlike regular wage earners, who often see debt as a liability, billionaires strategically use it to fund their lifestyles, expand their financial empires, and minimize tax liabilities—all without selling a single share of stock or piece of real estate. This system enables them to live in luxury while avoiding the high tax rates that ordinary people face on their earned income.

How the Rich Borrow Against Their Investments

Instead of Selling

The average person earns money through wages or salaries, which are heavily taxed. The wealthy, on the other hand, **borrow against their investments**, allowing them to live off their assets without triggering taxable events. This means that instead of liquidating stocks, real estate, or businesses—which would result in capital gains taxes—they use those assets as collateral to secure loans. Because loans are not considered income, they are **not subject to income or capital gains taxes**.

For example:

- A billionaire with $1 billion in stock can take out a **loan for $100 million** secured by their shares.
- This loan provides them with cash for personal or investment purposes.
- Because it is a loan and **not earned income**, they do not pay income tax on it.
- Their assets continue to appreciate in value, making future borrowing even easier.

This allows the wealthy to avoid selling assets, retain ownership, and continue growing their net worth without facing tax consequences. Moreover, they can reinvest the borrowed money into additional appreciating assets, compounding their financial advantages even further.

Loans vs. Taxable Income: Why Borrowing Money Is Better Than Earning Wages

For most people, earning a salary means paying taxes on that income before they can use it. But for the wealthy, borrowing against assets offers a more efficient way to access cash. Here's why borrowing is superior to earning taxable income:

- **Loans are not taxed**: Unlike wages, which are subject to income tax, loans are not considered taxable income.

- **Lower interest rates**: Ultra-wealthy individuals can secure loans at extremely low interest rates, often **below the rate of inflation.**

- **Retained ownership**: By borrowing against stocks, real estate, or businesses, billionaires can keep their assets, which continue to appreciate over time.

- **Tax-deductible interest**: In many cases, the interest paid on loans can be **deducted from taxable income**, further reducing tax liabilities.

Consider this comparison:

- A high-earning executive receives a **$10 million salary** and pays **up to 50% in taxes**, leaving them with **$5 million.**

- A billionaire borrows **$10 million** against their assets, pays **0% in income tax**, and only pays minimal interest (often deductible).

Over time, this strategy ensures that wealth is preserved, tax obligations are minimized, and financial power continues to grow. The ability to control taxable income through borrowing allows the ultra-wealthy to maintain liquidity without sacrificing long-term financial stability.

Leveraging Tax-Deductible Debt to Lower Tax Liabilities

Another advantage of using debt strategically is that **loan interest can often be deducted from taxable income**. This means that even if a billionaire generates income from investments, they can use interest payments on borrowed money to **offset their tax burden**.

For example:

- A billionaire earns $50 million from investments.
- They take out a $100 million loan at a 3% interest rate.
- The **$3 million in interest payments** can be deducted from taxable income, reducing their tax bill.

By continually refinancing and leveraging debt, the ultra-wealthy maintain liquidity while ensuring their taxable income remains as low as possible. This practice allows them to reinvest their borrowed funds into additional wealth-generating opportunities, further amplifying their financial advantage.

The Role of Luxury Purchases: How Billionaires Finance Yachts, Jets, and Mansions Using Borrowed Money

Billionaires don't pay cash for their extravagant lifestyles; they **finance their yachts, jets, and mansions using debt**. By structuring purchases through loans, they can access the luxury they desire without selling their appreciating assets or paying taxes on income.

- **Yachts & Private Jets**: Instead of purchasing outright, billionaires take loans secured by their assets. These loans can be structured in a way that reduces taxable income and provides liquidity. Many private jets are financed through corporate structures, allowing their cost to be written off as a business expense. Billionaires also register their jets in tax-friendly jurisdictions, avoiding hefty local taxes and regulatory costs.

- **Real Estate**: Mansions and luxury properties are often purchased using debt. In some cases, real estate loans are structured with **low or interest-only payments**, allowing the wealthy to maintain liquidity while benefiting from rising property values. For example, a billionaire may take out a mortgage on a $50 million property, making minimal payments while leveraging tax benefits from mortgage interest deductions.

- **Fine Art & Collectibles**: Many billionaires use art and collectibles as collateral for loans, allowing them to free up cash while still holding onto valuable assets that appreciate over time. Fine art financing has become an increasingly popular strategy, with high-net-worth individuals using pieces by famous artists as security for multimillion-dollar loans. These loans allow them to access liquidity without having to sell their valuable collections and incur capital gains taxes.

Additionally, many luxury purchases can be **classified as business expenses**, further reducing taxable income. For instance, a private jet used for business travel can be partially written off as a business expense, making it even more tax-efficient. Some billionaires even register their yachts and jets in tax-friendly jurisdictions to minimize costs and avoid higher taxes in their home countries. **By structuring these purchases correctly, they effectively finance their lifestyles while keeping taxable income low.**

How This Strategy Fuels a Cycle of Infinite Wealth

The use of debt as a tax shield is not just a one-time strategy; it is a perpetual cycle that allows the rich to maintain and expand their wealth indefinitely. Here's how the cycle works:

1. **Acquire appreciating assets** (real estate, stocks, businesses, luxury goods).
2. **Use those assets as collateral to borrow money** at low-interest rates.
3. **Use borrowed money to fund their lifestyles or reinvest** into new wealth-generating opportunities.
4. **Deduct loan interest from taxable income**, further reducing tax obligations.
5. **Allow assets to continue appreciating**, increasing net worth.
6. **Repeat the process**, compounding financial power over generations.

By leveraging this method, the ultra-wealthy ensure that their financial standing remains largely untaxed while their wealth continues to expand. This strategy is one of the most powerful mechanisms that separates the financial elite from the rest of the population.

The Debt Cycle That Keeps the Wealthy Untaxed

By leveraging debt as a financial tool, billionaires can live tax-free, retain ownership of their appreciating assets, and continually expand their wealth. This system allows them to avoid selling taxable investments, reduce their reported income, and legally minimize their tax liabilities.

While most people take on debt as a financial burden, the ultra-wealthy use it as a tax shield, turning borrowed money into a strategy for infinite financial growth. This financial loophole, which is largely inaccessible to the average person, is one of the key reasons why the rich continue to amass wealth while legally paying little to no taxes.

Borrowing Against Assets – Real Estate, Stocks, and Art

For the ultra-wealthy, borrowing against assets is one of the most powerful financial tools available. This strategy enables them to access liquidity without selling valuable holdings, thereby avoiding taxable events while continuing to grow their wealth. Financial institutions cater to these high-net-worth individuals by offering **low-interest, high-value loans**, backed by assets such as real estate, stocks, and art. This system allows the rich to unlock massive amounts of capital while keeping their investment portfolios intact and appreciating in value.

Real Estate: Refinancing Properties for Cash While Maintaining Ownership

Real estate is one of the most commonly leveraged assets among the wealthy. Instead of selling properties and triggering capital gains taxes, the ultra-rich **refinance their real estate holdings** to extract cash while keeping ownership.

- **Refinancing Luxury Properties**: Billionaires and large investors take out loans against their high-value properties, allowing them to tap into the growing equity without selling. This means they can access millions in cash while their real estate continues to appreciate in value.

- **Tax Advantages**: Mortgage interest on these loans is often **tax-deductible**, reducing taxable income and creating additional financial benefits.

- **Scaling Investments**: By continuously refinancing and borrowing against properties, wealthy investors can acquire additional real estate without ever liquidating their existing holdings, thereby compounding their wealth.

- **Example**: A real estate mogul with a $50 million property can take out a **$25 million loan** against it, use that cash for new investments, and continue generating rental or appreciation income from the property. This allows them to scale their investments **without ever selling the original asset.**

This cycle of refinancing, borrowing, and reinvesting enables real estate investors to **continuously expand their holdings**, ensuring they remain highly leveraged while maintaining long-term wealth growth.

Stocks: Using Margin Loans to Access Liquidity

Without Selling Shares

Another common strategy among the wealthy is **borrowing against stock portfolios** rather than selling shares. Selling stocks would trigger capital gains taxes, but using them as collateral for a margin loan avoids that tax hit while providing immediate liquidity.

- **Margin Loans**: High-net-worth investors use margin loans to borrow **up to 50-70% of their stock portfolio's value** at incredibly low interest rates, often below 3%.

- **Low Interest, High Leverage**: Since the stock market historically rises over time, the wealthy can continue to **borrow at low rates** while their portfolios appreciate, effectively making the interest costs negligible compared to the returns they generate.

- **Infinite Growth Potential**: By borrowing against stocks, the wealthy maintain full ownership of their assets while using borrowed funds to reinvest in other lucrative opportunities, compounding their returns over time.

- **Example**: A billionaire with a $500 million stock portfolio can borrow **$250 million at a 2% interest rate**. The loan provides immediate liquidity while the stock portfolio remains intact, growing in value. If the portfolio grows at an average rate of 8% annually, the billionaire is effectively earning more from their investments than they are paying in interest.

Banks and investment firms offer specialized financing products tailored to ultra-high-net-worth individuals, ensuring they can leverage their portfolios while retaining ownership of their assets.

This **creates a cycle of wealth accumulation that is nearly impossible for the average investor to replicate.**

Art & Collectibles: Monetizing Valuable Assets Through Specialized Loans

Art, fine wine, rare watches, and other collectibles are not just luxury items—they are **valuable financial assets** that can be leveraged for loans. Many of the world's wealthiest individuals use their art collections to secure financing, allowing them to maintain ownership while extracting cash for other investments or expenditures.

- **Art-Backed Loans**: Prestigious banks and specialized lenders offer loans secured by valuable art collections. These loans typically allow borrowers to access **50-60% of an artwork's appraised value.**

- **Non-Taxable Liquidity**: Since selling art would result in **high capital gains taxes**, using it as collateral for a loan provides liquidity without triggering a taxable event.

- **Long-Term Investment Strategy**: Many billionaires view art as both a financial investment and a way to hedge against inflation, leveraging their collections for liquidity while benefiting from long-term appreciation.

- **Example**: A billionaire who owns a **$100 million Picasso painting** can borrow **$50 million against it** at a low interest rate. This allows them to **access cash while retaining ownership** of a highly appreciating asset.

- **Trust & Secrecy**: Art-backed loans are often structured through **trusts and private banking services**, allowing for additional layers of financial privacy and protection against legal claims.

This strategy extends beyond artwork. Wealthy individuals also use **collectibles, luxury cars, and even rare jewelry** as collateral for loans, ensuring their capital remains active without selling off prized possessions.

How Lending Institutions Cater to the Ultra-Wealthy with Exclusive Loan Products

The financial industry has created an entire ecosystem of **specialized lending services** to cater to the rich. These loans come with **favorable interest rates, flexible repayment terms, and exclusive benefits**, ensuring the wealthy can access capital at a fraction of the cost that ordinary borrowers face.

- **Private Banking & Ultra-Exclusive Loan Terms**: Private banks offer exclusive lending products with **interest rates as low as 1-3%**, compared to the 6-8% rates that regular borrowers might face.

- **Collateral-Based Lending**: Instead of assessing income, these institutions evaluate an individual's **net worth and assets**, allowing for **larger loan amounts with minimal restrictions.**

- **Revolving Credit Lines**: The wealthy can establish ongoing credit lines secured by their assets, ensuring they always have **immediate access to liquidity**.

- **Secrecy & Asset Protection**: Many of these loans are structured through **trusts, shell corporations, and offshore banking** to protect privacy and shield assets from lawsuits, creditors, or government scrutiny.

How Borrowing Against Assets Fuels Perpetual Wealth Growth

The ability to borrow against real estate, stocks, and art provides the ultra-wealthy with an **endless cycle of liquidity and investment.** Unlike the average person, who must sell assets to access cash and pay taxes on those sales, the rich use their holdings as **perpetual collateral**, keeping their wealth intact and continually growing.

This method ensures that the ultra-wealthy:

1. **Never have to sell their appreciating assets.**
2. **Continue growing their net worth while maintaining liquidity.**
3. **Legally avoid capital gains and income taxes** by structuring loans strategically.
4. **Access luxury and investment opportunities that remain out of reach for regular investors.**

By leveraging their assets as collateral, the wealthy **maximize financial flexibility, reduce tax burdens, and continuously expand their wealth** in ways that most people can never access. This is one of the key reasons why the financial gap between the ultra-rich and the middle class continues to widen—because the rich know how to **borrow to grow**, while most people are forced to **earn and pay taxes.**

How Regular People Can Apply This Strategy

While the strategies used by the ultra-wealthy may seem exclusive, there are practical ways that non-billionaires can apply similar principles to build and protect wealth. By understanding how to leverage assets strategically, the average person can take advantage of some of the same financial benefits that the rich enjoy. However, careful planning and risk management are essential when implementing these methods.

Practical Ways Non-Billionaires Can Use Debt Strategically

1. Home Equity Loans and HELOCs (Home Equity Lines of Credit)

- **What It Is:** Homeowners can borrow against the equity in their homes through home equity loans or HELOCs.

- **Why It Works**: The interest on these loans is often tax-deductible, and the funds can be used for investments, education, or debt consolidation.

- **How It's Used by the Wealthy**: Many high-net-worth individuals use their real estate holdings as leverage to access capital while keeping ownership. They then reinvest this borrowed money into income-generating ventures.

- **Example**: A homeowner with a property valued at **$500,000** and **$200,000** in equity can take out a **$100,000 HELOC** and use the funds for further real estate investments, stock purchases, or business expansion—all without selling the home. This allows the homeowner to continue building wealth while benefiting from property appreciation.

2. Margin Investing: Borrowing Against Stocks

- **What It Is**: Investors can take out margin loans against their stock portfolios to gain liquidity without selling stocks.

- **Why It Works**: The borrowed funds can be reinvested, and because stocks appreciate over time, investors can grow their portfolio while maintaining ownership.

- **How It's Used by the Wealthy**: Billionaires frequently use margin loans to finance personal expenditures and new investments without triggering capital gains taxes.

- **Example**: An investor with a **$50,000 stock portfolio** can borrow **up to $25,000 at a low interest rate**, reinvesting it into more stocks, real estate, or businesses while still benefiting from long-term stock appreciation. If the portfolio grows at **8% annually**, the investor profits while repaying the loan at a much lower interest rate.

3. Business Credit and Leveraging Company Assets

- **What It Is**: Small business owners can borrow against their business assets or establish business credit lines.

- **Why It Works**: Business loans often have lower interest rates than personal loans, and loan interest can be tax-deductible.

- **How It's Used by the Wealthy**: Many wealthy individuals finance their luxury lifestyles through business credit, allowing them to write off expenses as business costs.

- **Example**: A business owner with a **$200,000 business property** can take out a loan against it to expand operations, generating more income without selling the asset. Similarly, they can purchase vehicles, travel, or fund investments through their business credit instead of using personal funds, maximizing tax advantages.

Other Ways to Leverage Debt for Wealth-Building

4. Using Life Insurance as Collateral for Loans

- **What It Is**: Permanent life insurance policies, such as whole life or universal life, accumulate cash value over time, which can be borrowed against.

- **Why It Works**: Borrowing against life insurance allows access to funds without selling other assets or triggering taxable events.

- **Example**: A person with a **$500,000 life insurance policy** with **$100,000 in cash value** can borrow against that amount at a low interest rate to invest in stocks, real estate, or business ventures.

Risks and Considerations: When Borrowing Against Assets Can Backfire

While leveraging debt can be a powerful tool, it comes with risks that must be carefully managed.

- **Over-Leverage Risk**: Borrowing too much against assets can lead to financial trouble if asset values decline. This can result in being forced to sell assets at a loss or facing financial distress when cash flow is insufficient to cover loan payments.

- **Interest Rate Fluctuations**: Some loans, such as margin loans or adjustable-rate HELOCs, come with variable interest rates that can increase over time. A rise in rates can make repayments more expensive and erode potential gains from investments.

- **Market Downturns**: If stocks or real estate values fall, lenders may require additional collateral, leading to potential financial strain. Borrowers may face a margin call, forcing them to sell investments at a loss to cover the debt.

- **Liquidity Risks**: If too many assets are leveraged, a borrower may struggle to cover loan repayments if income sources decline. This is especially risky during economic downturns or job losses.

- **Example of Risk**: A person who takes a **margin loan** on stocks and experiences a market crash could be forced to sell assets at a loss to cover the loan. Similarly, a real estate investor who borrows too aggressively may struggle if property values drop, leading to negative equity. In extreme cases, failing to manage debt properly could lead to foreclosure, bankruptcy, or the loss of valuable assets.

The Loophole That Keeps the Rich Getting Richer

The ability to borrow against appreciating assets without triggering taxable events is a fundamental reason why the wealthy continue to expand their financial advantage. This strategy enables them to access cash, invest further, and minimize tax burdens, all while retaining ownership of valuable assets.

How This System Maintains Wealth Inequality

- The rich have access to **low-interest, high-value loans**, whereas regular people often face higher borrowing costs and fewer opportunities.

- Wealthy individuals can avoid selling assets (which triggers capital gains taxes), while lower-income individuals must often sell assets to access liquidity.

- The financial system favors those with assets, providing them with **exclusive lending opportunities** that are not accessible to the average person.

- Many of the financial products available to the ultra-wealthy—such as non-recourse loans, offshore lending, and tax-exempt borrowing structures—are inaccessible to the middle class, further widening the wealth gap.

The Debate Over Whether Tax Laws Should Change

- Some argue that tax policies should be revised to prevent excessive wealth concentration.
- Others claim that these strategies are simply smart financial planning and should remain legal.
- Proposals such as **higher capital gains taxes, wealth taxes, or closing inheritance loopholes** have been discussed as ways to address this imbalance.
- Governments struggle to regulate these strategies effectively due to the complex legal structures and lobbying influence of financial elites.

Final Takeaways: Learning from the Wealthy's Financial Playbook

While most people cannot replicate billionaire strategies exactly, understanding these principles allows for smarter financial decisions:

- **Invest in appreciating assets**: Real estate, stocks, and businesses are key wealth-building tools.
- **Use debt strategically**: Borrowing against assets can provide liquidity while avoiding unnecessary taxes.
- **Minimize tax liabilities legally**: Utilize tax deductions, home equity loans, and business credit efficiently.

- **Protect financial security**: Use life insurance, trusts, and diversified investments to safeguard wealth against economic downturns.

- **Think long-term**: Wealth-building is not about quick returns but about consistently growing and protecting assets over decades.

By applying these lessons, individuals can build and protect their wealth more effectively, leveraging financial systems that have traditionally benefited only the ultra-rich. The key is to **borrow wisely, invest strategically, and minimize unnecessary tax burdens**—a playbook that, when used correctly, can help close the financial gap between the average person and the ultra-wealthy.

Chapter 6: Real Estate & Shell Companies – The Wealth Shelter

Why Billionaires Park Wealth in Real Estate

For centuries, real estate has been one of the most favored methods for the wealthy to store and grow their wealth. Unlike stocks, bonds, or other financial instruments, real estate provides a tangible, appreciating asset that offers multiple advantages beyond just investment returns. From luxury homes to commercial properties and entire islands, billionaires have long recognized that real estate is more than just a place to live or conduct business—it is a powerful financial tool for wealth preservation, tax benefits, and secrecy.

The Appeal of Real Estate as a Stable, Appreciating Asset

One of the biggest reasons billionaires prefer real estate is its ability to appreciate in value over time. Unlike fiat currency, which can be devalued due to inflation, and stocks, which are prone to market volatility, real estate often increases in worth, providing a reliable store of wealth.

- **Inflation Hedge**: Real estate prices tend to rise along with inflation, meaning properties maintain or even increase their purchasing power over time.

- **Tangible Security**: Unlike digital assets or company shares, real estate is a physical asset that cannot simply disappear overnight due to a financial crisis or corporate bankruptcy.

- **Generational Wealth**: Families pass down real estate holdings to future generations, ensuring long-term financial security.

How Property Holdings Provide Both Luxury and Financial Security

Owning prime real estate is a symbol of status and power, but it also serves practical financial purposes:

- **Luxury and Lifestyle**: Billionaires buy multi-million-dollar homes, penthouses, and private islands as both investments and lifestyle upgrades. These assets offer exclusivity and can be leveraged for social influence.

- **Diversification**: Real estate holdings spread wealth across different asset classes, reducing financial risk.

- **Passive Income**: Rental properties, office buildings, and luxury vacation homes generate consistent, high-value revenue streams.

- **Legal and Tax Protections**: Many countries offer favorable tax treatment for real estate investments, including deductions on mortgage interest, depreciation, and the ability to defer capital gains taxes through mechanisms like 1031 exchanges in the U.S.

Case Studies of Billionaires Using Real Estate to Store Wealth

Case Study 1: Donald Trump and the Power of Property Holdings

Former U.S. President and billionaire real estate mogul Donald Trump built his fortune largely through strategic real estate investments. Through his company, The Trump Organization, he amassed a vast portfolio of hotels, office buildings, and luxury residences worldwide. His ability to leverage properties for financing, tax benefits, and branding turned his real estate empire into a financial fortress.

Trump's approach to real estate investment included purchasing properties in prime locations, securing high-profile deals, and utilizing debt strategically to expand his holdings. By leveraging his assets, he was able to secure loans to fund additional acquisitions while minimizing tax liabilities. Furthermore, his branding strategy allowed him to attach the Trump name to numerous developments, increasing their market value without direct ownership of many properties.

Case Study 2: The Rothschild Family's Real Estate Empire

The Rothschild banking dynasty has long been associated with vast wealth, much of which is locked in prime real estate across Europe and North America. Their holdings include historical estates, commercial buildings, and exclusive properties in cities like London, Paris, and New York, providing both financial security and geopolitical influence.

For centuries, the Rothschilds have carefully curated their real estate portfolio, investing in properties that not only appreciate in value but also serve as strategic assets for maintaining global influence. Their estates include centuries-old mansions and modern office buildings, often acquired through complex ownership structures that shield their identities. By utilizing trusts and offshore companies, the Rothschilds ensure their holdings remain discreet while benefiting from favorable tax treatments.

Case Study 3: Russian Oligarchs and Luxury Real Estate

Russian billionaires, often referred to as oligarchs, have used real estate as a way to secure their fortunes outside of Russia. Many have purchased multi-million-dollar mansions in London, New York, and Monaco through offshore companies to protect their wealth from potential government seizures. This practice highlights how real estate is often used as a defense mechanism against political and economic instability.

For instance, figures like Roman Abramovich and Oleg Deripaska have invested heavily in high-end real estate, often using layers of shell companies to obscure ownership. These investments not only provide financial security but also grant access to Western financial systems, residency privileges, and an insurance policy against potential political fallout in their home country. The use of anonymous LLCs and tax havens ensures that these properties remain protected from scrutiny and legal actions.

Case Study 4: Jeff Bezos and Amazon-Fueled Property Expansion

Amazon founder Jeff Bezos has made strategic real estate purchases that complement his business empire. From acquiring massive warehouse spaces to luxury homes in prime locations, Bezos has used real estate as both a personal investment and a business necessity. His real estate holdings are worth billions and provide a diversified asset base that continues to appreciate.

Bezos owns an extensive portfolio that includes high-end homes in Beverly Hills, a massive estate in Washington, D.C., and penthouses in Manhattan. Additionally, Amazon's real estate investments, including fulfillment centers and corporate office spaces, allow Bezos to control critical infrastructure supporting his company's operations. These acquisitions not only enhance Amazon's logistics network but also serve as valuable, income-generating assets that increase in worth over time.

Real Estate as the Ultimate Wealth Shelter

For the ultra-wealthy, real estate is more than just an investment—it is a sophisticated tool for financial security, secrecy, and influence. Whether through luxury properties, commercial developments, or hidden offshore holdings, billionaires have mastered the art of using real estate to preserve and expand their wealth. Understanding these strategies allows individuals at all levels to rethink how they view property investment, potentially applying similar principles to their own financial plans.

Using LLCs and Offshore Firms to Hide Property Ownership

For the ultra-wealthy, real estate is more than just an investment—it is a powerful tool for secrecy, tax efficiency, and asset protection. By utilizing shell companies, limited liability companies (LLCs), and offshore firms, billionaires and corporations can obscure ownership details, shield assets from legal scrutiny, and minimize tax liabilities. These structures create a nearly impenetrable veil of secrecy, making it difficult for governments, creditors, or even the public to determine the true owners of high-value properties.

How Shell Companies and LLCs Obscure Ownership

One of the most effective methods used to hide property ownership is the establishment of LLCs and shell companies. These entities act as legal intermediaries, allowing individuals to own property without their names appearing in public records. Here's how the process works:

- **Layered Ownership Structures:** Wealthy individuals often create a chain of LLCs, each owned by another entity, making it nearly impossible to trace ownership back to the ultimate beneficiary.

- **Anonymous Registrations:** Many jurisdictions allow LLCs to be registered without disclosing the names of their owners, further obscuring the connection between the property and its true owner.

- **Nominee Directors & Shareholders:** Some jurisdictions permit the use of nominee directors and shareholders who appear as the official owners but act on behalf of the true owner, adding another layer of secrecy.

- **Trusts & Foundations:** In some cases, the wealthy place real estate holdings within trusts or private foundations, which are even harder to trace and provide additional legal protection.

The Role of Offshore Jurisdictions in Real Estate Secrecy

Certain countries and territories specialize in offering legal frameworks that protect asset confidentiality. These offshore jurisdictions are popular among the wealthy because they provide legal structures that keep ownership details private while offering favorable tax treatments. Some of the most well-known offshore havens include:

- **British Virgin Islands (BVI):** Known for allowing anonymous corporate ownership, making it difficult to trace real estate transactions.

- **Delaware, USA:** A domestic tax haven, Delaware permits the creation of LLCs without requiring the disclosure of beneficial owners.

- **Switzerland:** Historically famous for banking secrecy, Switzerland also offers trusts and legal structures that help shield property ownership.

- **Cayman Islands & Panama:** These jurisdictions facilitate the creation of offshore firms that own property while offering significant tax benefits and anonymity.

- **Dubai & Singapore:** Emerging as real estate secrecy hubs, these locations provide wealth-friendly regulations and private ownership protections.

By using these offshore jurisdictions, billionaires and corporations can move their wealth into real estate assets while ensuring that their names never appear in property records.

Famous Cases of Hidden Real Estate Empires

Over the years, multiple high-profile cases have exposed how the ultra-wealthy—including celebrities, politicians, and business magnates—use LLCs and offshore firms to amass extensive real estate portfolios in secrecy.

1. **The Russian Oligarchs' Hidden Mansions**
   Investigations have revealed that several Russian billionaires own vast real estate holdings in London, New York, and Monaco through offshore shell companies. The Panama Papers leak in 2016 exposed how these individuals funneled wealth into luxury properties while keeping their identities hidden.
2. **Donald Trump's Real Estate Empire**
   Former U.S. President Donald Trump and his organization have been known to use LLCs to acquire and manage properties across the globe. Many of his high-profile real estate deals were structured through a web of LLCs, making it difficult to determine actual ownership and financial dealings.
3. **Celebrities and Luxury Real Estate**
   Celebrities like Beyoncé and Jay-Z, as well as Kim Kardashian and Kanye West, have been reported to

purchase multimillion-dollar mansions through LLCs. This strategy protects their privacy and shields their properties from potential legal claims.

4. **The 1MDB Scandal & Luxury Properties**
   The 1MDB scandal, one of the biggest financial corruption cases in history, involved Malaysian financier Jho Low, who allegedly laundered billions of dollars through real estate purchases in the U.S. and Europe using shell companies.

These cases highlight how real estate, when paired with anonymous corporate structures, becomes a major vehicle for wealth concealment, money laundering, and tax avoidance.

The use of LLCs and offshore firms to hide property ownership is a widespread practice among the world's wealthiest individuals and corporations. While these strategies are often legal, they raise significant ethical and regulatory concerns. Governments and transparency advocates continue to push for stricter disclosure laws, but the wealthy still have ample tools at their disposal to keep their real estate holdings hidden from public view. Understanding these financial maneuvers is key to exposing the hidden wealth mechanisms that shape the global economy.

Real Estate as a Tool for Money Laundering

Real estate has long been one of the most effective vehicles for money laundering, providing a means for criminals and corrupt individuals to clean illicit funds while gaining valuable assets. Unlike other forms of wealth storage, real estate offers stability, anonymity, and the ability to appreciate in value over time. This makes it an attractive option for money launderers seeking to integrate illicit funds into the legitimate economy. Governments around the world have attempted to combat this practice, but the loopholes in the global real estate market continue to provide ample opportunities for criminals to exploit.

The Process: Buying High-Value Property with Illicit Funds

Money laundering through real estate typically follows a multi-step process to obscure the origins of illicit money and integrate it into the financial system legally. The general steps involved include:

1. **Placement:** The illicit funds are introduced into the real estate market, often through intermediaries like offshore accounts or anonymous shell companies. This allows the criminal to distance themselves from the transaction while still retaining control over the asset.
2. **Layering:** Multiple transactions, including flipping properties, overpaying or underpaying, and using different legal structures, help obscure the origin of the money. Shell companies often buy and sell properties amongst themselves to further complicate tracking.
3. **Integration:** The property can now be sold or rented out, generating seemingly legitimate income and allowing criminals to use the funds without raising suspicion. This step finalizes the laundering process, allowing the money to enter the legal economy completely cleansed of its illicit origins.

Why Real Estate is a Preferred Method for Cleaning Dirty Money

Real estate is a popular choice for money laundering due to several factors:

- **Lack of Transparency:** Many countries allow anonymous property ownership through LLCs and offshore entities, making it difficult for authorities to track ownership. This secrecy protects criminals from detection.

- **High-Value Transactions:** Large sums of money can be laundered in a single transaction, reducing the number of steps needed to clean illicit funds. Unlike cash-based businesses, real estate provides an easy way to legitimize millions of dollars at once.

- **Low Scrutiny:** Compared to the banking sector, real estate transactions often face less scrutiny, especially in jurisdictions with weak anti-money laundering (AML) regulations. Many real estate professionals are not required to report suspicious transactions, making it easier to move dirty money through properties.

- **Market Volatility Protection:** Real estate typically appreciates over time, allowing money launderers to not only clean their money but also grow their wealth. This makes it a dual-purpose asset: both a laundering tool and an investment vehicle.

- **Physical Asset:** Unlike cash or cryptocurrencies, real estate is a tangible asset that provides long-term security. Criminals favor real estate because it cannot be easily seized or devalued like other financial instruments.

Examples of Major Money-Laundering Cases Through Real Estate

1. The 1MDB Scandal

The 1Malaysia Development Berhad (1MDB) scandal stands as one of the most notorious and complex financial fraud cases in history. Orchestrated by Malaysian financier Jho Low, along with complicit government officials and business associates, the scheme allegedly siphoned over $4.5 billion from Malaysia's sovereign wealth fund. To obscure the origins of these stolen funds, Low established an intricate web of offshore accounts and shell companies, channeling illicit wealth into high-end real estate acquisitions across the United States and Europe.

Among his extravagant purchases were luxury penthouses in New York's Time Warner Center, multimillion-dollar estates in Beverly Hills, and even high-profile assets such as a private jet and the superyacht Equanimity. The scandal not only exposed how criminals exploit real estate for money laundering but also unveiled the roles played by major financial institutions, law firms, and real estate professionals in facilitating these transactions—either through willful complicity or lax oversight.

As the scandal unraveled, international investigations revealed systemic corruption, leading to a global effort to recover stolen assets. Authorities in the U.S., Switzerland, and Singapore conducted extensive probes, resulting in the U.S. Department of Justice filing multiple lawsuits to reclaim misappropriated funds. These efforts ultimately led to the seizure of over $1 billion in assets, including luxury properties, fine art, and designer goods linked to the scheme. The 1MDB scandal remains a landmark case, illustrating how high-value real estate transactions can serve as a critical conduit for international money laundering and financial crime.

2. Russian Oligarchs and Luxury Properties

Numerous Russian oligarchs have used real estate to launder money, particularly in major cities like London, New York, and Miami. Investigations have revealed that many of these properties are owned through layers of anonymous shell companies, offshore trusts, and complex legal structures, making it nearly impossible to trace the original source of funds. Many of these assets include luxury penthouses, sprawling mansions, and commercial properties, often acquired at inflated prices to mask illicit transactions.

Financial networks involving secretive banking institutions in jurisdictions like Switzerland, Cyprus, and the British Virgin Islands facilitate these transactions. These institutions provide discreet services that enable oligarchs to transfer vast sums through offshore accounts before investing in real estate, effectively obscuring their financial footprints. Additionally, high-end law firms and real estate brokers have played a role in structuring these purchases to ensure compliance with minimal oversight while maintaining secrecy.

The U.S. Treasury Department and UK authorities have increasingly targeted these hidden real estate empires, implementing beneficial ownership registries and imposing sanctions that freeze assets linked to questionable sources. For example, after Russia's invasion of Ukraine, Western governments sanctioned numerous Russian elites, leading to the seizure of multimillion-dollar properties in London's upscale neighborhoods and Manhattan's luxury real estate market. Some oligarchs attempted to circumvent these restrictions by transferring ownership to family members or restructuring ownership through additional offshore entities.

Sanctions imposed on Russian elites following geopolitical conflicts have further exposed the role of real estate in global money laundering schemes, demonstrating how deeply embedded financial secrecy mechanisms are in the industry. Despite these crackdowns, many of these individuals continue to find new ways to exploit legal loopholes, using real estate as a key vehicle to safeguard their wealth and evade financial scrutiny.

3. The Vancouver Real Estate Boom and Drug Money

In Canada, particularly in Vancouver, authorities have uncovered a vast network of drug cartels laundering money through real estate, leading to what has been dubbed the "Vancouver Model" of money laundering. Criminal organizations would funnel millions of dollars in illicit drug profits into multi-million-dollar homes, leveraging real estate as both a laundering mechanism and a long-term investment vehicle. To further obscure the money trail, many of these transactions were facilitated through anonymous shell companies and nominee buyers who acted as proxies for the actual criminals.

A key component of this laundering scheme involved integrating casino gambling as an intermediary step. Criminals would deposit large amounts of cash into casinos, gamble for a short period, and then cash out in the form of clean casino checks. These funds were then used to purchase high-value properties, allowing illicit money to seamlessly enter the legitimate financial system. This process, often referred to as "trade-based laundering," created a complex web of transactions that made it difficult for authorities to track the true origins of the money.

In response to these revelations, Canadian authorities implemented stricter anti-money laundering (AML) measures, including mandatory disclosure of beneficial ownership for real estate purchases and increased scrutiny on high-value transactions. The federal government also introduced new legislation targeting money-laundering loopholes in the real estate and casino sectors. Despite these efforts, experts argue that loopholes still remain, and criminals continue to find innovative ways to exploit the system.

4. The Panama Papers Revelations

The Panama Papers leak exposed how politicians, business executives, and criminals worldwide used offshore companies to buy luxury real estate, often through intricate financial networks designed to obscure ownership. Many of these transactions were deliberately structured to evade taxes and bypass anti-money laundering regulations, making it nearly impossible to trace the true beneficiaries. The leaked documents provided an unprecedented glimpse into the secretive world of real estate-based money laundering, revealing how high-profile figures—including government officials, corporate executives, and criminal syndicates—channeled illicit wealth into luxury properties.

These financial networks often relied on a combination of shell companies, nominee directors, and offshore trusts based in secrecy-friendly jurisdictions such as the British Virgin Islands, Panama, and Switzerland. The wealth was funneled through a web of accounts, sometimes disguised as legitimate business investments, before being used to purchase high-end real estate in major financial hubs like London, New York, and Dubai.

Among the assets exposed in the leak were multimillion-dollar penthouses in Manhattan, sprawling estates in Beverly Hills, and lavish hotels in Europe, all purchased through layers of anonymous corporate entities. One of the most striking cases involved high-ranking political leaders whose relatives and close associates secretly owned properties worth tens of millions.

In response to the revelations, global investigations were launched, leading to crackdowns on illicit financial flows. Governments worldwide enacted stricter disclosure laws for property ownership and financial institutions, while authorities seized high-value properties linked to illicit transactions. Despite these efforts, critics argue that loopholes remain, allowing the ultra-wealthy and criminals to continue using real estate as a primary vehicle for money laundering.

5. Chinese Capital Flight and Overseas Real Estate

China has strict capital controls limiting how much money individuals can transfer out of the country. However, wealthy Chinese elites have been able to bypass these controls through a sophisticated web of underground banking networks, offshore shell companies, and secretive financial intermediaries. These individuals often funnel large sums of money through Hong Kong-based financial firms, cryptocurrency exchanges, and foreign currency traders, effectively skirting official restrictions.

Once the funds reach offshore accounts in tax havens such as the British Virgin Islands or the Cayman Islands, they are further layered through complex legal structures before being used to purchase high-value properties in major cities like Los Angeles, Sydney, and Toronto. The properties acquired range from luxury penthouses and sprawling estates to commercial real estate investments, often bought outright in cash or through private lending arrangements that avoid traditional banking oversight.

This trend has raised significant concerns about the role of foreign real estate investment in inflating housing prices and laundering money overseas. Investigations by financial watchdogs and real estate regulatory bodies have uncovered cases where multimillion-dollar properties were purchased under the names of family members or anonymous LLCs, effectively hiding the true ownership and source of funds.

Governments in various countries have since responded with stricter foreign buyer taxes, enhanced beneficial ownership registries, and increased scrutiny of high-value real estate transactions. Despite these measures, illicit capital flight from China continues, with new methods constantly emerging to exploit legal loopholes and avoid financial tracking. Global investigations have highlighted the need for stronger international cooperation to combat money laundering in real estate and prevent illicit wealth from distorting housing markets worldwide.

Real estate remains a highly effective method for laundering money due to its stability, anonymity, and high-value nature. While governments and financial watchdogs have attempted to curb these practices through stricter regulations and transparency initiatives, the wealthy and criminals alike continue to exploit loopholes. Real estate money laundering is a global issue that affects not only financial markets but also the affordability of housing for regular citizens. Understanding how these schemes operate is crucial for policymakers and the general public to push for stronger financial oversight and accountability in the global real estate market. Without increased transparency and enforcement, luxury properties will continue to serve as one of the most attractive money-laundering tools available.

Asset Protection Through Real Estate Holdings

Real estate is one of the most powerful tools for asset protection among the wealthy. By utilizing legal structures such as trusts, shell companies, and offshore entities, high-net-worth individuals (HNWIs) can shield their assets from creditors, lawsuits, and government intervention. This strategy ensures that wealth is preserved across generations while maintaining privacy and financial security. Unlike other asset protection methods, real estate provides tangible value, legal advantages, and tax benefits, making it an essential part of wealth management for the elite.

Using Trusts and Legal Structures to Shield Assets

Trusts and legal entities are commonly used to hold real estate assets, providing both legal protection and tax benefits. The most frequently used structures include:

- **Revocable and Irrevocable Trusts**: A revocable trust allows the owner to maintain control over the assets while providing legal separation. An irrevocable trust, on the other hand, places the assets beyond the reach of creditors and legal claims, ensuring that they are preserved for beneficiaries. These trusts can also help in estate planning by reducing inheritance taxes and facilitating the seamless transfer of wealth to heirs.

- **Limited Liability Companies (LLCs)**: Many wealthy individuals purchase real estate through LLCs, which protect personal assets from liability claims and provide a layer of anonymity. An LLC separates the individual from the property, making it difficult for creditors to seize personal wealth. Additionally, multiple LLCs can be used to own different properties, further reducing exposure to risk.

- **Offshore Entities and Foundations**: Jurisdictions such as the Cayman Islands, Panama, and Liechtenstein offer financial structures that allow property ownership without direct personal association, making it difficult for governments or creditors to track and seize assets. Offshore structures also provide tax benefits and reduce reporting obligations in certain cases, further protecting wealth from scrutiny.

- **Family Limited Partnerships (FLPs)**: These allow families to collectively own real estate while limiting exposure to estate taxes and legal claims against individual members. FLPs provide an effective way to transfer wealth while maintaining control over properties and reducing vulnerability to lawsuits.

These structures are not only used for privacy but also provide strategic ways to legally reduce tax burdens, secure wealth transfers, and prevent forced liquidation of properties due to financial disputes. Many financial advisors recommend layering these structures to enhance asset protection, making it nearly impossible for external parties to determine true ownership.

Real Estate as a Financial Safe Haven

Owning real estate in countries with strong property rights and stable legal frameworks is a preferred method for securing wealth. Some key advantages include:

- **Stability in Economic Uncertainty**: During economic downturns, real estate often retains its value better than other asset classes like stocks or bonds. Physical assets provide security that digital or paper-based investments cannot, making real estate a preferred choice during financial crises.

- **Legal Protections Against Expropriation**: Countries such as the United States, Switzerland, and the United Kingdom have strong legal protections for private property, making real estate ownership a secure investment. Unlike cash in banks, which can be frozen or seized, real estate is far more difficult for governments to confiscate.

- **Currency and Inflation Hedging**: Investing in real estate in stable economies protects against currency devaluation and inflation, ensuring that wealth is preserved over time. Real estate values typically appreciate, serving as a long-term hedge against economic fluctuations.

- **Residency and Citizenship Benefits**: Many nations offer residency or citizenship through real estate investment programs, such as Portugal's Golden Visa or the U.S. EB-5 Immigrant Investor Program, allowing investors to secure personal and financial benefits. These programs provide tax advantages, global mobility, and legal protections that further enhance wealth preservation.

- **Diversification of Wealth**: By holding properties in multiple countries, investors mitigate risks associated with political instability, economic crises, or sudden regulatory changes. Diversifying real estate holdings allows for greater financial security and access to international markets.

Challenges for Creditors and Governments in Seizing Protected Real Estate

Governments and creditors face significant challenges when attempting to seize real estate that has been structured through protective legal frameworks. Some key obstacles include:

- **Complex Ownership Structures**: Multiple layers of trusts, LLCs, and offshore accounts make it difficult to identify the true owner of a property. Often, different entities in various jurisdictions are used to mask ownership, making legal action cumbersome.

- **Jurisdictional Limitations**: Assets held in offshore jurisdictions with strong privacy laws are often beyond the reach of foreign court rulings and government orders. Countries such as the British Virgin Islands and Monaco have strict financial privacy laws that shield real estate owners from external claims.

- **Legal Barriers**: Many legal frameworks protect property owners from unjust seizure, requiring extensive litigation and proof of wrongdoing before assets can be accessed. In cases where real estate is held in offshore structures, local courts often have no jurisdiction over the properties.

- **Time-Consuming and Costly Legal Battles**: Creditors and governments must navigate long and expensive legal proceedings, often discouraging attempts to seize protected assets. Many legal experts are adept at using delays, appeals, and jurisdictional disputes to protect real estate holdings.

- **Anonymity and Privacy Measures**: Some jurisdictions do not require public disclosure of beneficial ownership, making it nearly impossible to link properties to their true owners. This ensures that even in high-profile legal cases, the actual asset holders remain hidden from scrutiny.

Emerging Trends in Real Estate Asset Protection

As global regulations tighten, wealthy individuals are exploring new methods to enhance real estate asset protection. Some emerging trends include:

- **Blockchain-Based Real Estate Transactions**: Some investors are leveraging blockchain technology to tokenize property ownership, making it even more challenging for authorities to track assets.

- **Dual Citizenship and Diplomatic Protections**: Wealthy individuals are increasingly acquiring second citizenships in countries with strong asset protection laws, allowing them to benefit from diplomatic protections.

- **Private Lending Structures**: Instead of purchasing real estate outright, some individuals use private lending agreements where the property is technically owned by a lender, further shielding it from legal claims.

- **Strategic Property Leases:** Long-term leasing agreements with related entities can serve as an alternative to direct ownership, making properties harder to seize.

Despite global efforts to increase transparency and crack down on financial secrecy, real estate remains one of the most effective means of asset protection. Understanding these strategies provides insight into how the ultra-wealthy secure their wealth while maintaining financial privacy. The combination of legal structures, international diversification, and strategic investment in stable economies ensures that real estate remains a cornerstone of asset protection for those who can afford it.

The Global Crackdown on Hidden Real Estate Wealth

As governments and regulatory bodies worldwide recognize the role of real estate in financial secrecy, new measures are being implemented to curb hidden wealth. Authorities are targeting anonymous ownership structures, enforcing stricter financial reporting, and imposing penalties on non-compliance. However, the ultra-wealthy continue to adapt, leveraging new methods to maintain their financial privacy while avoiding regulatory scrutiny. These ongoing developments have created a complex landscape in which real estate is both an asset protection tool and a point of contention for policymakers.

New Regulations on Property Ownership Transparency

To address the misuse of real estate for illicit financial activities, many countries have introduced laws that increase transparency in property ownership. Key regulations include:

- **Beneficial Ownership Registries**: Governments in jurisdictions like the United States, United Kingdom, and European Union now require disclosure of the true owners behind shell companies and trusts that hold real estate. These registries aim to prevent money laundering and tax evasion by making ownership information publicly accessible. Many of these registries are connected to broader financial databases, allowing for greater cross-border scrutiny.

- **Know Your Customer (KYC) and Anti-Money Laundering (AML) Compliance**: Real estate agents, lawyers, and financial institutions are now required to conduct due diligence on buyers, ensuring that funds used for property transactions are legitimate. AML regulations mandate verification of buyers' identities and sources of income before transactions can proceed. Failure to comply with these standards results in heavy fines, legal penalties, and, in some cases, business license revocation.

- **Foreign Buyer Restrictions and Taxes**: Countries such as Canada and Australia have imposed foreign ownership taxes and outright bans on certain non-resident property purchases to prevent real estate from being used as a money-laundering vehicle. These measures aim to curb speculative buying and ensure housing affordability for local populations. In addition, some governments have introduced cooling-off periods and additional taxation on properties left unoccupied for extended periods.

- **Automatic Exchange of Financial Information (AEOI)**: Under agreements such as the Common

Reporting Standard (CRS), tax authorities in over 100 countries now exchange financial information, making it harder for individuals to hide wealth through international real estate transactions. The expansion of AEOI frameworks means that individuals attempting to obscure their assets face increasing risk of exposure.

Efforts by Governments to Close Loopholes

While new regulations have increased transparency, the ultra-wealthy have historically found ways to navigate legal loopholes. Governments are now taking additional steps to close these gaps:

- **Tightening Offshore Structures**: Many tax havens that previously allowed anonymous real estate ownership are now facing international pressure to implement stricter disclosure rules. For example, the British Virgin Islands and the Cayman Islands have been forced to enhance transparency in their financial systems. As a result, some real estate investors are shifting assets to jurisdictions with more lenient regulations or investing in alternative asset classes.

- **Enhanced Enforcement Mechanisms**: Law enforcement agencies and financial regulators are increasing their collaboration to track illicit funds. Governments are investing in forensic accounting teams and artificial intelligence-driven systems to detect suspicious real estate transactions. These advanced data analytics tools allow authorities to flag irregular financial activity with greater accuracy and efficiency.

- **Sanctions and Asset Freezes:** In response to geopolitical events, governments have imposed sanctions on oligarchs and political figures suspected of using real estate to shield illicit wealth. The freezing of assets in cities like London and New York has demonstrated the effectiveness of such measures. However, legal battles over ownership rights and diplomatic protections continue to create challenges in enforcing asset seizures.

- **Requiring Disclosure of Legal and Financial Advisors:** To counteract the role of lawyers, accountants, and real estate agents in facilitating financial secrecy, authorities now require professionals to report suspicious transactions under AML laws. These measures increase personal liability for advisors, forcing many to rethink their involvement in high-risk transactions.

- **Digital Tracking and Blockchain Analysis:** Governments are beginning to leverage blockchain forensic tools to track real estate ownership changes in digital asset transactions. With the rise of tokenized property investments, regulatory agencies are developing new ways to monitor and control blockchain-based real estate deals.

How the Ultra-Rich Are Adapting to Stay Ahead of Regulation

Despite the tightening regulatory environment, the ultra-wealthy continue to find innovative ways to protect their assets. Some emerging strategies include:

- **Using Nominee Owners and Complex Legal Structures**: Instead of direct ownership, high-net-worth individuals transfer properties to relatives, business associates, or employee-controlled trusts, creating additional layers of secrecy. This strategy makes it difficult to establish legal ownership ties in court proceedings.

- **Tokenization of Real Estate**: Some investors are turning to blockchain technology to fractionalize property ownership, making it harder to track ownership through traditional legal frameworks. By leveraging decentralized ownership structures, real estate assets can be shielded from prying regulatory eyes.

- **Private Lending and Mortgage Schemes**: Rather than owning real estate outright, some wealthy individuals use private lending structures where property titles remain under lenders' names, reducing the risk of seizure. These arrangements allow individuals to retain control over properties without being the direct legal owners.

- **Dual Citizenship and Diplomatic Immunity**: By acquiring second citizenships in countries with strong financial secrecy laws, the wealthy can protect their real estate holdings from foreign legal action. Diplomatic status can also serve as a shield against property seizures in some jurisdictions.

- **Investing in Legal Battles**: Some ultra-wealthy individuals hire top-tier legal teams to challenge regulatory actions and delay enforcement through prolonged court cases. The complexity and duration of these legal battles often discourage authorities from pursuing asset seizure cases to their full extent.

- **Shifting to Alternative Investment Vehicles**: Instead of holding direct real estate investments, some high-net-worth individuals are increasingly investing in real estate-backed funds, REITs, and private equity structures, which offer similar benefits while reducing the risk of direct ownership exposure.

Can Real Estate Wealth Ever Be Fully Traced?

The global effort to increase transparency in real estate ownership represents a significant shift in financial regulation. However, a balance must be struck between financial privacy and public accountability. While beneficial ownership registries and AML laws improve oversight, enforcement remains challenging due to jurisdictional limitations and the adaptability of the ultra-rich.

For regular investors, these developments highlight important lessons in financial structuring and legal asset protection. While governments are closing loopholes for illicit actors, legitimate strategies remain available for those seeking to lawfully preserve wealth through real estate investments.

Looking ahead, real estate will continue to serve as a wealth protection tool, but increasing regulatory pressure will make it harder to exploit legal blind spots. The future will likely see an ongoing game of cat and mouse between regulators and the wealthy, with financial secrecy evolving in response to new laws and technological advancements. Additionally, governments may begin to introduce more severe penalties for non-disclosure, potentially making real estate ownership a less attractive asset protection strategy for some high-net-worth individuals.

While authorities are making progress, the ability of the ultra-wealthy to adapt remains a key factor in whether real estate wealth can ever be fully traced. As technology advances and regulations tighten, only time will tell how effective these measures will be in curbing financial secrecy within global real estate markets.

Chapter 7: Insider Trading & Market Manipulation – When the Rules Don't Apply to the Rich

Financial markets are often perceived as a level playing field where anyone with capital can participate and profit. However, the reality is far from fair. Wealthy individuals, hedge funds, and corporate insiders frequently exploit loopholes and gray areas in financial regulations to gain an advantage, often with little to no consequences. While ordinary investors face severe penalties for even minor infractions, financial elites continue to manipulate markets in ways that often go unnoticed—or worse, are considered standard practice. This chapter explores how insider trading and market manipulation operate in practice, why they are illegal for ordinary investors but frequently overlooked for the wealthy, and the systemic power imbalances that make true market fairness nearly impossible.

Definition of Insider Trading and Market Manipulation

Insider trading refers to the buying or selling of stocks based on non-public, material information. When corporate executives, government officials, or fund managers use privileged access to make financial decisions before the public is aware, they gain an unfair advantage over everyday investors. While laws exist to prevent such behavior, enforcement is inconsistent, and the consequences for the ultra-rich are often negligible.

Market manipulation, on the other hand, involves artificially influencing stock prices through deceptive or unethical means. This can include spreading false information, coordinating large trades to create the illusion of demand, executing high-frequency trades that distort market behavior, or exploiting technical loopholes to gain a trading edge. Market manipulation can take many forms, such as "pump-and-dump" schemes, where influential figures inflate the value of a stock before selling at a profit, or "spoofing," a tactic used by sophisticated traders to create false demand signals. Such practices undermine investor confidence and further tilt the scales in favor of those with financial power and industry connections.

Why These Practices Are Illegal for Ordinary Investors but Often Overlooked for the Wealthy

While strict laws exist to prosecute insider trading and market manipulation, enforcement disproportionately targets small-scale offenders while allowing the wealthiest market players to operate with relative impunity. The reasons for this include:

- **Legal Gray Areas**: Many high-level financial maneuvers exist in a regulatory gray zone, where laws are either too ambiguous or too leniently enforced to apply to billionaires and hedge funds. What is illegal for a small-time trader is often repackaged as a "strategic investment" when executed by a high-profile investor.

- **Regulatory Capture**: Agencies like the Securities and Exchange Commission (SEC) are often staffed by former Wall Street professionals who may hesitate to aggressively prosecute their peers. In some cases, regulators leave government jobs to take lucrative positions at hedge funds and investment banks, creating conflicts of interest that weaken oversight.

- **Influence Over Policy**: Wealthy individuals and corporations spend millions lobbying for favorable regulations and loopholes that enable them to continue profiting from questionable practices. This influence extends to lawmakers who pass financial regulations that often contain hidden exemptions benefiting major market players.

- **Minimal Consequences**: When financial elites are caught engaging in illegal activities, they often settle for fines that are merely a fraction of their ill-gotten gains, allowing them to continue operating with little disruption. In contrast, smaller investors caught engaging in similar behavior face criminal charges, reputational ruin, and even prison sentences.

- **The Burden of Proof**: Prosecuting insider trading cases requires proving that an individual had material non-public information and acted on it. However, financial elites often hide behind intermediaries and complex networks of communication, making direct evidence hard to obtain. As a result, many high-profile cases collapse due to insufficient proof.

The Power Imbalance in Financial Markets and Regulatory Enforcement

The stock market is often described as a meritocracy, but in practice, it operates as a highly uneven battlefield. Ordinary retail investors rely on public information, react to market changes after they occur, and face strict penalties for even minor infractions. Meanwhile, the ultra-wealthy have access to privileged networks, legal teams that shield them from prosecution, and high-speed trading technology that gives them an edge over the average investor.

Regulatory bodies are often outmatched in their ability to enforce financial laws against well-funded corporate players. High-profile insider trading cases that lead to convictions are the exception rather than the rule, and penalties for white-collar financial crimes rarely include prison time.

The Role of Hedge Funds, Dark Pools, and High-Frequency Trading Hedge funds and institutional investors engage in market activities that resemble insider trading but remain legal due to regulatory loopholes. "Dark pools," private stock exchanges that operate outside of public markets, allow large trades to occur without the transparency required in standard trading environments. This enables institutions to move significant amounts of money without revealing their intentions to the broader market.

High-frequency trading (HFT), used by major financial firms, allows for thousands of trades per second, often leveraging algorithms to detect and exploit microsecond-level price differences. While legal, this practice puts retail investors at a disadvantage since their trades execute much slower, leaving them vulnerable to price fluctuations created by algorithmic trading.

Case Studies of Financial Crimes with Little to No Consequences

There have been several notable cases where high-profile individuals and institutions were caught engaging in market manipulation or insider trading yet faced minimal consequences:

- **The 2008 Financial Crisis**: Leading up to the crisis, major banks and hedge funds engaged in deceptive mortgage securities trading, profiting off the collapse they helped create. Despite clear evidence of wrongdoing, few executives faced legal repercussions.

- **Steven Cohen & SAC Capital**: Billionaire hedge fund manager Steven Cohen ran SAC Capital, which was found guilty of insider trading. The firm paid a $1.8 billion fine, but Cohen himself avoided prison and later rebranded his company as Point72 Asset Management, continuing to operate in the financial sector.

- **Elon Musk and Tesla Tweets**: In 2018, Elon Musk tweeted that he was considering taking Tesla private at $420 per share, causing the stock to spike. The SEC fined him $20 million for market manipulation, but he remained CEO and faced no criminal charges.

- **Congressional Insider Trading**: Members of the U.S. Congress are often privy to market-moving information through legislative proceedings. Despite periodic scandals involving lawmakers trading stocks based on this knowledge, very few have ever been held accountable.

Insider trading and market manipulation remain persistent issues in financial markets, benefiting the wealthy while punishing smaller investors. While governments continue to introduce stricter regulations, enforcement remains uneven, with financial elites often avoiding serious consequences. Until regulatory agencies gain the resources and independence needed to challenge these entrenched advantages, the financial playing field will remain tilted in favor of those with the means to exploit it.

Understanding these mechanisms allows ordinary investors to be more aware of the risks and challenges they face in markets that are not as fair as they seem. Future discussions on financial regulation must address these disparities if true market integrity is ever to be achieved.

How Billionaires Legally and Illegally Influence Stock Markets

The "Legal" Side of Insider Information

Billionaires and powerful investors have access to a level of market influence that ordinary traders can only dream of. While outright insider trading is illegal, the wealthy often operate within a gray area that allows them to legally benefit from privileged information, shaping markets to their advantage in ways that everyday investors cannot.

Private Meetings and Closed-Door Discussions with Regulators and Politicians

The ultra-rich frequently engage in private meetings with government officials, policymakers, and central bank leaders. These discussions, often disguised as "economic advisory" or "industry consultations," provide key insights into upcoming regulatory changes, interest rate shifts, and policy decisions that can significantly impact stock prices. Unlike the general public, these individuals can adjust their investment strategies before the information becomes public knowledge.

For instance, during the 2008 financial crisis, executives from major financial institutions met with U.S. Treasury officials to discuss bailout strategies. While the public remained largely unaware of the imminent government intervention, many insiders were able to reposition their portfolios to benefit from the forthcoming stimulus measures. This practice continues today, as top Wall Street executives maintain close relationships with government decision-makers to stay ahead of economic shifts.

Strategic Lobbying and Policy Influence That Benefits Specific Investments

Wealthy investors and corporate leaders spend billions on lobbying efforts to shape policies that favor their financial interests. Whether it's securing tax breaks, deregulating industries, or influencing trade agreements, these strategic moves can drastically impact market trends.

For example, pharmaceutical giants and biotech hedge funds often lobby the Food and Drug Administration (FDA) to accelerate drug approvals. By obtaining early knowledge of favorable decisions, they can buy or short stocks ahead of the market reaction, effectively capitalizing on insider information while staying within legal boundaries. Similarly, energy companies lobby for favorable environmental regulations that impact their stock valuations, ensuring they can adjust investment strategies before new laws take effect.

The Role of Financial Media in Shaping Stock Movements

Billionaires and hedge fund managers have direct access to financial media outlets, using their influence to shape narratives around certain stocks or sectors. By making strategic appearances on business news networks or publishing bullish or bearish reports, they can drive public sentiment in their desired direction.

Elon Musk's tweets about Tesla, Dogecoin, and Bitcoin serve as prime examples. His statements—often casual or meme-driven—have caused dramatic fluctuations in stock and cryptocurrency prices, benefiting those who act on the information first. Similarly, hedge fund managers may release reports targeting specific companies, short-selling their stocks before driving negative media coverage that pushes prices lower. These tactics blur the line between legal market influence and unethical manipulation.

Illegal Insider Trading: A Double Standard

While many forms of market influence remain in a legal gray zone, outright insider trading—where non-public, material information is used for personal gain—remains illegal. However, enforcement is often inconsistent, and high-profile offenders frequently receive minimal consequences compared to the profits they make.

How Executives, Hedge Funds, and Politicians Use Privileged Information

Corporate executives routinely trade their own company's stock, sometimes in ways that raise ethical concerns. CEOs and board members may conveniently sell shares before negative earnings reports or regulatory actions, avoiding losses that ordinary investors cannot anticipate.

Hedge funds often obtain insider information through "expert networks," where industry specialists provide privileged insights. While some of these networks claim to operate within compliance standards, many have been implicated in high-profile insider trading cases. These networks act as intermediaries, allowing traders to access valuable information while maintaining a degree of separation that provides plausible deniability.

Politicians, too, have been caught using confidential legislative knowledge to trade stocks. Despite public outrage, congressional members have repeatedly avoided significant repercussions for stock trades based on upcoming policy decisions. The STOCK Act, intended to prevent insider trading by lawmakers, has proven difficult to enforce, allowing these practices to persist. Many lawmakers continue to trade stocks in industries directly affected by legislation they oversee, raising serious ethical concerns.

The Minimal Consequences for High-Profile Offenders

When billionaires or hedge fund managers are caught engaging in insider trading, the penalties they face are often minor compared to their overall wealth. Fines may amount to a fraction of their illicit gains, and prison sentences, if given at all, tend to be short.

One of the most notorious cases involved Raj Rajaratnam, the hedge fund billionaire behind Galleon Group. Convicted in 2011 for orchestrating one of the largest insider trading schemes in history, he received an 11-year prison sentence. However, many argue that this was an exception rather than the rule, as other financial elites often evade serious punishment.

Martha Stewart, a household name in business and media, was sentenced to just five months in prison for insider trading related to her sale of ImClone stock in 2001. Despite the conviction, her career rebounded, demonstrating how reputational damage can be short-lived for the wealthy. Other cases, such as those involving corporate executives, often result in settlements where individuals pay a fine without admitting wrongdoing.

Case Studies of Major Insider Trading Scandals

1. **Raj Rajaratnam and Galleon Group** – Rajaratnam orchestrated one

of the most sophisticated insider trading networks in Wall Street history, leveraging a web of corporate insiders, consultants, and fellow traders to obtain confidential financial information. His hedge fund, Galleon Group, profited by hundreds of millions of dollars by trading stocks based on privileged insights into mergers, acquisitions, and earnings reports before they became public knowledge. Rajaratnam's network included executives from major firms like Goldman Sachs and Intel, as well as well-placed insiders in various industries. His 2011 conviction led to an 11-year prison sentence and a $150 million forfeiture, marking one of the largest insider trading cases ever prosecuted. However, his case remains an anomaly, as many hedge funds and institutional traders have since adapted their strategies, making insider trading even more discreet and harder to prosecute. The use of encrypted messaging, offshore entities, and indirect information-sharing methods has allowed similar schemes to persist with fewer legal repercussions.

1. **Martha Stewart and ImClone** – In December 2001, Martha Stewart sold nearly 4,000 shares of ImClone Systems based on a tip from her broker, Peter Bacanovic, who had learned that the company's CEO, Sam Waksal, was attempting to sell his own shares ahead of an impending negative FDA decision. The agency was about to reject ImClone's highly anticipated cancer drug, Erbitux, which would cause the stock to plummet. By selling early, Stewart avoided losses of approximately $45,000.

The scandal erupted in 2002, leading to a high-profile investigation by the SEC and the FBI. Stewart was convicted of conspiracy, obstruction of justice, and making false statements to investigators in 2004. She was sentenced to five months in prison, five months of house arrest, and two years of probation. Despite the conviction,

Stewart's brand rebounded after her release. She leveraged the media attention, returning to television and business ventures, ultimately regaining her status as a successful entrepreneur.

1. **Congressional Stock Trading Scandals** – Numerous U.S. lawmakers have been accused of trading stocks based on non-public legislative information. Despite public outrage, enforcement remains lax, allowing politicians to benefit from privileged knowledge without facing serious legal consequences. Investigations have revealed that members of Congress frequently trade stocks in companies directly impacted by legislation they oversee.

One of the most glaring examples occurred in early 2020, when several U.S. senators, including Richard Burr, Kelly Loeffler, Dianne Feinstein, and Jim Inhofe, sold significant stock holdings following private briefings on the severity of the impending COVID-19 pandemic. These lawmakers offloaded millions in stocks before the market crashed in March 2020, raising suspicions that they used privileged government information for personal financial gain. Although investigations were launched, no charges were filed, reinforcing the perception that lawmakers operate under a different set of rules than the general public.

Another case that sparked controversy involved Nancy Pelosi's husband, Paul Pelosi, whose well-timed stock trades in companies like Nvidia, Tesla, and Alphabet fueled speculation about whether he had access to confidential legislative information. While there is no direct evidence linking Pelosi's trades to insider knowledge, the frequency of profitable trades among lawmakers and their families continues to raise ethical concerns.

These scandals underscore the difficulties in enforcing insider trading laws against politicians. While corporate executives and hedge fund managers occasionally face prosecution, lawmakers enjoy legal loopholes and weak regulatory oversight, allowing them to continue trading with minimal accountability. Public pressure has led to calls for stricter regulations, such as banning lawmakers from owning or trading individual stocks, but meaningful reform has yet to materialize.

1. **The SAC Capital Advisors Scandal** – Billionaire hedge fund manager Steven A. Cohen's firm, SAC Capital Advisors, was one of the most infamous insider trading cases in Wall Street history. The firm was found guilty of insider trading and paid a record $1.8 billion in fines, one of the largest penalties ever imposed for such violations. Between 1999 and 2010, SAC employees engaged in a pattern of illegal trading, using confidential corporate information obtained from insiders to gain an unfair market advantage. The U.S. government charged several SAC employees, leading to multiple convictions and prison sentences. Despite the overwhelming evidence against the firm, Cohen himself avoided criminal charges, as prosecutors were unable to directly link him to the illicit activities. Instead, he settled civil charges with the SEC and was temporarily banned from managing outside investor funds. However, Cohen made a swift comeback, founding a new hedge fund, Point72 Asset Management, and later acquiring the New York Mets baseball team. His return to

the financial elite underscored how wealth and influence often shield high-profile figures from lasting consequences, reinforcing the perception that the ultra-rich operate under different rules than ordinary investors.

These cases highlight the disparity in how insider trading laws are enforced. While the occasional high-profile individual is prosecuted, many wealthy investors and politicians continue to exploit privileged information with minimal risk. The financial system remains structured in a way that allows those with influence and connections to profit, often at the expense of everyday investors.

Hedge Funds, Dark Pools, and High-Frequency Trading

Hedge Funds and Market Control

Hedge funds play a dominant role in financial markets, often wielding immense power to influence stock prices, corporate valuations, and overall market trends. These elite investment firms engage in a variety of tactics, both overt and covert, to maximize their profits and manipulate market dynamics in ways that are often inaccessible to retail investors. Their ability to operate with minimal regulatory oversight and access to vast amounts of capital allows them to dictate market movements with precision.

The Role of Hedge Funds in Shorting, Pumping, and Dumping Stocks

Hedge funds frequently engage in aggressive short-selling tactics to drive down the price of stocks they believe are overvalued. This can involve spreading negative sentiment through financial media or orchestrating coordinated short attacks to profit from a stock's decline. Shorting involves borrowing shares, selling them at the current price, and then buying them back later at a lower price to return to the lender, pocketing the difference as profit. In some cases, hedge funds collaborate with financial journalists or research firms to release damaging reports on a company, influencing investors to sell their shares and drive the price lower.

On the flip side, hedge funds also engage in "pumping and dumping," where they accumulate shares in a company, generate positive publicity, and then sell off their holdings at inflated prices before retail investors catch on. This tactic can be especially effective when hedge funds use social media influence or align with prominent financial influencers to hype up a stock. Once the price reaches an artificial peak, the hedge fund quietly sells off its holdings, leaving retail investors holding the bag when the stock inevitably crashes.

Private Deals, Backroom Agreements, and Friendly Analysts

One of the key advantages hedge funds have over ordinary investors is their ability to secure exclusive private deals. These firms often engage in off-the-record discussions with company executives, investment banks, and even regulators, giving them an edge in making informed decisions. Hedge funds use their deep industry connections to gain insights into potential mergers, earnings reports, or regulatory changes before they become public knowledge.

Additionally, hedge funds cultivate relationships with financial analysts who issue favorable ratings or downgrade stocks in alignment with the hedge fund's positions, influencing broader market sentiment. Analysts at major banks and brokerage firms often provide preferential coverage to companies in which hedge funds hold significant positions, subtly steering market opinion in favor of the fund's strategy.

How Hedge Funds Influence IPOs and Takeovers

Initial Public Offerings (IPOs) and corporate takeovers present lucrative opportunities for hedge funds. Through pre-IPO placements, hedge funds gain access to shares at discounted rates before they are available to the public. These early investments often come with sweetheart deals, such as guaranteed profits regardless of market performance. Hedge funds can also manipulate IPOs by creating artificial demand, pushing stock prices higher on opening day, only to exit their positions before the price stabilizes.

Similarly, hedge funds play a role in mergers and acquisitions, either by facilitating deals behind the scenes or leveraging their holdings to pressure management into favorable decisions. They may accumulate shares in a company targeted for acquisition and use their voting power to sway the outcome in a way that benefits their interests. Their influence ensures that hedge funds are often in control of the most profitable market moves long before retail investors become aware of them.

Dark Pools: The Hidden Stock Market

Dark pools are private exchanges where institutional investors conduct trades away from the public eye. These secretive trading venues allow elite investors to buy and sell massive quantities of stocks without affecting the market price, providing an unfair advantage over retail traders.

What Dark Pools Are and How They Allow Elite Investors to

Trade in Secrecy

Unlike public stock exchanges such as the NYSE or NASDAQ, dark pools operate with minimal disclosure requirements. This means that major investors can execute large transactions without revealing their intentions to the broader market. These hidden transactions enable hedge funds, institutional traders, and ultra-wealthy investors to buy or sell shares in bulk without alerting retail traders, who would otherwise react to significant market moves.

The Impact of Dark Pools on Market Transparency and Retail Investors

Dark pools undermine market transparency by allowing significant trades to occur without public knowledge. As a result, stock prices do not always reflect true market sentiment, leaving retail investors at a disadvantage. These undisclosed transactions also contribute to sudden and unexplained price fluctuations, making it difficult for everyday investors to make informed decisions.

By the time information about large trades becomes public, the market has often already adjusted, meaning ordinary investors miss out on potential gains or fall victim to price manipulation. The advantage dark pools provide to institutional investors ensures that retail traders are constantly one step behind in the market.

How Market-Moving Trades Happen Before the Public Even Knows

One of the biggest criticisms of dark pools is their ability to facilitate market-moving trades before they appear on public exchanges.

Hedge funds and institutional investors use these platforms to quietly accumulate or offload massive positions, influencing stock prices behind the scenes. By the time these trades are reported, retail investors are left reacting to changes they had no way of anticipating. In some cases, market-moving trades executed in dark pools may only be disclosed after a significant price shift has already occurred, making it nearly impossible for retail traders to compete.

High-Frequency Trading (HFT) and the Speed Advantage

High-frequency trading (HFT) firms utilize powerful computer algorithms to execute trades at speeds far beyond human capability. These firms exploit tiny market inefficiencies to generate millions in profits each day, often at the expense of traditional investors.

The Use of Algorithmic Trading to Front-Run Retail Investors

HFT firms deploy sophisticated algorithms that analyze market data and execute trades within fractions of a second. These algorithms detect large incoming trades and strategically place orders ahead of them, a practice known as "front-running." This allows HFT firms to profit from price movements before retail investors even have a chance to react.

How HFT Firms Use Microseconds to Profit from Market Inefficiencies

The advantage of high-frequency traders comes down to speed. By leveraging cutting-edge technology, HFT firms can spot arbitrage opportunities—instances where a stock is priced slightly differently on two exchanges—and exploit these inefficiencies before human traders can respond. Some firms even pay for co-location services, which allow their servers to be physically placed next to exchange servers, reducing trade execution times to microseconds.

The sheer volume of trades executed in microseconds adds up to significant profits over time. With thousands of trades occurring within a single second, even minuscule price discrepancies can result in millions of dollars in gains for HFT firms.

Regulatory Loopholes That Allow HFT to Operate Freely

Despite the controversial nature of HFT, regulatory bodies such as the SEC have struggled to implement effective oversight. Many HFT strategies exist in legal gray areas, where firms exploit loopholes to operate without violating explicit regulations. Additionally, the financial industry's deep ties to policymakers often result in resistance to stricter regulations, ensuring that high-frequency trading continues to thrive with minimal interference.

Hedge funds, dark pools, and high-frequency trading collectively highlight the systemic imbalances in financial markets. While these mechanisms provide immense advantages to the ultra-wealthy and institutional investors, they also pose significant challenges to market fairness and transparency. Understanding these tactics is crucial for retail investors seeking to navigate an increasingly complex financial landscape. As technology and financial instruments evolve, so too do the methods used by elite investors to maintain their dominance over the stock market.

The Loopholes in SEC Regulations That Favor the Wealthy

How Corporate Executives Legally Sell Stock Before Bad News Is Announced

One of the most controversial yet legal practices in financial markets is the ability of corporate executives to sell company stock before negative news becomes public. Executives often have access to material non-public information (MNPI) regarding their company's performance, regulatory issues, or pending litigation. Despite strict insider trading laws, executives exploit legal avenues to offload stock before bad news impacts the share price, ensuring they escape the financial fallout that ordinary investors face.

10b5-1 Trading Plans: A Loophole for Executives

SEC Rule 10b5-1 was designed to allow corporate insiders to establish pre-planned stock sales to avoid accusations of insider trading. However, these plans have become a shield for executives to legally time their sales to avoid losses or even maximize gains.

- **Executives can modify or cancel plans without disclosure:** Some executives create multiple 10b5-1 plans and selectively execute the most favorable one.

- **Suspicious trading patterns:** Studies show that many executives' stock sales under these plans coincide with stock price peaks and precede negative earnings announcements.

- **Minimal oversight:** The SEC rarely enforces strict compliance, and penalties for abuse are minimal.

- **Executives exploit loopholes to front-run earnings reports:** By strategically setting up plans months in advance, executives can still time trades advantageously, even under the guise of automated scheduling.

The Revolving Door Between Wall Street and Regulators

Regulatory agencies, such as the SEC, are meant to enforce financial laws and protect investors. However, the constant movement of personnel between regulatory agencies and Wall Street firms creates conflicts of interest that benefit the wealthy. This revolving door ensures that those making and enforcing regulations are often the same individuals who stand to benefit from regulatory loopholes.

How the Revolving Door Works

- **Regulators take lucrative jobs in finance:** Many SEC officials leave public service for high-paying positions at hedge funds, banks, and investment firms, often joining the very companies they previously regulated.

- **Lax enforcement against financial giants:** Knowing they may one day work for Wall Street firms, regulators may be hesitant to impose harsh penalties or regulations that could damage future job prospects.

- **Policy influence and deregulation:** High-ranking officials who transition into finance bring insider knowledge of regulatory processes and can lobby to weaken rules that constrain market manipulation.

- **Regulatory capture:** When agencies meant to oversee financial institutions are effectively controlled by the very industry they regulate, enforcement becomes symbolic rather than substantive.

Political Donations and Their Influence on Financial Regulations

The financial sector spends billions of dollars lobbying and donating to political campaigns, ensuring that regulations favor wealthy investors and corporations. This financial influence distorts policymaking and ensures that those with the deepest pockets shape the rules of the game.

The Influence of Campaign Contributions

- **Super PACs and dark money:** Hedge funds, banks, and billionaire investors contribute to political action committees (PACs) that support lawmakers who oppose stricter regulations.

- **Legislation shaped by corporate donors:** Financial industry lobbyists draft bills that reduce oversight, delay new regulations, or create exemptions for powerful firms.

- **Weak enforcement mechanisms:** Political influence ensures that regulatory agencies remain underfunded, limiting their ability to investigate and prosecute financial crimes effectively.

- **Financial deregulation disguised as economic growth initiatives:** Lawmakers often justify reducing oversight by claiming it fosters investment and job creation, when in reality, it allows for increased financial exploitation.

Why Penalties for Market Manipulation Are Often Just a "Cost of Doing Business"

Financial institutions and wealthy investors repeatedly engage in market manipulation, insider trading, and other illicit activities, yet the consequences are often negligible compared to their profits. This lack of meaningful punishment enables systemic corruption and allows financial elites to continue gaming the system without fear of significant repercussions.

Fines That Do Not Deter Crime

- **Multibillion-dollar settlements with no admissions of wrongdoing:** Large banks and hedge funds frequently settle SEC charges for fractions of their illicit profits, avoiding trials and preventing further scrutiny.

- **Executives rarely face prison time:** While lower-level employees may take the fall, top executives often avoid prosecution due to legal settlements and lobbying influence.

- **Repeat offenses with no meaningful consequences:** Major financial institutions, such as JPMorgan Chase, Goldman Sachs, and Citadel, have faced multiple fines over the years but continue operating with little change in behavior.

- **Regulatory fines absorbed as operational expenses:** Many firms factor SEC penalties into their budgets, treating them as minor costs rather than deterrents.

- **Deferred prosecution agreements:** Instead of criminal charges, many firms receive leniency through agreements that impose temporary compliance measures rather than strict penalties.

The loopholes in SEC regulations allow the ultra-wealthy to manipulate markets with minimal risk. From executive stock sales to regulatory capture and political influence, these advantages ensure that the rules apply differently to the rich than to everyday investors. Without significant reform, these systemic issues will continue to erode trust in financial markets and deepen economic inequality. Increased transparency, stricter enforcement, and regulatory independence are necessary to level the playing field and restore faith in a financial system that currently prioritizes the elite over ordinary participants.

Examples of Financial Crimes with Little to No Consequences

Elon Musk and Twitter Market Manipulation

Elon Musk, the billionaire CEO of Tesla and SpaceX, has repeatedly demonstrated his ability to influence financial markets through social media. His tweets, often spontaneous and controversial, have moved billions in stock market value, sometimes resulting in allegations of market manipulation.

How Musk's Tweets Move Markets

- In August 2018, Musk tweeted that he was considering taking Tesla private at $420 per share and had "funding secured." This caused Tesla's stock to soar, only for the claim to later be revealed as false. The SEC sued Musk for securities fraud, leading to a settlement where Musk stepped down as Tesla's chairman and paid a $20 million fine—an amount negligible compared to his net worth.

- In 2021, Musk tweeted about Dogecoin, a meme-based cryptocurrency, causing its value to skyrocket by over 800% in just weeks. His promotion of Dogecoin and Bitcoin through tweets significantly impacted cryptocurrency markets, benefiting those who acted early but leaving others with substantial losses when the value eventually crashed.

- Despite multiple SEC warnings and settlements, Musk has continued making market-moving statements with little consequence beyond minor fines. The SEC's enforcement measures have done little to deter him, showcasing how billionaire influencers can manipulate financial markets with impunity.

- Musk's ability to affect market movements extends beyond tweets—his public statements and interviews have also led to significant stock fluctuations in Tesla and other companies where he holds influence.

- Investors and analysts increasingly question whether Musk's market-moving tactics blur the line between free speech and financial misconduct, with little regulatory intervention to hold him accountable.

The 2008 Financial Crisis and the Lack of Accountability

The 2008 financial crisis remains one of the largest economic disasters in modern history, yet very few top executives faced any legal consequences. Major banks engaged in reckless financial practices, including subprime mortgage lending and the creation of toxic financial products, which ultimately led to the collapse of the global economy.

The Role of Major Banks in Market Manipulation and Fraud

- Banks such as Lehman Brothers, Goldman Sachs, and JPMorgan Chase knowingly sold mortgage-backed securities filled with risky loans, misleading investors about their safety.

- Financial institutions engaged in fraudulent rating practices, working with credit rating agencies to assign high ratings to risky investments, which misled investors and pension funds into purchasing doomed financial products.

- When the crisis unfolded, taxpayers bailed out these banks through the $700 billion Troubled Asset Relief Program (TARP), while millions of Americans lost their homes, jobs, and savings.

- Institutions like AIG played a critical role in amplifying the crisis by insuring these risky financial products, leading to a government bailout of $182 billion.

- Large banks have since paid billions in fines related to their misconduct leading up to the crisis, yet no senior executives have served significant prison sentences.

Why Almost No Top Executives Went to Jail

- Despite widespread evidence of financial fraud, almost no high-level executives were prosecuted. Most institutions settled with regulators by paying large fines without admitting wrongdoing.

- The Justice Department and SEC preferred settlements over criminal prosecutions, fearing the impact on the financial system.

- The only major conviction related to the crisis was Kareem Serageldin, a mid-level banker at Credit Suisse, while CEOs and top executives of major firms walked away with millions in bonuses.

- Former executives from firms like Lehman Brothers and Countrywide Financial have since gone on to lucrative careers, highlighting the minimal personal repercussions for those responsible for the financial meltdown.

- The crisis led to reforms like the Dodd-Frank Act, but loopholes and regulatory rollbacks have since weakened many of the measures meant to prevent future abuses.

Steven Cohen and SAC Capital: The Insider Trading Scandal That Barely Touched a Billionaire

Steven Cohen, a legendary hedge fund manager, built SAC Capital Advisors into one of the most profitable and aggressive hedge funds in Wall Street history. However, behind its success was a massive insider trading operation that relied on non-public information to generate billions in illicit profits.

How SAC Capital Gained an Unfair Edge

SAC Capital's trading strategy heavily depended on what prosecutors later called a "culture of corruption." The fund paid analysts and portfolio managers to gather non-public corporate information—sometimes obtained directly from insiders at pharmaceutical, technology, and financial companies. This confidential data allowed SAC Capital to make near-flawless bets in the stock market, profiting from earnings announcements, mergers, and FDA drug approvals before they were made public.

A key example was the case of Mathew Martoma, a portfolio manager at SAC Capital. Martoma obtained inside information about a clinical trial for an Alzheimer's drug being developed by Elan and Wyeth. Knowing in advance that the trial results would be disappointing, SAC Capital sold its $700 million position in the stocks, avoiding massive losses and profiting from the stock's decline. This single illegal trade netted SAC Capital over **$275 million**, making it one of the largest insider trading profits in history.

The Legal Fallout: A Firm Takes the Fall, But Cohen Walks Free

In 2013, SAC Capital pleaded guilty to insider trading charges and agreed to pay a record-breaking **$1.8 billion in fines and penalties**. However, despite the widespread misconduct within his firm, **Steven Cohen himself was never criminally charged**. Instead, Cohen paid a separate **$135 million fine** and was temporarily barred from managing outside money for two years.

While many of SAC Capital's traders, including Martoma, were convicted and sentenced to prison, Cohen simply rebranded. In 2018, he launched a new hedge fund, **Point72 Asset Management**, which now manages billions of dollars with no restrictions.

Why Cohen Escaped Major Consequences

1. **Legal Loopholes & Lack of Direct Evidence** – While insider trading was rampant at SAC Capital, prosecutors failed to find direct evidence that Cohen personally directed or knowingly engaged in the illegal trades. He maintained plausible deniability by delegating stock trades to his portfolio managers.
2. **Financial and Political Influence** – Cohen had an army of top-tier lawyers and a vast network of financial and political connections. His legal team used aggressive defense tactics to ensure that criminal charges never reached him directly.
3. **The "Too Big to Jail" Effect** – Just like the banks involved in the 2008 financial crisis, SAC Capital was so large and systemically important that regulators opted for financial penalties rather than criminal prosecution.

The Takeaway: Insider Trading Penalties Are Just a Cost of Doing Business

The SAC Capital case highlights a fundamental truth about Wall Street: **for the ultra-wealthy, financial crimes often lead to fines rather than prison time**. Even though SAC Capital was shut down, Cohen's fortune remained intact, and he continued to thrive in the financial industry. Today, Point72 Asset Management operates as a leading hedge fund, proving that even billion-dollar insider trading scandals do little to stop the rich from getting richer.

Congressional Insider Trading

While insider trading is illegal for regular investors, members of Congress have been found to trade stocks based on privileged information related to upcoming legislation and government policies.

How Lawmakers Trade Stocks Based on Policies They Vote On

- Congressional members receive classified briefings on economic conditions, regulatory changes, and industry-specific developments before the public.

- Many lawmakers have made suspiciously timed trades, such as selling off stocks before economic downturns or investing in industries set to benefit from upcoming legislation.

- In early 2020, several U.S. senators sold millions in stocks after receiving classified briefings on the impending

COVID-19 pandemic, avoiding major losses before the market crashed.

- Despite public outcry, most lawmakers involved in suspicious stock trades have faced no serious consequences, raising concerns about accountability and ethical standards in government.

- Some members of Congress strategically invest in industries they regulate, benefiting from the very policies they help shape.

The Stock Act and Its Limited Impact

- The Stop Trading on Congressional Knowledge (STOCK) Act, passed in 2012, aimed to curb insider trading among lawmakers by requiring them to disclose stock transactions.

- However, enforcement of the law has been weak, and penalties for violations are minimal.

- Many lawmakers continue to trade stocks actively, raising concerns about conflicts of interest and the lack of accountability.

- Public trust in government transparency has eroded due to repeated examples of politicians benefiting financially from their legislative positions.

- Calls for stronger restrictions, including banning lawmakers from trading individual stocks, have gained traction but face resistance from those who benefit from the status quo.

The financial elite have repeatedly engaged in market manipulation, insider trading, and fraudulent activities with little to no consequences. While ordinary investors face strict penalties for financial misconduct, billionaires, top executives, and politicians often escape with minor fines or settlements.

Can Markets Ever Be Fair, or Are They Permanently Rigged for the Rich?

- The lack of meaningful penalties for financial crimes perpetuates a system where the wealthy can operate with impunity.
- Regulatory agencies like the SEC need stronger enforcement mechanisms to prevent market manipulation.
- Until significant reforms take place, financial markets will continue to favor the wealthy while leaving regular investors at a disadvantage.
- The intersection of finance, politics, and regulation creates a system where those in power set the rules to benefit themselves, with little accountability to the public.

Lessons Retail Investors Can Learn from Hedge Funds and the Ultra-Wealthy

- Stay informed about market trends and regulatory changes to avoid being caught in manipulated markets.
- Diversify investments to mitigate risk from market manipulation.
- Be cautious of hype-driven investments fueled by influential figures.
- Consider passive investing strategies and long-term financial planning instead of chasing short-term gains influenced by market manipulators.

The Future of Regulation and Whether Real Change Is Possible

- Stronger laws, better enforcement, and increased transparency are necessary to restore trust in financial markets.
- Political and public pressure may drive future reforms, but only if systemic financial abuses are continuously exposed and challenged.
- Without significant changes, financial crime among the ultra-wealthy will remain an accepted part of the system rather than an exception.

- Increasing independent oversight and holding financial elites accountable through stricter penalties could begin to level the playing field for all market participants.

PART 3:

THE HIDDEN TOOLS OF CONTROL

Chapter 8: Psychological Warfare – How the Wealthy Influence Public Perception

Financial elites wield immense influence over public perception, using a range of psychological tactics to shape how people think about wealth, markets, and economic policy. From media manipulation to political funding and educational control, these strategies ensure that the masses remain financially uninformed while the wealthy maintain and expand their power. This chapter explores how the ultra-rich control the flow of information and use psychological warfare to maintain their dominance.

By strategically influencing public opinion, the wealthy are able to justify economic inequality, resist regulatory changes, and ensure that financial systems continue to serve their interests. Whether through shaping news coverage, promoting misleading economic theories, or controlling narratives on social media, these tactics reinforce a financial landscape where the rich stay rich while the average person struggles to get ahead.

The Role of Media in Shaping Economic Narratives

How Financial Elites Fund and Control Major Media Outlets

Mainstream media plays a crucial role in controlling economic narratives, and much of it is owned by billionaires or large corporate conglomerates. Wealthy individuals and corporations fund major news networks, financial journals, and digital media platforms, ensuring that economic stories are framed in ways that benefit them.

Media coverage tends to downplay corporate misconduct while amplifying messages that support free markets and deregulation. Through ownership and sponsorship, the rich shape public discourse on financial matters, often promoting policies that protect their interests.

Additionally, media control extends beyond news networks to include think tanks, research institutions, and economic publications. Many of these organizations receive funding from financial elites, producing reports and studies that reinforce their preferred economic policies. By controlling both mainstream and academic narratives, the wealthy ensure that alternative viewpoints—such as wealth redistribution, corporate accountability, or stricter financial regulation—remain marginalized.

The Selective Reporting of Economic Crises and Financial Crimes

Economic downturns and financial crimes are often reported in a way that obscures the role of the wealthy in causing or benefiting from them. During financial crises, media outlets focus on systemic issues like market volatility or government intervention, rather than highlighting how elite investors profited from the collapse. Financial crimes, such as insider trading or tax evasion, are sometimes covered as isolated incidents rather than as part of a broader pattern of exploitation. This selective reporting keeps the public misinformed and prevents widespread backlash against the financial elite.

Furthermore, when financial scandals do make headlines, coverage often centers on a few individuals rather than the larger structures that enable corruption. For example, while certain corporate executives may face public scrutiny, the broader mechanisms that allow financial crimes to persist—such as weak regulatory oversight, legal loopholes, and lobbying efforts—are rarely addressed in depth. This approach creates the illusion that financial misconduct is rare rather than systemic, ensuring that public anger remains unfocused and ineffective.

Media as a Tool for Manufacturing Market Sentiment (Bull vs. Bear Markets)

Stock market trends are heavily influenced by media coverage. Financial networks and publications create narratives that drive investor behavior, often aligning with the interests of hedge funds, investment banks, and billionaire investors. During a bull market, media outlets push stories about economic optimism, encouraging retail investors to pour money into the market—often at the peak of the cycle. Conversely, during bear markets, negative media coverage can trigger panic selling, allowing institutional investors to buy stocks at lower prices. This manipulation of sentiment benefits those with insider knowledge and the capital to take advantage of market swings.

This psychological strategy is especially evident in financial journalism, where exaggerated predictions of market crashes or rallies can shift public perception overnight. Billionaire investors often use media appearances to subtly hint at their market positions, influencing stock prices before making their own trades. By understanding how sentiment is engineered, the financial elite can capitalize on fear, greed, and speculation while everyday investors are left vulnerable to sudden market shifts.

The Rise of Financial Influencers and Controlled Narratives on Social Media

The digital age has given rise to financial influencers who shape public investment strategies, often under the hidden influence of major financial players. Many of these influencers receive undisclosed sponsorships from hedge funds, stock trading platforms, and cryptocurrency firms, subtly promoting specific investments while downplaying risks. Meanwhile, social media algorithms favor content that aligns with mainstream financial interests, suppressing critical perspectives that challenge the existing system. This digital influence keeps retail investors engaged in the markets but often misinformed about the real forces at play.

Social media platforms also serve as a battleground for financial propaganda. Bots and paid accounts flood discussions with pro-market messaging, while dissenting voices face shadow bans or algorithmic suppression. This digital manipulation creates an environment where the average investor believes they are making independent financial decisions, when in reality, they are being guided by carefully curated content. The result is a generation of retail investors who participate in the stock market without truly understanding the structural advantages that the wealthy maintain.

Beyond individual influencers, large investment firms and financial institutions have developed sophisticated digital marketing strategies that subtly promote their interests. Free stock trading apps, for example, often market themselves as empowering retail investors while steering them toward risky trading behaviors that ultimately benefit institutional players. By shaping the financial education landscape online, the ultra-rich ensure that everyday investors remain susceptible to psychological manipulation, speculation, and financial dependency.

Through these media-based psychological tactics, the wealthy maintain their dominance over financial markets and economic discourse. By controlling the information people consume, they shape public perception in a way that justifies existing wealth inequalities and discourages meaningful financial reform. Understanding these tactics is the first step toward financial empowerment—recognizing the forces that influence our economic decisions allows us to question the narratives we are fed and make more informed choices about our financial futures.

How Financial Elites Fund Politicians to Maintain Their Advantage

Super PACs, Lobbying, and Campaign Donations Shaping Financial Policies

Financial elites wield enormous influence over political decision-making through vast financial contributions. Super PACs (Political Action Committees) enable billionaires and corporations to donate unlimited sums of money to political campaigns, ensuring that the policies enacted favor their financial interests. Lobbying further strengthens this influence, with corporate-funded lobbyists working directly with legislators to draft laws that benefit large financial institutions. This direct financial pipeline between Wall Street and Washington ensures that politicians remain accountable to their wealthiest donors rather than the broader electorate.

For instance, during the 2008 financial crisis, major banks that had contributed significantly to political campaigns were granted billions in taxpayer-funded bailouts, while everyday citizens faced foreclosure, unemployment, and financial ruin. Similarly, tax policies overwhelmingly reflect the interests of the wealthy, with capital gains taxes remaining significantly lower than income taxes—providing a disproportionate advantage to high-net-worth individuals who derive most of their wealth from investments rather than wages.

The Revolving Door Between Wall Street and Washington

A deeply entrenched pathway exists between the financial sector and government regulatory agencies, known as the "revolving door." High-ranking officials in the Treasury Department, Federal Reserve, and Securities and Exchange Commission (SEC) often have backgrounds in major investment banks, hedge funds, or private equity firms. This phenomenon allows financial elites to maintain direct influence over the very institutions designed to regulate them, creating conflicts of interest that shape economic policy in favor of the wealthy.

One of the most notorious examples is the revolving door between Goldman Sachs and the U.S. government. Over multiple administrations, former Goldman Sachs executives have occupied key government positions, from Treasury Secretary to presidential economic advisors. This overlap ensures that regulations favor large financial institutions, often at the expense of smaller businesses and consumers. Critics argue that this dynamic leads to policies that prioritize corporate profits while minimizing oversight and accountability, effectively granting major financial institutions a competitive edge over ordinary investors.

How Regulatory Agencies Are Influenced by Corporate Interests

Despite their intended role in regulating financial markets and protecting consumers, agencies such as the SEC and the Commodity Futures Trading Commission (CFTC) frequently fall under the sway of corporate interests. A combination of budget constraints, political pressure, and industry-funded research makes it difficult for these agencies to impose stringent regulations. Regulatory capture—a phenomenon in which regulatory agencies prioritize the interests of the industries they are meant to oversee—further undermines enforcement efforts.

A glaring example of this is the SEC's handling of the 2008 financial crisis. Despite widespread evidence of fraudulent lending practices, deceptive financial instruments, and market manipulation by major banks, penalties were typically limited to fines that represented only a fraction of the profits generated by these unethical practices. Instead of facing criminal charges or significant regulatory action, many financial executives received multimillion-dollar bonuses, reinforcing the perception that the ultra-wealthy operate under a different set of rules.

Furthermore, corporate lobbying and campaign donations have systematically weakened financial regulations. The rollback of crucial provisions of the Dodd-Frank Act—legislation designed to prevent another financial crisis—was largely driven by lobbying efforts from Wall Street firms. The result has been a regulatory environment in which large financial institutions continue to take excessive risks with minimal accountability.

Case Studies of Political Donations Leading to Favorable Policies

1. **The 2008 Financial Bailouts**: Major banks like JPMorgan Chase, Citigroup, and Goldman Sachs collectively contributed millions to political campaigns, ensuring they had strong political allies in Washington. When the financial crisis struck, these institutions, despite their direct role in creating the economic collapse, were rewarded with generous bailout packages amounting to hundreds of billions of dollars in taxpayer money. Meanwhile, smaller

banks, businesses, and homeowners faced foreclosures, job losses, and economic ruin with little to no assistance from the government. The justification for these bailouts was the concept of "too big to fail," suggesting that allowing major financial institutions to collapse would have catastrophic consequences for the global economy. However, critics argue that the decision to prioritize large banks over ordinary citizens showcased the immense influence of Wall Street over policymaking. Additionally, instead of using bailout funds to support economic recovery, many banks allocated significant portions of the money toward executive bonuses and stock buybacks, further enriching top executives while the general public bore the brunt of the financial downturn. This crisis exposed the stark reality that financial elites operate under different rules, where political contributions buy not only access but also preferential treatment in times of economic distress.

2. **Tax Cuts for the Wealthy (2017 Tax Reform)**: The Tax Cuts and Jobs Act, championed by corporate donors and lobbyists, significantly reduced corporate tax rates from 35% to 21%, leading to massive financial gains for corporations and high-net-worth individuals. Political contributions from billionaires and large business interests played a crucial role in ensuring the passage of these tax cuts, despite public opposition and concerns about widening income inequality. The legislation also included loopholes that disproportionately benefited real estate investors and hedge fund managers, allowing them to minimize their tax burdens significantly. While the wealthy reaped the benefits, the long-term impact included a growing national deficit and reduced government funding

for social programs such as healthcare, education, and infrastructure. Supporters of the tax cuts argued that they would stimulate economic growth and job creation, but critics pointed out that much of the corporate tax savings went toward stock buybacks, further enriching executives and shareholders rather than benefiting the broader economy.

3. **Deregulation of Financial Markets**: Hedge funds, private equity firms, and banking giants have historically funneled money into campaigns supporting deregulation. A prime example is the lobbying push to roll back key provisions of the Dodd-Frank Act, which was originally enacted to prevent reckless financial behavior following the 2008 crash. The lobbying efforts were aggressive, with Wall Street firms spending hundreds of millions of dollars to sway legislators through campaign contributions, policy research, and direct meetings with lawmakers. The successful rollback allowed major financial institutions to engage in riskier trading activities with fewer restrictions, increasing the likelihood of future market instability. The changes also benefited high-frequency traders and hedge funds, which capitalized on regulatory gaps to engage in speculative practices that amplified market volatility. Critics argue that the deregulation not only increased systemic risks but also reinforced the notion that financial elites can shape the rules to protect their interests while the broader public remains vulnerable to economic downturns. This case underscores how strategic political donations and persistent lobbying efforts enable financial institutions to dismantle regulations designed to prevent financial crises, ultimately prioritizing profits over long-term economic

stability.

4. **Pharmaceutical and Healthcare Lobbying**: While not exclusive to Wall Street, the pharmaceutical industry's lobbying efforts provide another example of how political donations shape policy. Major drug companies contribute heavily to campaigns, ensuring that legislative efforts to regulate drug prices or expand healthcare access are stifled. For instance, in 2019 alone, the pharmaceutical industry spent over $300 million on lobbying efforts in the United States, targeting key lawmakers to prevent the passage of drug pricing reforms. One of the most notable cases was the prolonged battle over Medicare's ability to negotiate drug prices, a policy strongly opposed by pharmaceutical giants despite overwhelming public support. Additionally, major pharmaceutical firms employ former government officials as lobbyists, leveraging their political connections to influence legislation in their favor. This dynamic mirrors the financial sector's ability to control policy outcomes that safeguard their profits at the expense of the public interest, ensuring that corporate interests take precedence over public health and affordability.

These examples illustrate how financial elites manipulate political systems to protect and expand their wealth, often at the expense of economic fairness and transparency. The ability to legally influence political decisions through vast sums of money remains one of the most powerful tools of control in modern finance, ensuring that the rules governing markets continue to favor those with the most resources.

The Myth of the "Self-Made Billionaire"

How Generational Wealth, Tax Loopholes, and Government Subsidies Help the Ultra-Rich

The narrative of the "self-made billionaire" is one of the most persistent myths in modern society. While stories of rags-to-riches success dominate media portrayals, many billionaires owe their fortunes to generational wealth, tax loopholes, and government support. In reality, financial advantages such as inherited wealth, tax incentives, and state-backed programs provide a significant head start that most ordinary people do not have.

Generational wealth plays a crucial role in wealth accumulation. Many of today's most well-known billionaires were born into wealthy families that provided them with elite education, financial literacy, and direct access to influential networks. Hefty inheritances, trust funds, and family-run businesses ensure that wealth remains concentrated within the same social circles. Additionally, estate planning strategies like tax-exempt trusts and offshore accounts allow wealthy families to preserve their fortunes across generations with minimal taxation.

Government subsidies and tax loopholes further enable the wealthy to amass and protect their wealth. Programs designed to encourage business growth, such as tax credits and low-interest government loans, disproportionately benefit individuals with existing capital. Billionaires also take advantage of sophisticated tax avoidance strategies, including offshore accounts, shell companies, and deductions that significantly lower their effective tax rates. These tactics create an environment where billionaires pay a smaller percentage of their income in taxes than the average middle-class worker.

Beyond direct financial support, policies such as deregulation and tax incentives allow major corporations to reduce labor costs and maximize profits at the expense of workers. Large-scale corporations owned by billionaires benefit from laws that favor stock buybacks, minimizing tax burdens while boosting their net worth. These advantages make it clear that financial success at the billionaire level is rarely a product of individual effort alone.

The Media's Glorification of Billionaire Success Stories While Ignoring Systemic Advantages

The mainstream media often celebrates billionaire success stories, reinforcing the idea that extreme wealth is the result of sheer determination and hard work. Business magazines, news outlets, and social media platforms promote the idea that billionaires are uniquely talented, innovative, and deserving of their fortunes. However, these narratives often omit the structural advantages that facilitated their rise to the top.

For example, media coverage of tech entrepreneurs frequently highlights their ingenuity while ignoring the massive financial backing they received in the early stages of their ventures. Many so-called self-made billionaires attended elite universities, had access to venture capital through family connections, and benefited from government-funded research and development. This creates a misleading impression that success is purely merit-based rather than heavily influenced by pre-existing advantages.

Moreover, billionaire-funded media outlets shape public perception by downplaying discussions of wealth inequality and systemic privilege. Through ownership stakes in major publications, funding of think tanks, and sponsorship of political commentary, financial elites control narratives that sustain the myth of the self-made billionaire. By focusing on inspirational success stories and omitting discussions about inherited wealth, they reinforce the illusion that anyone can achieve billionaire status with enough effort.

Media portrayal of billionaires also serves as a distraction from policies that protect and grow their wealth. Coverage of billionaire philanthropy, for example, often highlights their charitable donations while failing to mention the tax benefits they receive for these actions. Similarly, the focus on extravagant lifestyles and luxury spending further glamorizes extreme wealth while diverting attention from economic policies that allow billionaires to maintain their fortunes.

The Truth Behind Startup Funding, Insider Deals, and Elite Networking

While many billionaires are credited with building their empires from scratch, a closer examination of their journeys reveals significant external support. Startup funding, insider deals, and elite networking play a crucial role in wealth creation, giving financial elites an enormous advantage over the average entrepreneur.

Venture capital is often framed as a level playing field where anyone with a good idea can secure funding. In reality, funding decisions are largely influenced by personal connections and existing wealth. Many of the most successful startups were backed by investors with ties to elite financial institutions, family offices, or politically connected individuals. Founders from wealthy backgrounds have an easier time securing capital, as investors tend to favor those with pre-existing financial security and industry connections.

Insider deals further enable the wealthy to multiply their fortunes. Many billionaires have access to exclusive investment opportunities, such as pre-IPO shares, private equity deals, and government contracts, which are not available to ordinary investors. These arrangements allow financial elites to capitalize on opportunities before they become accessible to the public, ensuring exponential returns on investment.

Elite networking is another crucial factor in billionaire success. High-net-worth individuals attend exclusive gatherings, join influential organizations, and form strategic partnerships that give them direct access to policymakers, regulators, and business leaders. These networks provide inside knowledge on economic trends, regulatory changes, and lucrative investment opportunities, ensuring that financial elites stay ahead of the curve while the general public remains uninformed.

Another overlooked aspect is the role of financial institutions in billionaire wealth creation. Banks and investment firms often offer preferential loan terms, insider stock access, and risk-free investments to individuals with significant wealth. These exclusive opportunities ensure that billionaires continue to profit with minimal financial risk, further widening the gap between them and the average entrepreneur.

Case Study: The Hidden Financial Backing Behind "Self-Made" Billionaires

A closer look at some of the most famous "self-made" billionaires reveals hidden financial backing that contradicts the narrative of individual perseverance. One prominent example is Elon Musk, often portrayed as a self-made entrepreneur who built Tesla, SpaceX, and other ventures through sheer determination and brilliance.

Musk's financial journey, however, began with significant advantages. His father was a wealthy engineer and businessman in South Africa, affording him access to a privileged upbringing and private schooling. Additionally, Musk received early financial support from family members, including a reported six-figure investment from his father to launch his first venture, Zip2.

When Musk transitioned to Tesla and SpaceX, he benefited from extensive government support. Tesla received billions in government subsidies and tax credits, helping the company achieve financial viability. SpaceX secured lucrative government contracts from NASA and the U.S. military, allowing the company to develop its technology without bearing the full cost of research and development. These government-backed opportunities were instrumental in Musk's wealth accumulation but are rarely acknowledged in the self-made narrative surrounding him.

Another example is Jeff Bezos, whose early success with Amazon was facilitated by a $250,000 investment from his parents. This seed capital provided Bezos with a significant cushion to grow his company without facing the financial struggles that most entrepreneurs encounter. Additionally, Amazon has benefited from various tax breaks, regulatory advantages, and government contracts over the years, further solidifying Bezos's status as one of the world's richest individuals.

Other billionaires, such as Mark Zuckerberg and Bill Gates, also had substantial financial and educational advantages. Gates's mother was an executive with IBM, helping to secure key business partnerships for Microsoft, while Zuckerberg attended an elite preparatory school and Harvard University, gaining access to exclusive tech funding networks. These advantages significantly contributed to their ability to scale their businesses, yet they are often omitted from their success stories.

These examples illustrate how the myth of the self-made billionaire distorts public perception of wealth creation. By obscuring the role of generational wealth, government support, and insider opportunities, this narrative reinforces the illusion that extreme financial success is purely a result of personal effort rather than systemic advantages.

Psychological Tactics Used to Keep the Masses Financially Illiterate

The Promotion of Consumerism and Debt Culture

One of the most effective ways financial elites maintain control is by promoting consumerism and a culture of debt. Through targeted advertising, media influence, and societal norms, the masses are encouraged to spend beyond their means, trapping them in cycles of financial dependency. Credit cards, buy-now-pay-later schemes, and personal loans are aggressively marketed as tools for financial freedom, while in reality, they serve to keep individuals tied to financial institutions through high-interest payments and mounting debt obligations.

Consumer culture is reinforced through the portrayal of luxury lifestyles as symbols of success. Social media influencers, Hollywood celebrities, and billionaire-backed brands push the idea that true success is reflected in expensive cars, designer clothing, and extravagant vacations. This illusion of prosperity pressures people into spending rather than saving or investing, ultimately benefiting corporations and financial institutions that profit from consumer debt.

Furthermore, the financial industry thrives on keeping individuals dependent on loans and credit products. Mortgage lending, auto loans, and student debt are structured to extract maximum interest payments over extended periods, ensuring long-term profitability for lenders. As a result, the average person spends much of their life working to pay off debt rather than accumulating wealth.

The Education System's Failure to Teach Financial Literacy

A key reason financial illiteracy persists is the deliberate omission of financial education from traditional schooling. Despite the importance of money management in everyday life, most educational institutions provide little to no instruction on personal finance, investing, or economic systems. Instead, schools focus on outdated curricula that prioritize theoretical knowledge over practical financial skills.

This lack of education leaves individuals vulnerable to financial exploitation. Without a solid understanding of compound interest, inflation, and investment strategies, people are more likely to fall prey to high-interest loans, suboptimal savings accounts, and predatory financial products. In contrast, the wealthy ensure their children receive financial education from an early age, giving them a head start in wealth-building strategies such as real estate investing, tax optimization, and asset protection.

The financial illiteracy gap is further widened by the influence of financial institutions in policy making. Banks, credit card companies, and lenders benefit from a population that remains uninformed about how financial systems work. Efforts to introduce financial literacy programs in schools often face opposition from industries that profit from widespread economic ignorance.

How Complex Financial Systems Keep Average Investors at a Disadvantage

Financial markets, tax codes, and investment strategies are intentionally designed to be complex and difficult for the average person to navigate. By making financial systems opaque, elites maintain control over wealth accumulation while keeping ordinary investors at a disadvantage.

For example, the stock market is often portrayed as a tool for wealth-building, yet it is dominated by institutional investors, hedge funds, and high-frequency trading algorithms that have access to information and technology unavailable to retail investors. These entities use advanced data analytics, automated trading strategies, and exclusive investment opportunities to maximize profits, while the average investor is left to navigate volatile markets with limited resources and knowledge.

Additionally, tax codes are written in ways that favor the wealthy, offering deductions, loopholes, and offshore structures that allow billionaires to minimize their tax burdens. Meanwhile, middle-class workers are subject to payroll taxes, limited deductions, and minimal access to tax-advantaged wealth-building strategies. The complexity of these systems discourages ordinary individuals from fully engaging with financial markets, reinforcing economic inequality.

Behavioral Economics: How People Are Psychologically Manipulated into Bad Financial Decisions

The field of behavioral economics has revealed that people's financial decisions are heavily influenced by psychological biases that can be manipulated by financial institutions and corporations. By exploiting cognitive biases, companies ensure that consumers continue to make financial choices that benefit the wealthy elite.

One such bias is **instant gratification**, where individuals prioritize immediate rewards over long-term benefits. This is why credit cards and payday loans are structured to offer immediate spending power while obscuring the long-term costs of debt. Similarly, gambling-like features in stock trading apps encourage impulsive, high-risk investing rather than disciplined wealth-building.

Another common bias is **loss aversion**, where people fear financial losses more than they value equivalent gains. Financial institutions use this to their advantage by promoting "safe" investment products with low returns, such as savings accounts and bonds, while the wealthy capitalize on higher-risk, high-reward investments like real estate, private equity, and hedge funds.

Additionally, the concept of **financial paralysis** ensures that people remain inactive in their financial decision-making due to the overwhelming complexity of investment options. By making financial planning appear daunting, banks and investment firms position themselves as indispensable advisors, charging fees and commissions for managing money that individuals could handle themselves with proper education.

Through consumerism, financial illiteracy, market complexity, and psychological manipulation, financial elites ensure that the masses remain economically disadvantaged. The average person is encouraged to spend rather than save, remain dependent on credit, and avoid engaging with complex financial strategies that could improve their financial standing. Meanwhile, the wealthy exploit these very systems to their advantage, securing and expanding their economic dominance.

Understanding these tactics is the first step toward breaking free from financial control. By prioritizing financial education, questioning mainstream financial advice, and seeking out wealth-building strategies used by the elite, individuals can begin to shift the balance of economic power in their favor. The challenge lies in overcoming a system designed to keep people uninformed—but with knowledge and strategic action, financial independence is within reach.

Chapter 9: The Debt Trap – How the Financial System Keeps You Struggling

Debt is often presented as a necessary tool for financial progress, a stepping stone to homeownership, education, and business success. However, beneath the surface lies a system intentionally designed to keep people financially trapped. From student loans to credit card debt and mortgages, the mechanisms of borrowing are structured in a way that benefits banks and financial institutions far more than the individuals taking on the debt.

Over the past few decades, personal debt has skyrocketed, leaving millions struggling to stay afloat. Governments and corporations promote the idea that borrowing is a normal and even responsible financial decision, but in reality, debt has become a cornerstone of economic control. The more individuals rely on borrowed money to maintain their standard of living, the more power financial institutions wield over their lives.

This chapter explores how debt functions as a mechanism of control, rather than a tool for economic advancement. It delves into the psychological and economic effects of long-term debt, revealing how the financial system keeps individuals struggling to pay off loans while ensuring a steady stream of profits for banks and lenders.

Understanding the true nature of debt is the first step in breaking free from the financial traps that have been carefully constructed to benefit the wealthy and powerful. By examining the deceptive marketing tactics, unfair lending practices, and systemic inequalities that underpin the debt economy, we can begin to take back control of our financial futures.

How Credit and Debt Are Designed to Keep People Financially Enslaved

Debt has long been positioned as a necessary tool for economic growth, both on an individual and societal level. Governments, banks, and corporations encourage borrowing, branding it as a stepping stone toward prosperity—whether through homeownership, education, or business investment. However, beneath the surface lies a more sinister reality: the modern credit and debt system is strategically designed to keep people financially trapped, ensuring they remain bound to lenders for decades, if not for life. The longer individuals remain in debt, the more profit financial institutions generate, creating a system that thrives on economic dependence rather than empowerment.

The Historical Evolution of Consumer Debt

The origins of consumer debt can be traced back centuries, but its role in modern capitalism has expanded exponentially in recent decades. Prior to the mid-20th century, borrowing was largely reserved for businesses and governments. The idea of consumer credit on a mass scale was introduced with the rise of installment plans in the early 1900s, allowing individuals to purchase goods with structured payments. However, the widespread use of credit cards in the latter half of the century transformed personal debt into a fundamental aspect of everyday life, normalizing borrowing as an essential financial tool.

The expansion of consumer debt was further fueled by aggressive marketing campaigns from financial institutions, convincing people that credit equated to financial security. Banks, eager to profit from interest payments, introduced more accessible lending options, making credit cards, personal loans, and mortgages available to larger segments of the population. The 1950s and 1960s saw the introduction of consumer-friendly lending, where banks encouraged individuals to take on debt under the guise of wealth-building opportunities. This shift led to an increase in household borrowing, further embedding debt into the fabric of economic life.

In the wake of economic downturns and financial crises, governments and banks have often promoted borrowing as a means of economic recovery. The post-World War II era saw the rise of mortgage-backed homeownership, while the 1980s and 1990s ushered in an explosion of credit card availability. More recently, the aftermath of the 2008 financial crisis saw central banks lower interest rates, encouraging individuals to take on even more debt as a means of sustaining consumer spending. The COVID-19 pandemic further accelerated consumer reliance on credit, as many people turned to loans and credit cards to survive economic uncertainty, deepening their financial vulnerability.

Despite the increasing reliance on credit, debt has created significant financial disparities. While financial institutions package loans as stepping stones to a better life, many borrowers find themselves trapped in long-term repayment cycles. The ease of acquiring credit has made overspending more common, while high-interest rates and complex repayment structures ensure that individuals remain in debt for extended periods. With rising living costs, stagnant wages, and increasing inflation, many people find themselves relying on credit for basic necessities rather than wealth-building. This systemic entrapment in debt serves as a powerful tool of control, ensuring a continuous flow of profits for banks and financial corporations while limiting economic mobility for the average person.

Encouraging Excessive Borrowing Through Easy

Credit Access

Financial institutions aggressively market credit as a means of achieving life's milestones, from buying a home to funding higher education. Banks and credit card companies dangle enticing offers, such as zero-interest introductory rates, high spending limits, and rewards programs, luring consumers into debt. However, once individuals are locked into these financial commitments, they often find themselves subjected to fluctuating interest rates, hidden fees, and complex repayment terms that make escaping debt difficult. In many cases, promotional offers expire quickly, leaving borrowers stuck with much higher interest rates than they initially anticipated. Additionally, banks use psychological tactics such as gamified rewards systems and purchase incentives to encourage excessive spending, making it easy to accumulate debt before realizing its long-term financial impact.

Moreover, credit rating systems reinforce the necessity of borrowing. A high credit score, a measure supposedly designed to reflect financial responsibility, is primarily built through taking on and managing debt. This paradox means that those who avoid borrowing altogether may actually be penalized when seeking financing for major purchases. The system is designed to make credit-seeking behavior appear responsible while discouraging financial independence. Lenders prioritize a borrower's credit history over their actual savings or net worth, making it difficult for individuals who have practiced disciplined financial habits to access better loan terms. As a result, individuals are subtly coerced into maintaining a cycle of borrowing and repayment, further entrenching themselves in the system.

Another deceptive practice is the normalization of minimum payments. Many credit card companies set low minimum payment requirements, leading consumers to believe they are making progress in repaying their debt when, in reality, they are primarily covering interest rather than principal. This keeps borrowers in a perpetual loop of repayment, with some individuals paying several times the original loan amount over the years due to compounding interest. Financial institutions also structure payments in a way that prioritizes high-interest debt first, ensuring that customers remain in debt for as long as possible. Additionally, many credit agreements contain clauses that allow lenders to retroactively apply higher interest rates or penalty fees if a borrower misses even a single payment, further exacerbating their financial struggles. Through these tactics, banks and credit companies ensure a steady stream of revenue, reinforcing a financial system that benefits lenders while keeping borrowers financially constrained.

The Illusion of "Good Debt" vs. "Bad Debt"

Society often distinguishes between "good debt"—mortgages, student loans, business loans—and "bad debt," such as credit card balances and payday loans. However, this distinction primarily serves to legitimize borrowing that benefits financial institutions rather than individuals. While mortgages and student loans are touted as investments in the future, they often come with long-term burdens that make wealth accumulation challenging, leaving borrowers in a state of perpetual financial strain.

For example, student loans are promoted as a pathway to higher earning potential, yet many graduates find themselves saddled with debt for decades due to high interest rates and predatory repayment structures. The student loan crisis in many countries, particularly in the United States, has left millions of borrowers struggling with monthly payments that consume a significant portion of their income. The structure of these loans often leads to ballooning debt balances due to capitalized interest and limited relief options. Meanwhile, government-backed lending ensures that universities and banks continue to profit, regardless of whether students can actually afford the debt they take on. Additionally, private lenders exploit the gaps in federal aid by offering high-interest loans with little consumer protection, further trapping students in financial hardship.

Similarly, homeownership is considered a pillar of financial security, yet the 2008 housing crisis demonstrated how banks manipulate mortgage lending to their advantage, leading to mass foreclosures and financial ruin for millions. Adjustable-rate mortgages (ARMs), subprime lending, and predatory refinancing tactics have all contributed to homeowners being trapped in unfavorable loan agreements that put them at risk of financial devastation. Mortgage-backed securities and collateralized debt obligations (CDOs) created artificial demand, pushing banks to lend recklessly and bundle risky loans into complex financial products. When the housing bubble burst, it was everyday homeowners, not the banks, who suffered the most. To this day, lenders continue to push aggressive mortgage terms, often targeting lower-income and minority borrowers with high-interest loans under the guise of accessibility, keeping vulnerable populations in cycles of debt and instability.

The distinction between "good debt" and "bad debt" ultimately masks the systemic exploitation within the financial system. Even so-called beneficial loans can be structured in ways that disproportionately benefit lenders while keeping borrowers financially dependent. The reality is that debt, regardless of its type, is a powerful mechanism for control—one that ensures financial institutions maintain their dominance while individuals struggle to break free from the cycle of repayment.

Debt Dependence and Financial Mobility

Debt is often framed as a tool for financial mobility, but in reality, it frequently has the opposite effect. Instead of enabling individuals to build wealth, debt dependency ensures that a significant portion of their income is directed toward interest payments rather than savings or investments. This creates a financial environment where individuals struggle to accumulate assets, leaving them vulnerable to economic downturns. The obligation to service debt can also prevent people from pursuing entrepreneurial ventures or career changes, as they must prioritize steady paychecks over risk-taking and innovation.

Furthermore, debt disproportionately affects lower-income individuals, exacerbating economic inequality. While the wealthy strategically use borrowing to leverage investments, take advantage of tax breaks, and grow their assets, the average person is often forced into debt merely to cover basic expenses like housing, healthcare, and education. The result is a system in which those who can least afford to be in debt end up paying the highest interest rates, reinforcing a cycle of financial struggle. In contrast, high-net-worth individuals benefit from lower interest rates, better loan terms, and access to capital markets, further widening the wealth gap.

Additionally, predatory lending practices specifically target vulnerable populations. Payday loans, which often come with exorbitant interest rates exceeding 400%, trap low-income borrowers in cycles of debt that are nearly impossible to escape. Many of these loans are structured so that borrowers can only afford to pay the interest, rolling over the principal repeatedly, leading to long-term financial instability. Similarly, subprime auto loans feature excessive financing terms, balloon payments, and hidden fees, ensuring that borrowers ultimately pay far more than the actual value of their vehicles. Credit card companies also employ deceptive tactics, such as retroactive interest hikes and penalty fees, further exploiting consumers who may already be financially strapped.

Beyond traditional lending institutions, newer forms of debt traps have emerged, including buy-now-pay-later schemes and predatory student loan refinancing. These modern financial products are marketed as convenient and flexible but often come with hidden costs that make repayment burdensome in the long run. The rise of digital lending platforms has also introduced algorithmic bias, where automated systems disproportionately approve high-interest loans for low-income borrowers while offering better rates to those with pre-existing financial advantages.

The long-term impact of these financial practices is a society where economic mobility is severely restricted. Rather than serving as a tool for financial progress, debt has become a mechanism of control, ensuring that the lower and middle classes remain reliant on banks and lenders. Without significant policy changes and increased financial literacy, the debt trap will continue to serve as one of the most effective tools for maintaining economic disparity.

The modern debt system is not merely a financial instrument but a mechanism of control designed to keep individuals reliant on banks and lenders. By understanding the historical development of consumer credit, the deceptive marketing tactics of financial institutions, and the hidden costs of borrowing, individuals can make more informed financial choices. Breaking free from the debt trap requires a shift in mindset—one that prioritizes financial independence over the illusion of prosperity through borrowed money.

While personal responsibility plays a role in financial decision-making, the larger issue lies in systemic structures designed to maximize lender profits at the expense of borrowers. A fundamental reevaluation of the financial system, including regulatory reforms and increased financial education, is necessary to create an economy that genuinely empowers individuals rather than keeping them shackled to debt. Awareness is the first step, but action—both on an individual and collective level—is required to challenge the institutions that profit from financial dependence.

Student Loans, Mortgages, and Credit Card Traps

Student Loans:

How skyrocketing tuition costs and predatory lending trap students for decades.

Higher education was once a pathway to economic mobility, but today, it has become a financial burden that follows individuals for much of their lives. Over the last few decades, tuition fees have increased at a rate far exceeding inflation and wage growth, leaving students with no choice but to rely on massive loans to afford college. These loans, marketed as investments in the future, often come with interest rates and repayment terms that heavily favor lenders over borrowers.

Predatory lending practices further exacerbate the problem. Many student loan borrowers sign agreements with high-interest rates, limited refinancing options, and rigid repayment schedules. Upon graduation, many find themselves trapped with six-figure debts while struggling to secure well-paying jobs. Those who fail to complete their degrees are in an even worse situation—left with substantial debt but without the credential necessary to increase their earning potential.

For example, a student who borrows $100,000 at an interest rate of 6% can end up paying nearly double the original amount over a 20-year repayment period. This means that even if they secure a job immediately after graduation, their disposable income is significantly reduced, limiting their ability to invest in assets like homes or retirement funds. Worse, if they face financial hardship or job instability, interest accrues rapidly, creating a scenario where borrowers remain in debt for most of their working lives.

The government's role in perpetuating student loan dependency.

While federal loans are often perceived as more manageable compared to private loans, the government itself plays a significant role in the student debt crisis. The U.S. government holds over $1.7 trillion in student debt, making it one of the largest creditors in the country. Federal student loans come with interest rates that generate billions in revenue, ensuring that student debt remains a highly profitable sector.

Additionally, student loans are one of the few forms of debt that are nearly impossible to discharge through bankruptcy. This legal structure ensures that borrowers remain on the hook for repayment no matter their financial circumstances, making student debt one of the most inescapable financial obligations in modern society.

A prime example is the case of Navient, a major student loan servicer, which has faced multiple lawsuits for misleading borrowers about repayment options and steering them into costly forbearance plans instead of more manageable income-driven repayment programs. Such practices prolong debt repayment, further enriching lenders at the expense of borrowers.

Why student debt relief is controversial despite clear economic benefits.

Advocates for student debt relief argue that it would boost the economy by increasing disposable income and homeownership rates while allowing young professionals to invest in their futures. However, opponents claim that debt forgiveness is unfair to those who have already repaid their loans and could contribute to inflation. The political divisions surrounding student debt relief have resulted in gridlock, leaving millions of borrowers in limbo while interest continues to accumulate on their outstanding balances.

Despite evidence that student loan forgiveness could stimulate economic growth, political opposition remains strong. For instance, in 2022, President Biden's attempt to forgive $10,000–$20,000 in student loans for eligible borrowers faced significant legal challenges and resistance from conservative lawmakers. While relief measures were temporarily implemented, many borrowers found themselves back in repayment after court rulings blocked long-term forgiveness efforts.

Mortgages:

How the 30-year mortgage structure benefits banks more than homeowners.

The 30-year mortgage is the most common home loan in the United States, but it overwhelmingly benefits banks rather than borrowers. While the longer repayment term keeps monthly payments lower, it also means that homeowners end up paying two to three times the actual price of their home due to accrued interest. Banks and lending institutions profit significantly from this extended repayment period, ensuring that most borrowers remain in debt for decades.

Lenders also manipulate mortgage structures to further benefit their interests. Many banks impose prepayment penalties, which discourage borrowers from paying off their loans early. Additionally, banks often offer lower interest rates on shorter-term loans, but because most people cannot afford the higher monthly payments, they are steered toward the longer 30-year option. Over time, these interest payments can exceed the original loan amount, ensuring that banks make enormous profits while homeowners continue paying.

Furthermore, lenders often design mortgages to make refinancing an attractive but costly option. Borrowers looking to reduce their interest rates or monthly payments may be hit with fees, penalties, and additional closing costs, further reinforcing the financial advantage banks hold over homeowners. Refinancing can also reset the loan term, extending the repayment period and leading to even more interest payments in the long run.

The deceptive nature of adjustable-rate mortgages and housing market crashes.

Adjustable-rate mortgages (ARMs) were a major factor in the 2008 financial crisis. Banks lured borrowers in with low introductory interest rates, only for these rates to increase dramatically after a few years. As a result, many homeowners were suddenly unable to afford their mortgage payments, leading to a wave of foreclosures that ultimately collapsed the housing market. Despite increased regulatory oversight, risky mortgage products still exist, leaving future homeowners vulnerable to similar financial disasters.

Credit Cards:

The psychology behind minimum payments and high-interest rates.

Credit card companies strategically design their repayment structures to keep consumers in debt. The minimum payment system allows borrowers to make small monthly payments, often covering only a fraction of the principal balance, ensuring that they remain indebted for years while accumulating massive interest charges. This structure creates the illusion of affordability while maximizing profits for credit card companies. For instance, if a borrower carries a $5,000 balance with an 18% interest rate and only makes the minimum payment each month, they could end up paying over $10,000 in total by the time the balance is fully paid off.

Credit card companies also exploit psychological tendencies such as loss aversion and optimism bias to keep consumers trapped in debt. Many borrowers believe they will be able to pay off their balance soon, leading them to underestimate the long-term cost of carrying debt. Additionally, marketing tactics such as rewards programs and cashback incentives encourage spending, making it more difficult for consumers to manage their balances effectively.

How hidden fees, penalties, and variable interest rates trap consumers.

Credit cards often come with an array of hidden costs, including late fees, balance transfer fees, annual fees, and penalties for exceeding credit limits. While many cards advertise attractive introductory rates or rewards, they often conceal clauses that allow lenders to hike interest rates drastically after an initial period. Additionally, some credit cards impose penalty interest rates—if a borrower misses just one payment, their interest rate can jump significantly, leading to much higher long-term costs.

Another predatory aspect of credit cards is the structure of balance transfers. Some companies offer 0% interest balance transfers but include fees that can offset any potential savings. If a borrower fails to pay off the transferred balance before the promotional period ends, they can be hit with a much higher interest rate, leading to even greater debt accumulation. A real-world example of this trap is the 2008 financial crisis, where aggressive lending practices, including deceptive credit card agreements, contributed to widespread consumer financial distress.

Moreover, many consumers assume their credit card interest rates are fixed, only to discover that they fluctuate based on market conditions. Variable interest rates mean that a borrower who started with a 14% interest rate could see it rise to 24% or more without warning, making it difficult to manage monthly payments and leading to deeper financial strain. These hidden mechanisms ensure that consumers who rely on credit cards as a financial safety net often end up paying significantly more in the long run.

Student loans, mortgages, and credit cards are marketed as tools for financial growth, but in reality, they serve as mechanisms for wealth extraction by financial institutions. The structure of these financial products is designed to keep borrowers in perpetual debt, limiting economic mobility and reinforcing wealth inequality. Understanding these traps is the first step toward financial independence and breaking free from the cycle of debt dependency.

The Impact of Inflation and Stagnant Wages

Inflation and stagnant wages have long been tools that silently erode the financial well-being of the working and middle class while benefiting financial elites. Understanding the mechanics of inflation and the myth of wage growth is essential to recognizing how the system is structured to keep ordinary people struggling while wealth continues to concentrate at the top.

How Inflation Erodes Purchasing Power and Disproportionately Affects the Working Class

Inflation, the general rise in prices over time, reduces the value of money and weakens the purchasing power of wages. While modest inflation is considered normal in a growing economy, the problem arises when wages fail to keep pace with rising costs. Essentials like housing, healthcare, education, and food become increasingly expensive, making it harder for the average person to maintain their standard of living.

For example, in the last 40 years, housing prices have increased exponentially, yet wages have remained relatively stagnant when adjusted for inflation. This means that while people may technically be earning more in nominal terms, their real purchasing power has significantly declined. In the 1970s, a single-income household could afford a home, healthcare, and education with relative ease. Today, dual-income households still struggle to make ends meet, with many finding it nearly impossible to save for retirement or unexpected expenses.

Lower-income households feel the impact of inflation more acutely because a larger percentage of their income is spent on necessities. When prices rise, they have little to no flexibility to cut back on expenses, forcing many to rely on credit just to afford basic needs—further trapping them in a cycle of debt. For example, when food and gas prices increase, lower-income families must either cut other critical expenses, such as healthcare or childcare, or take on additional debt to maintain their current standard of living.

Additionally, inflation creates a wealth transfer effect. Those with significant assets—such as stocks, real estate, or commodities—often see their investments appreciate in value, offsetting the negative impact of inflation. In contrast, individuals who primarily rely on wages experience a continuous decline in their purchasing power, exacerbating economic inequality.

The Myth of "Wage Growth" and Why It Hasn't Kept Up with Rising Living Costs

One of the biggest misconceptions propagated by policymakers and financial institutions is that wages have been steadily increasing. While there have been nominal wage increases, the reality is that these raises have not kept up with inflation.

In real terms, wages have stagnated for decades, meaning that the average worker today has less purchasing power than workers in previous generations. For instance, while the federal minimum wage has remained at $7.25 per hour in the U.S. since 2009, the cost of rent, healthcare, and education has skyrocketed. A minimum-wage worker today would need to work multiple jobs just to afford a modest apartment in most major cities—something that was not the case just a few decades ago.

Moreover, companies have shifted compensation structures away from direct salary increases to bonuses, stock options, and performance-based incentives—benefits that are often unreliable and do little to improve workers' ability to handle rising costs. These alternative compensation models disproportionately benefit executives and higher-level employees while leaving lower-wage workers vulnerable to economic instability.

Additionally, wage suppression tactics, such as union-busting efforts, outsourcing jobs to lower-cost regions, and reliance on gig and contract work, have further hindered meaningful wage growth. The rise of automation and artificial intelligence also threatens job security, making it even more difficult for workers to demand higher wages or long-term stability.

How Central Banks Manipulate Interest Rates and Inflation to Serve Financial Elites

Central banks, such as the Federal Reserve, play a critical role in controlling inflation and interest rates. However, their policies often prioritize the interests of the financial elite over those of ordinary citizens.

For example, during economic downturns, central banks lower interest rates to encourage borrowing and spending. While this may temporarily stimulate the economy, it also makes it cheaper for corporations and the wealthy to take out massive loans for investments—driving up asset prices like stocks and real estate. This means that those who already own assets become even wealthier, while those who don't are left behind. During the COVID-19 pandemic, for instance, the Federal Reserve's aggressive interest rate cuts fueled a stock market boom, disproportionately benefiting wealthy investors while millions of everyday workers struggled with job losses and financial insecurity.

Conversely, when inflation gets too high, central banks raise interest rates, making borrowing more expensive. This disproportionately harms middle and lower-income individuals, who are more likely to rely on credit for everyday expenses, while the wealthy—who already own assets—benefit from higher returns on their investments. A prime example of this was the 1980s, when the Federal Reserve raised interest rates to combat inflation, leading to widespread layoffs and economic hardship for working-class Americans.

Furthermore, many central banks operate under a dual mandate: to control inflation and to maximize employment. However, in practice, inflation control often takes precedence, leading to policies that suppress wage growth and job security in favor of maintaining low inflation rates that benefit bondholders, banks, and large corporations.

The Cycle of Borrowing Just to Keep Up with the Cost of Living

For millions of people, stagnant wages and rising costs have created an endless cycle of borrowing just to survive. As inflation drives up the prices of necessities, those who don't see wage increases are forced to take on debt to cover basic expenses.

Credit card debt, payday loans, and personal loans have become lifelines for many struggling individuals, yet the interest on these debts quickly compounds, making repayment increasingly difficult. In contrast, wealthy individuals have access to low-interest loans, financial advisors, and tax loopholes that allow them to maintain and grow their wealth without the same financial burdens.

For instance, a family earning a modest income may turn to credit cards to cover an unexpected medical bill. If they can only afford to make the minimum payment, high-interest rates quickly cause their debt to spiral out of control. Meanwhile, a wealthy individual facing a financial setback can secure a low-interest loan against their assets, avoiding exorbitant fees and maintaining their financial stability.

This system ensures that those who already have wealth continue to accumulate more, while those struggling to get by remain stuck in perpetual financial insecurity. Without systemic changes to wage policies, inflation control, and financial regulations, the gap between the rich and the working class will only continue to widen.

Understanding these mechanisms is crucial for individuals seeking to protect themselves from financial exploitation. By demanding wage increases tied to inflation, advocating for fair monetary policies, and learning to navigate financial markets more effectively, people can push back against a system designed to keep them economically disadvantaged.

How Banks Profit Off Your Financial Struggles

Banks and financial institutions thrive on a system that ensures consumers remain in a perpetual state of debt. Instead of empowering individuals to achieve financial independence, the banking industry is structured to maximize profits by encouraging borrowing, imposing high-interest rates, and penalizing those who struggle to repay. The result is a system where financial distress becomes a revenue-generating tool for banks, ensuring that wealth continues to concentrate at the top while everyday people remain financially burdened.

The Business Model of Perpetual Debt: Why Banks Prefer You to Stay in Debt Rather Than Pay It Off

The modern banking system does not benefit from financially secure, debt-free individuals. Instead, its business model is built on keeping consumers locked into cycles of borrowing and repayment, ensuring a continuous stream of revenue through interest and fees.

For example, credit cards offer the illusion of financial flexibility, but banks design them to encourage long-term debt dependency. With minimum payment requirements set deliberately low, many consumers end up paying only a fraction of their total balance each month, allowing interest to accumulate exponentially. A $5,000 credit card balance at an interest rate of 20% can take decades to pay off if only minimum payments are made, with the borrower ultimately paying more in interest than the original balance itself.

Similarly, mortgages and auto loans are structured to generate maximum profit for lenders. A 30-year mortgage, while making homeownership accessible, also ensures that homeowners pay nearly double the original loan amount due to interest accumulation. Refinancing options, late fees, and penalty charges add further layers of profitability for banks while keeping borrowers financially tethered for extended periods. Additionally, balloon payments and adjustable-rate mortgages allow lenders to extract even more money from borrowers by changing the terms in ways that often lead to long-term financial hardship.

Predatory Lending Practices and How They Disproportionately Target the Lower and Middle Classes

Banks and financial institutions deliberately market high-interest loans and risky financial products to those with the least financial stability. Payday loans, subprime mortgages, and high-fee checking accounts are disproportionately offered to lower-income individuals who may lack access to better financial tools.

For example, payday lenders often target financially vulnerable individuals with short-term loans that carry exorbitant interest rates—sometimes exceeding 400% APR. The structure of these loans makes repayment nearly impossible, forcing borrowers to continually roll over their debt, racking up fees that far exceed the original loan amount.

Similarly, subprime mortgages were a significant factor in the 2008 financial crisis. Lenders issued high-risk loans to individuals who could not afford them, often using deceptive practices such as adjustable-rate mortgages (ARMs) that started with low introductory rates before skyrocketing, pushing borrowers into foreclosure. These unethical lending practices devastated millions of families while the banks that caused the crisis were bailed out by taxpayer money.

Additionally, predatory lending disproportionately affects marginalized communities. Studies have shown that racial minorities, low-income families, and individuals with limited financial literacy are often targeted by these exploitative financial products. Banks and lenders use deceptive advertising, misleading terms, and aggressive sales tactics to lure vulnerable individuals into high-cost loans, deepening cycles of poverty and economic inequality.

The Role of Debt Collection Agencies and How They Profit from Financial Distress

When borrowers fall behind on payments, banks sell their debts to third-party debt collection agencies for pennies on the dollar. These agencies then aggressively pursue debtors, using tactics that range from relentless phone calls to legal action. Their goal is to extract as much money as possible from individuals who are already in financial distress.

Debt collection agencies profit immensely from this business model. By purchasing debt at steep discounts—sometimes as low as 5% of the original balance—they can collect only a fraction of the amount owed and still make a significant profit. Additionally, these agencies often tack on additional fees and interest, further increasing the financial burden on the debtor.

In some cases, collectors have been known to use unethical and even illegal tactics, such as harassing calls, threats, and misrepresentation of legal consequences. Because many consumers lack the financial literacy or legal resources to challenge these practices, they often end up paying more than they legally owe. Some debt collectors even resort to "zombie debt" tactics, attempting to collect on old or expired debts that consumers may no longer be legally required to pay. This predatory behavior highlights the extent to which the financial system exploits those already struggling.

How Financial Literacy Gaps Ensure Continued Profits for Lenders

A key factor enabling banks to maintain their grip on consumers is the widespread lack of financial education. Schools rarely teach essential financial skills such as budgeting, managing debt, understanding credit scores, or negotiating loan terms. As a result, many individuals enter adulthood unprepared to navigate the financial system, making them easy targets for exploitative banking practices.

For example, many consumers do not fully understand how compound interest works. Banks take advantage of this by structuring loans and credit products in ways that appear affordable in the short term but become financially crippling over time. Similarly, the fine print on banking agreements often includes hidden fees, fluctuating interest rates, and penalty clauses that can significantly increase a borrower's financial obligations.

Financial illiteracy also plays a crucial role in keeping people reliant on banking institutions. Without proper knowledge, individuals are less likely to invest, build wealth, or take advantage of tax-saving strategies that could improve their financial situations. Instead, they remain trapped in paycheck-to-paycheck cycles, relying on credit to make ends meet, which further benefits banks and lenders.

The modern banking system is designed to maximize profits at the expense of consumers, particularly those in lower and middle-income brackets. By encouraging perpetual debt, imposing high-interest rates, and preying on financial illiteracy, banks ensure that millions remain trapped in cycles of borrowing and repayment.

Breaking free from this system requires both individual action and systemic change. Consumers can take steps to educate themselves on financial management, prioritize debt repayment, and advocate for fair lending practices. On a broader level, financial regulations must be strengthened to prevent predatory lending, enforce transparent banking practices, and ensure that individuals have access to fair and equitable financial resources. Governments should implement stronger consumer protection laws, promote financial education in schools, and regulate high-interest loans to prevent widespread economic exploitation.

Until these changes occur, the banking industry will continue to profit from financial struggles while the average person remains economically disadvantaged. The more people understand how the system is designed to work against them, the better they can protect themselves and demand changes that lead to a fairer financial system for all.

Chapter 10 – The Education Scam: Why Schools Don't Teach Financial Literacy

Education is often presented as the key to success, yet one of the most crucial life skills—financial literacy—is largely absent from mainstream school curriculums. Students graduate with knowledge of historical events, algebraic equations, and literary analysis but remain unprepared to handle real-world financial responsibilities like budgeting, investing, or managing debt. This glaring omission is not a coincidence but a feature of an outdated education system designed to maintain the status quo rather than empower individuals financially.

In today's rapidly changing economic landscape, where inflation, rising living costs, and job instability are becoming the norm, financial literacy is more important than ever. Yet, it remains overlooked in schools, leaving students vulnerable to financial pitfalls such as debt, poor credit decisions, and inadequate savings. Meanwhile, the wealthy ensure their children receive an elite education that includes lessons on wealth-building, investing, and financial independence. This disparity creates a system where financial knowledge is reserved for the privileged few, keeping wealth concentrated among the elite while the rest struggle to navigate complex financial systems.

This chapter explores why financial literacy is intentionally ignored in standard education, who benefits from this lack of knowledge, and how the wealthy gain an unfair advantage by teaching these principles to their own. Additionally, we will examine the rise of alternative financial education methods, including self-education, online courses, and social media influencers dedicated to bridging the financial literacy gap. By understanding the reasons behind this educational failure, individuals can take proactive steps to equip themselves with the knowledge necessary to achieve financial independence and break free from systemic economic control.

The Outdated School System and Why Financial Literacy Is Ignored

The modern school system remains rooted in a structure designed during the Industrial Revolution, a time when the primary goal of education was to produce disciplined workers for factories and offices rather than independent entrepreneurs, investors, or financially empowered citizens. This outdated model persists, ensuring that financial literacy remains an afterthought—if it is addressed at all.

Historically, education systems were created to provide basic skills in reading, writing, and arithmetic—essentials for industrial and clerical jobs. However, as economies evolved and financial systems became more complex, school curriculums failed to adapt to these changes. Today, students graduate with the ability to solve quadratic equations but often lack the knowledge to file taxes, understand interest rates, invest wisely, or manage their credit effectively.

Standardized curriculums reinforce this gap by prioritizing theoretical knowledge over real-world financial skills. Traditional subjects like algebra, history, and literature dominate the curriculum, while practical lessons on budgeting, savings, and financial planning remain largely ignored. Even when personal finance is introduced, it is often presented in a shallow or optional manner rather than as a core educational requirement. Key concepts such as compound interest, tax management, and investment strategies are frequently excluded, leaving students unprepared for critical financial decisions in adulthood.

The lack of financial literacy education is not accidental—it benefits financial institutions, corporations, and even governments that thrive on a population reliant on loans, credit cards, and employer-based retirement plans. A financially uninformed public is more likely to accumulate debt, live paycheck to paycheck, and remain dependent on traditional employment rather than pursuing wealth-building opportunities like entrepreneurship or smart investing. By keeping individuals unaware of how financial systems work, banks continue to profit from high-interest loans, credit card fees, and financial mismanagement.

Additionally, financial illiteracy creates a cycle of lifelong dependency. Without a strong foundation in money management, individuals are prone to making costly mistakes, such as taking on excessive student debt, failing to build credit responsibly, or neglecting long-term financial planning. This dependency benefits banks, which profit from high-interest loans and overdraft fees, and employers, who retain a workforce that lacks the financial freedom to leave jobs or start independent ventures.

Meanwhile, elite private schools and prestigious institutions catering to the wealthy often provide students with an entirely different education—one that includes lessons on investment strategies, tax optimization, asset protection, and wealth accumulation. This systemic disparity ensures that financial knowledge remains concentrated among the privileged while the majority of the population remains financially disempowered. The rich continue to pass down generational wealth, while those without financial literacy struggle to break free from cycles of debt and financial insecurity.

The deliberate omission of financial education from mainstream schooling raises a fundamental question: Who truly benefits from an uninformed public? As long as financial literacy remains absent from the core curriculum, the cycle of financial dependency and economic inequality will persist. To create a financially empowered society, schools must prioritize real-world financial education, equipping students with the knowledge and skills necessary to navigate an increasingly complex economic landscape.

Who Benefits from Keeping the Public Uninformed?

The exclusion of financial literacy from mainstream education is not merely an oversight—it is a calculated decision that benefits powerful institutions at the expense of the average person. Banks, corporations, and even governments all have vested interests in keeping the majority of the population financially illiterate. A lack of financial knowledge leads individuals to rely heavily on credit, accumulate debt, and struggle with financial insecurity, all while benefiting those who control the system. By maintaining widespread economic ignorance, these entities ensure a constant flow of dependent consumers, indebted workers, and uninformed taxpayers, reinforcing structures that perpetuate wealth inequality and economic control.

The Financial Industry

Financial institutions, including banks, credit card companies, and lenders, thrive on a financially uneducated public. Without a strong understanding of interest rates, fees, and loan structures, many individuals fall into debt traps that are difficult to escape. Banks generate billions in profits from high-interest credit cards, payday loans, and mortgage lending practices designed to keep borrowers locked into long-term repayment cycles. The less the public understands about personal finance, the easier it is for these institutions to charge exorbitant fees and implement predatory lending policies without scrutiny. Many banks deliberately obscure loan terms with complex jargon, making it difficult for consumers to grasp the full financial consequences of borrowing. Hidden fees, compounding interest, and misleading promotional rates further ensnare individuals who lack the financial knowledge to navigate these pitfalls.

Moreover, financial institutions lobby aggressively against widespread financial education reforms. If more people understood how to effectively manage their finances, there would be fewer high-interest credit card users, fewer borrowers taking out risky subprime loans, and fewer individuals paying excessive banking fees. To maintain their profit margins, banks and lenders invest in marketing campaigns that downplay the risks of debt while promoting consumer spending. They encourage the normalization of living paycheck to paycheck, making financial struggle appear as an unavoidable reality rather than a consequence of a deliberately engineered system.

A striking example of this is the student loan industry. Young borrowers are often enticed into taking on substantial debt under the assumption that higher education will guarantee financial success. However, many graduates find themselves struggling with decades of repayment, often unable to buy homes or save for retirement due to overwhelming student loan burdens. Meanwhile, banks, private lenders, and government-backed loan providers continue profiting off their financial struggles, ensuring that the cycle of debt dependency persists across generations.

Ultimately, financial illiteracy is not just a byproduct of an outdated education system—it is a deliberately maintained mechanism that ensures banks and lenders continue to profit at the expense of an uninformed public.

The Corporate World

Businesses benefit from a workforce that is focused on earning wages rather than building independent wealth. When employees lack financial education, they are less likely to negotiate salaries, seek higher-paying opportunities, or invest in wealth-building assets. This ensures a steady supply of laborers who remain reliant on employment rather than achieving financial independence. Additionally, companies profit from consumer ignorance by promoting lifestyle inflation—convincing people to take on unnecessary debt for material possessions, luxury goods, and non-essential services. Employers also leverage financial insecurity to maintain control over their workforce. When workers live paycheck to paycheck and lack financial literacy, they are less likely to take risks, demand better benefits, or explore alternative income streams. Instead, they remain tied to jobs that offer little upward mobility, fearing the financial consequences of leaving.

Many corporations also suppress discussions about financial literacy within the workplace. While companies may offer retirement plans or employee stock options, they rarely provide the education necessary to help workers maximize these benefits. As a result, many employees fail to take full advantage of employer-matching contributions, investment opportunities, or tax-efficient savings strategies, further entrenching their dependence on wages rather than wealth accumulation.

An example of corporate-driven financial illiteracy can be seen in retail and service industries, where employees are often encouraged to participate in employee discount programs rather than focus on long-term savings or investment opportunities. While these discounts create a sense of financial benefit, they ultimately encourage spending rather than wealth-building behaviors, reinforcing cycles of consumer debt and economic dependency.

Ultimately, a financially uneducated workforce is a controllable workforce—one that remains dependent on steady employment, hesitant to challenge unfair labor practices, and more willing to accept stagnant wages due to financial insecurity. By limiting financial knowledge, corporations ensure that power and wealth remain concentrated at the top while the average worker remains locked in a cycle of dependency and economic vulnerability.

Government Interests

Governments also have a stake in keeping financial knowledge scarce. Taxation systems are deliberately complex, making it difficult for the average person to maximize deductions, utilize tax-advantaged accounts, or build tax-efficient investment portfolios. The tax code, filled with intricate loopholes and exemptions primarily designed for corporations and the wealthy, remains nearly impossible for the average taxpayer to navigate without professional assistance. A financially illiterate population is less likely to challenge unfair tax policies or seek out legal loopholes used by the wealthy to minimize their tax burdens. Additionally, reliance on government social programs increases when people lack the financial knowledge to manage their money effectively, creating a dependent electorate that can be influenced by political incentives. Governments benefit from this lack of knowledge, as it ensures continued tax revenue from individuals who are unaware of legal strategies to minimize their liabilities. Furthermore, financial illiteracy allows policymakers to introduce policies that sound beneficial on the surface but ultimately fail to address systemic wealth disparities. For example, stimulus checks or one-time relief programs are often presented as solutions to financial hardships, but they do little to address the root causes of economic instability, such as rising inflation, stagnant wages, and increasing consumer debt. By keeping citizens financially uninformed, governments maintain control over economic narratives while perpetuating cycles of financial dependence.

Case Studies of Deliberate Financial Misinformation

1. **The Payday Loan Trap:** Payday loans are aggressively marketed as a fast and convenient way to cover emergency expenses, but beneath the surface lies a predatory financial scheme designed to exploit the most vulnerable borrowers. These short-term loans often come with exorbitant interest rates—sometimes exceeding 400% APR—which, rather than providing relief, trap individuals in a cycle of perpetual debt. Borrowers, particularly those from low-income backgrounds, are drawn in by the appeal of instant cash, only to realize that repayment terms are nearly impossible to meet without taking out additional loans. As a result, many are forced into a continuous loop of rollovers and mounting fees, ultimately paying far more in interest than the original loan amount. Lenders deliberately prey on financial illiteracy and the desperation of those in urgent need of funds, ensuring a steady stream of profits from individuals who can least afford the cost of borrowing. The payday loan industry thrives on this cycle, systematically keeping borrowers dependent while presenting itself as a necessary financial service for those with limited options.
2. **The Myth of the "Perfect Credit Score":** Credit bureaus and banks reinforce the misconception that achieving a high credit score necessitates frequent credit card usage and maintaining revolving balances. Many consumers are misled into believing that making only the minimum payment each month benefits their financial standing, when in fact, it extends their repayment period, accumulates substantial interest, and increases overall debt

burden. Financial institutions capitalize on this misunderstanding by generating revenue through late fees, penalty interest rates, and compounding interest, ensuring a steady stream of profits at the expense of uninformed consumers. Meanwhile, effective strategies such as responsible credit utilization, timely full payments, and diversification of credit types remain largely uncommunicated, keeping individuals trapped in costly financial cycles.

3. **Student Loan Debt as a "Good Investment":** Students are frequently encouraged to take on massive loans under the assumption that a college degree guarantees financial security. However, tuition costs have skyrocketed far beyond wage growth, leaving many graduates saddled with decades of repayments and limited financial mobility. Government-backed student loan programs ensure that lenders get paid regardless of a borrower's financial struggles, while borrowers face predatory repayment terms and little recourse. Meanwhile, universities and loan providers continue to profit from an education system that prioritizes financial gain over student success.
4. **Adjustable-Rate Mortgage (ARM) Scams:** Leading up to the 2008 financial crisis, banks and mortgage lenders aggressively pushed adjustable-rate mortgages (ARMs) as an affordable path to homeownership. Homebuyers, lured by initially low interest rates, later faced drastic payment increases when rates adjusted upward. Many borrowers, unaware of the risks, found themselves unable to keep up with ballooning payments, leading to mass foreclosures. Banks profited immensely from these misleading loan structures, while millions of families lost their homes and financial stability.

5. **The "Buy Now, Pay Later" Phenomenon:** Modern retail and e-commerce platforms heavily promote "Buy Now, Pay Later" (BNPL) schemes, encouraging consumers to make purchases without immediate financial consequences. While marketed as a budget-friendly option, these installment-based payment plans often come with hidden fees, high interest rates for missed payments, and a tendency to encourage overspending. Consumers who lack financial literacy underestimate the cumulative impact of multiple BNPL purchases, leading to increased financial strain and unnecessary debt. Retailers and lenders, in turn, benefit from higher consumer spending and recurring fees.

These case studies expose how financial misinformation is deliberately propagated to keep consumers ensnared in cycles of debt and economic dependency. To resist these manipulative tactics, individuals must take proactive steps in educating themselves about personal finance, critically evaluate financial products, and demand greater transparency from financial institutions and policymakers.

A closer look at these financial pitfalls reveals that widespread financial illiteracy is not a mere lapse in the education system but a deliberately maintained structure that benefits those in positions of power. Escaping this cycle requires individuals to take ownership of their financial education, seek trustworthy resources, and challenge the exploitative financial mechanisms that profit from economic ignorance. Only through collective awareness and informed financial choices can individuals regain control over their economic well-being and disrupt the systems that reinforce financial inequality.

How Elite Schools Teach Wealth-Building Secrets to the Privileged

The stark contrast between public school curriculums and the education provided at elite institutions highlights a fundamental divide in financial knowledge. While most public schools focus on producing disciplined workers who follow traditional career paths, elite schools and Ivy League universities instill financial strategies designed to preserve and expand wealth. This disparity ensures that the upper class maintains economic dominance while the average individual struggles with financial literacy gaps, further entrenching systemic inequality in wealth distribution and economic mobility.

The Contrast Between Public and Elite Education

Public education prioritizes subjects such as mathematics, literature, and history but rarely incorporates comprehensive financial education. In contrast, elite schools integrate wealth-building concepts into their curriculum, teaching students how to leverage investments, reduce tax liabilities, and build generational wealth. These schools operate on the principle that financial acumen is as crucial as academic excellence, ensuring that graduates leave with the skills necessary to manage and grow wealth effectively.

For instance, while a public school student may be taught basic arithmetic and budgeting in a limited personal finance class, a student at an elite institution might learn about asset diversification, hedge funds, private equity, and real estate investment. They are introduced to topics such as compound interest, risk assessment, and financial independence strategies, which the majority of the population learns only through trial and error in adulthood. This knowledge gap perpetuates financial inequality, as those without access to these resources are left navigating a complex financial world without proper guidance, limiting their ability to make informed economic decisions and achieve financial stability.

Financial Strategies Taught at Ivy League Schools and Exclusive Institutions

Elite institutions provide an education that extends far beyond textbooks and lectures. Courses at Ivy League universities and prestigious private schools cover topics such as:

- **Investment Strategies:** Students are introduced to stock market fundamentals, venture capital, and risk management techniques, allowing them to develop sophisticated investment portfolios early in life.

- **Tax Avoidance Techniques:** Understanding tax loopholes, offshore accounts, and legal structures that minimize tax liability, enabling them to legally protect their assets and maximize financial returns.

- **Entrepreneurship and Business Scaling:** Unlike public school curriculums that focus on securing a stable job, elite schools emphasize building businesses, generating passive income, and leveraging financial instruments to scale enterprises quickly.

- **Networking and Social Capital:** Beyond financial concepts, these institutions emphasize the power of connections. Students are often introduced to influential mentors, industry leaders, and exclusive business networks that provide access to high-paying opportunities, investments, and insider knowledge about emerging markets.

For example, Harvard and Stanford offer programs that teach students about hedge fund management and angel investing, while public schools rarely touch on topics beyond basic saving and budgeting. Additionally, students at these institutions participate in high-profile competitions, case studies, and simulations that expose them to real-world financial decision-making processes. This creates an inherent advantage for those who have access to such privileged education, as they are equipped with the tools to accumulate and sustain wealth more effectively than their peers in standard educational settings.

How Generational Wealth is Maintained Through Insider Knowledge and Private Networks

Generational wealth is not solely about passing down money—it is about transferring financial knowledge, strategic investment skills, and access to exclusive opportunities. Wealthy families ensure that their children receive the necessary education and mentorship to maintain their economic status.

Private schools and elite universities serve as breeding grounds for financial elites, fostering environments where students are immersed in advanced economic concepts from an early age. Many of these institutions offer courses taught by hedge fund managers, venture capitalists, and seasoned entrepreneurs, giving students direct insight into high-level financial strategies. These lessons often take place in private workshops, case studies, and even networking retreats, where students develop business acumen through direct mentorship.

Additionally, legacy admissions play a significant role in preserving generational wealth. Many elite schools prioritize applicants whose family members are alumni, ensuring that wealth-building education remains within a select group. These students benefit from networking events, internships, and investment opportunities unavailable to the general public. Their access to capital, combined with an in-depth understanding of financial markets and risk management, sets them apart from their peers in traditional educational settings.

For example, a child from a wealthy family may receive personal tutoring on tax strategies, be introduced to investment opportunities through family connections, or even be gifted seed capital to start a business. In contrast, a middle-class or lower-income student without these advantages is left to navigate financial systems independently, often learning through trial and error. The cumulative effect of these disparities ensures that wealth remains concentrated within a privileged class while others struggle to access the same resources and opportunities.

Real Examples of How Wealthy Families Teach Financial Strategies While the Average Student Remains Uninformed

1. **The Rockefeller Family** - The Rockefeller family, one of the wealthiest dynasties in American history, has long emphasized financial education within their lineage. Members of the family receive training on investment strategies, wealth preservation, and philanthropic financial planning from an early age. They are taught how to leverage trust funds, charitable foundations, and real estate investments to maintain their fortune for future generations. Family wealth advisors ensure that financial literacy remains a priority, offering strategic guidance on maintaining and expanding wealth through sophisticated investment techniques. Additionally, they are educated on economic cycles and global markets, helping them make calculated decisions that secure their wealth across multiple generations.

2. **Warren Buffett's Approach** - Despite being one of the world's richest individuals, Warren Buffett has emphasized teaching his children about financial discipline, investment strategies, and the power of compound interest. Unlike the average student who may never hear about the stock market in school, Buffett's children grew up learning about value investing, capital allocation, and long-term wealth-building principles. These principles allow them to make strategic financial decisions that ensure wealth longevity across generations. Buffett's emphasis on delayed gratification and frugality also instills in them a mindset of sustainable financial management rather than reckless spending.
3. **Elite Internships and Exclusive Opportunities** - Many wealthy families secure high-level internships and job placements for their children within prestigious firms, often through personal connections rather than merit-based applications. These internships provide early exposure to financial management, corporate strategy, and investment opportunities that are inaccessible to the majority of students. Exclusive mentorship programs and private training sessions further deepen their understanding of economic systems, providing a significant head start in wealth accumulation.
4. **Private Financial Advisors for Wealthy Families** - While middle-class families may rely on basic financial literacy from high school courses or online resources, the wealthy often employ personal financial advisors to educate and guide their children on investment decisions, estate planning, and tax strategies. This direct mentorship gives them a significant advantage in managing and growing their wealth. Many wealthy individuals also enroll in

private financial boot camps or receive one-on-one coaching from seasoned professionals to refine their understanding of global economic trends and financial instruments.

The disparity between public education and elite schooling creates an uneven playing field where financial literacy remains an exclusive privilege rather than a universal right. Bridging this gap requires a fundamental shift in educational priorities. Public schools must incorporate comprehensive financial literacy programs that teach real-world money management skills, investment strategies, and tax planning. Without these changes, financial inequality will continue to widen, ensuring that wealth remains concentrated within an elite minority while the rest of the population struggles to achieve financial security.

The Rise of Self-Education and Alternative Financial Learning

For decades, the traditional education system has neglected to provide individuals with the financial literacy necessary to navigate the complexities of modern economies. In response, there has been a dramatic rise in self-education, driven by accessible technology, alternative learning platforms, and a growing awareness of financial independence. This shift is empowering individuals to take control of their financial futures, bypassing traditional gatekeepers of wealth-building knowledge and creating new opportunities for financial empowerment.

The Growing Popularity of Financial Self-Education

With the rapid expansion of the internet, financial education is no longer restricted to elite institutions. Books, online courses, podcasts, and social media platforms have become primary sources for learning about investing, budgeting, wealth-building, and economic trends. Influential figures such as Robert Kiyosaki (*Rich Dad Poor Dad*), Ramit Sethi (*I Will Teach You to Be Rich*), and financial influencers on platforms like YouTube and TikTok have helped demystify complex financial concepts. These resources have empowered millions to take control of their financial futures, often providing insights that formal education ignores or de-emphasizes.

Financial self-education is particularly popular among younger generations, who are increasingly skeptical of traditional career and investment paths. Many young adults are turning to cryptocurrency, real estate, and stock market investing as alternatives to the conventional "work hard, save money, and retire" mindset. With rising tuition costs and stagnating wages, individuals are looking for ways to maximize wealth outside of traditional employment structures. Side hustles, freelancing, and passive income strategies have become widespread as people seek financial security in an uncertain economic landscape.

How Technology Has Made Financial Knowledge More Accessible

The democratization of financial education has been largely driven by technological advancements. The availability of user-friendly investment apps (such as Robinhood, E*TRADE, and Wealthfront), budget management tools (like Mint and YNAB), and online financial courses (Udemy, Coursera, and MasterClass) have removed traditional barriers to financial learning, making it easier than ever for individuals to educate themselves about money management.

Social media platforms also play a crucial role in spreading financial literacy. Financial influencers share bite-sized insights on topics such as debt management, investment strategies, and passive income generation. Online communities and forums like Reddit's r/personalfinance and r/wallstreetbets have created spaces where individuals can share experiences, discuss financial strategies, and learn from real-world examples. These platforms allow people from all backgrounds to access information that was once reserved for those with direct connections to financial professionals or elite institutions.

The Risks of Misinformation in the Self-Taught Financial Space

While self-education provides invaluable opportunities, it also comes with risks. The financial content available online is largely unregulated, leading to the spread of misleading or outright false information. Many so-called "financial gurus" capitalize on people's desperation for quick wealth by promoting get-rich-quick schemes, MLMs (multi-level marketing), or risky investment strategies without sufficient warnings about potential downsides. The allure of overnight success often blinds individuals to the importance of thorough research and risk management.

Furthermore, the oversimplification of complex financial concepts can lead to unrealistic expectations. For example, while day trading and cryptocurrency investments have made some individuals wealthy, they also come with high volatility and risks that many self-taught investors fail to understand. Without proper due diligence, individuals may fall victim to scams, misinformation, or financial losses that set them back rather than move them forward.

The rise of "finfluencers" (financial influencers) has also led to an influx of advice that prioritizes virality over accuracy, making it crucial for individuals to critically assess the credibility of their sources.

Steps Individuals Can Take to Educate Themselves and Bridge the Financial Knowledge Gap

1. **Start with Credible Sources:** Rely on well-reviewed books, reputable financial news websites, and expert-authored courses rather than social media hype.
2. **Diversify Learning Methods:** Engage in multiple learning approaches—read books, watch expert-led courses, attend webinars, and listen to podcasts for a well-rounded understanding of financial topics.
3. **Verify Information:** Cross-check financial advice from different sources before making major financial decisions, ensuring the information is accurate and applicable to your situation.
4. **Apply Knowledge Practically:** Use budgeting apps, start small investments, or practice simulated trading to apply what you learn in a controlled environment, allowing for hands-on experience without significant financial risk.
5. **Seek Professional Guidance:** Consult financial advisors or certified professionals when making critical financial moves to ensure you are making informed decisions that align with your long-term goals.
6. **Stay Updated:** Financial markets and economic conditions change constantly. Keeping up with news, trends, and regulatory changes will help individuals adapt and make better financial decisions over time.

The traditional education system's failure to prioritize financial literacy has left generations vulnerable to debt, economic instability, and a cycle of financial dependence. However, the rise of self-education and alternative financial learning is changing this narrative. With technology making financial knowledge more accessible than ever, individuals now have the opportunity to take control of their wealth-building journey, regardless of their background or formal education.

By actively seeking knowledge, questioning financial norms, and leveraging the wealth of information available today, people can break free from financial ignorance and achieve economic empowerment. The future of financial education lies in a hybrid approach—one where traditional institutions integrate practical money management skills into their curriculums while individuals continue to harness self-learning tools to take control of their financial destinies. The movement toward widespread financial literacy reform is growing, but until then, self-education remains the most powerful tool for those seeking financial independence and security.

Chapter 11: The Hidden World of Elite Networking & Influence

Wealth and power are not just about money; they are about influence. The ultra-rich operate within exclusive circles, shaping global policies, economies, and even societal trends through their vast networks. These networks exist in the form of invitation-only conferences, private organizations, and financial alliances that allow the wealthy to consolidate their power while remaining largely invisible to the general public. Understanding these secretive groups is key to uncovering how influence truly operates behind the scenes. By controlling the flow of information, lobbying for favorable policies, and funding institutions that align with their interests, the elite maintain their dominance over political and economic systems worldwide.

Secret Billionaire Groups: Bilderberg, Davos, Bohemian Grove

Bilderberg Group

The Bilderberg Group is one of the most well-known yet highly secretive gatherings of the global elite. Established in 1954, this invitation-only conference convenes political leaders, billionaires, corporate executives, and media moguls for confidential discussions held annually in luxury venues. While the group insists that these meetings are informal platforms for dialogue, critics contend that major geopolitical and economic strategies are orchestrated within these closed-door sessions, far from public scrutiny. The lack of official records or media access fuels speculation about the group's influence over global affairs, with some alleging that it serves as a private policy-shaping forum for the world's most powerful individuals. Many prominent figures, including U.S. presidents, European prime ministers, and central bank heads, have participated in these gatherings, raising concerns about the extent of elite coordination beyond democratic oversight. The secrecy surrounding Bilderberg fuels ongoing debates about its role in shaping international policies, economic trends, and political landscapes.

World Economic Forum (Davos)

Held annually in Davos, Switzerland, the World Economic Forum (WEF) is another gathering where world leaders, CEOs, and top intellectuals discuss economic policies and future global trends. While the conference appears more open than Bilderberg, the true influence of Davos participants lies in the informal deals and partnerships forged behind closed doors. Critics argue that these discussions shape policies that benefit corporations and the ultra-rich, often at the expense of the general population. For example, economic policies such as globalization, deregulation, and technological automation—promoted at Davos—have increased inequality while boosting corporate profits.

Bohemian Grove

Bohemian Grove, a secluded retreat for the world's most influential men, serves as a convergence point for business, politics, and global decision-making. Nestled in the redwood forests of California, this invitation-only gathering has been attended by U.S. presidents, Fortune 500 executives, and banking moguls for over a century. While it presents itself as a casual and exclusive retreat for camaraderie, reports suggest that pivotal political strategies, economic alliances, and policy discussions occur away from public scrutiny. Notable past attendees include Ronald Reagan, Richard

Nixon, and Henry Kissinger, who were rumored to have forged political pacts in the Grove's private settings. Beyond discussions, the event is infamous for its elaborate rituals, including the "Cremation of Care" ceremony—an extravagant theatrical performance that critics argue symbolizes the detachment of the elite from the real struggles of ordinary citizens. The highly secretive nature of the gathering has fueled speculation about the extent of its influence on global affairs.

How the Rich Shape Policies Through Lobbying and Political Donations

The influence of wealth on politics is one of the most significant ways elites maintain control over society. Through lobbying, Super PACs (Political Action Committees), and direct political donations, the wealthy shape laws and policies in ways that serve their financial interests.

1. **Lobbying** - Corporate lobbyists work directly with lawmakers to draft legislation that benefits major industries, frequently at the expense of the general public. The financial sector, pharmaceutical companies, and defense contractors are among the most powerful lobbying forces in government. For instance, the pharmaceutical industry spends billions lobbying for favorable drug pricing policies, ensuring high medication costs that maximize corporate profits. Similarly, financial institutions lobby for deregulation, which often leads to economic instability and crises that disproportionately harm lower-income individuals while benefiting wealthy investors. This strategic lobbying effort ensures that industries can operate with minimal oversight, reinforcing economic disparities

and prioritizing corporate interests over public welfare.

2. **Super PACs and Dark Money** - Campaign financing laws have created a system where billionaires can exert disproportionate influence over elections through Super PACs, effectively determining which candidates have the financial backing to succeed. The 2010 Citizens United ruling further intensified this imbalance by enabling unlimited corporate spending in elections, granting a small group of ultra-wealthy individuals immense control over political campaigns and legislative priorities. As a result, policies that favor corporate interests and economic elites often take precedence over those that would benefit the broader population. This unrestricted flow of money in politics has led to a system where financial power translates directly into political power, making it increasingly difficult for ordinary citizens to have their voices heard in the democratic process.
3. **Revolving Door Between Politics and Business** - Many top government officials seamlessly transition into high-paying corporate roles after leaving office, creating a continuous cycle of influence that ensures business interests remain prioritized in political decision-making. This practice benefits both politicians, who secure lucrative post-political careers, and corporations, which gain insider access to regulatory and legislative processes. For instance, former lawmakers frequently join lobbying firms, corporate boards, or financial institutions, where they leverage their government experience and connections to push for policies favorable to big business. This revolving door perpetuates regulatory capture, where agencies meant to oversee industries instead serve their interests, often at the

expense of consumers and small businesses. High-profile examples include former U.S. Treasury officials joining Wall Street firms, ex-defense secretaries securing roles with military contractors, and energy regulators moving into executive positions within oil and gas companies—all reinforcing a system where financial and political power are deeply intertwined.

The Power of Foundations and Charities in Wealth Preservation

Many of the world's wealthiest individuals and families use philanthropic foundations and charitable organizations not just to give back, but also to maintain influence and protect their wealth. While philanthropy is often seen as a benevolent act, it frequently serves as a strategic tool for the elite.

- **Tax Advantages:** Many billionaires establish foundations as a way to shield their wealth from taxes while maintaining control over how the funds are allocated. By donating money to their own foundations, wealthy individuals can avoid paying taxes while directing funds toward causes that serve their long-term interests. Some high-profile examples include the Ford Foundation and the Walton Family Foundation, which not only provide tax relief but also keep wealth concentrated within elite circles.

- **Policy Influence:** Through charitable giving, elites fund research institutions, think tanks, and educational programs that align with their worldviews and interests. For example, major foundations like the Gates Foundation influence global health policies, while the

Koch Foundation funds libertarian economic research to promote deregulation and lower corporate taxes. These contributions help shape public narratives and policies that serve the donors' long-term economic and ideological goals.

- **Public Image Management:** Philanthropy also serves as a powerful PR tool, allowing billionaires to maintain a positive public image despite accumulating wealth through exploitative business practices. High-profile donations to causes such as climate change or poverty alleviation help deflect criticism of labor exploitation, monopolistic practices, or tax avoidance. Companies and executives who face backlash over poor working conditions or tax evasion often use philanthropy to rehabilitate their reputations while continuing to operate in ways that exacerbate inequality.

Elite networking is not just about socializing—it is about consolidating power, shaping policies, and maintaining financial dominance over the rest of society. While these exclusive gatherings and financial maneuvers remain hidden from public scrutiny, understanding how they operate allows us to question and challenge the structures that keep wealth and power concentrated at the top. The ability of elites to shape public policies through lobbying, political donations, and philanthropy demonstrates how influence is often wielded in ways that benefit the few while leaving the majority struggling with economic inequality.

As financial literacy and political awareness grow, individuals can take steps to hold the ultra-rich accountable and push for greater transparency in global economic and political decision-making.

Recognizing the mechanisms behind elite influence is the first step toward creating a more equitable society where wealth and power are not hoarded by a select few, but rather distributed in ways that benefit the broader population. The movement for financial and political reform must continue to challenge these hidden power structures and demand accountability from those who shape the world from behind the scenes.

PART 4:

THE FUTURE OF WEALTH & HOW YOU CAN PROTECT YOURSELF

Chapter 12: The Future of Money – Digital Currencies, AI, and the Next Wealth Shift

The financial world is undergoing a seismic transformation. Traditional banking, which has dominated the global economy for centuries, is now being challenged by digital assets, artificial intelligence, and decentralized finance (DeFi). These technological innovations are not just altering the way people store and invest money—they are redefining the very concept of wealth itself.

The emergence of cryptocurrencies, blockchain, and AI-driven financial systems has sparked a global debate about the future of money. Governments and central banks are scrambling to maintain control, while tech entrepreneurs and digital pioneers are pushing for a financial revolution. This chapter explores the battle between decentralized financial systems and state-backed digital currencies, examining how these shifts will impact everyday individuals, investors, and the wealthy elite. Understanding these changes is essential for financial survival in the rapidly evolving landscape.

At the heart of this transformation is the struggle between traditional financial institutions and emerging digital alternatives. Central banks are pushing for the adoption of Central Bank Digital Currencies (CBDCs), while blockchain-based systems promise financial independence and decentralization. Meanwhile, AI-driven financial markets are altering the nature of investment, with powerful algorithms managing billions of dollars in assets at lightning speed.

This chapter will break down the key elements of this financial revolution, including how cryptocurrencies impact wealth distribution, the growing role of artificial intelligence in the stock market, the potential dangers of government-controlled digital currencies, and the risks and rewards of DeFi. By the end of this chapter, you will have a clear understanding of the opportunities and threats posed by these changes and what steps you can take to protect and grow your wealth in the digital age.

How Cryptocurrency and Blockchain Impact Wealth Distribution

The Promise of Decentralization: Reducing Reliance on Traditional Banks

One of the most groundbreaking aspects of cryptocurrency and blockchain technology is their ability to function outside the constraints of traditional banking institutions. By facilitating peer-to-peer transactions without intermediaries, cryptocurrencies offer a lifeline to millions who are unbanked or underbanked, particularly in developing regions where access to financial services is limited. This decentralized model reduces reliance on centralized authorities that historically have dictated financial policies, imposed high transaction fees, and restricted access to capital. With the rise of decentralized finance (DeFi) platforms, individuals now have the ability to borrow, lend, and trade assets on a global scale without seeking approval from banks or financial regulators. Additionally, the transparency and immutability of blockchain technology enhance security, reducing instances of fraud and corruption that are prevalent in traditional banking systems. However, while decentralization offers these advantages, it also introduces new challenges, including regulatory uncertainty, cybersecurity risks, and the need for financial literacy to navigate the complex crypto landscape effectively.

How Bitcoin, Ethereum, and Other Cryptocurrencies

Have Created New Wealth Opportunities

The emergence of Bitcoin, Ethereum, and other digital assets has dramatically reshaped wealth distribution, creating financial opportunities for those who recognized their potential early. Bitcoin, often referred to as "digital gold," has surged in value since its creation in 2009, with early adopters amassing substantial fortunes. For instance, individuals who purchased Bitcoin when it was worth just a few cents have since seen its value skyrocket to tens of thousands of dollars per coin. Ethereum, on the other hand, introduced smart contract functionality, which has led to the rise of decentralized applications (dApps) and the expansion of blockchain-based finance. The explosion of initial coin offerings (ICOs) and decentralized finance (DeFi) platforms has enabled many to participate in alternative financial ecosystems outside of traditional banking networks. However, this new wealth distribution has been highly uneven, with those possessing advanced technical knowledge or insider access benefiting the most. Stories of crypto millionaires, such as the Winklevoss twins—who turned their Bitcoin holdings into billions—demonstrate the potential upside, while cases like the collapse of FTX reveal how even well-established figures in the space can suffer massive financial losses. The disruptive nature of cryptocurrency continues to challenge traditional financial institutions, offering new pathways to wealth while exposing participants to high levels of risk and volatility.

The Risks of Volatility, Fraud, and Government Crackdowns

Despite its potential, the cryptocurrency market is highly volatile. Prices can skyrocket or plummet within hours, often driven by speculation, regulatory announcements, or technological developments. For instance, Bitcoin has experienced price swings of over 50% within a matter of weeks, leading to both massive gains and catastrophic losses for investors.

Fraud is another significant issue plaguing the industry. Scams such as rug pulls, Ponzi schemes, and hacking incidents have resulted in billions of dollars in losses. A prime example is the OneCoin scandal, where investors were duped into a fraudulent cryptocurrency scheme that stole approximately $4 billion. Similarly, the collapse of the crypto exchange FTX in 2022 exposed the dangers of mismanagement and lack of transparency within the industry.

Furthermore, governments worldwide are grappling with how to regulate digital assets. Some countries, like China, have outright banned cryptocurrency trading, citing concerns over financial stability and illicit activities. Others, such as the United States, are taking a more measured approach, implementing stricter regulations and tax laws to govern the sector. These regulatory uncertainties often lead to sharp market fluctuations, creating an unpredictable investment environment that requires caution and extensive research from participants.. Prices can skyrocket or plummet within hours, making it a risky investment for those unfamiliar with its nature. Fraud is another significant issue—rug pulls, Ponzi schemes, and hacking incidents have resulted in substantial losses for investors. Furthermore, governments worldwide are grappling with how to regulate digital assets. Some countries, like China, have outright banned cryptocurrency trading, while others, such as the United States, continue to develop regulations that could impact market stability and investor confidence.

Examples of Early Crypto Adopters Who Built Fortunes—And Those Who Lost Everything

Several individuals have amassed incredible wealth through early cryptocurrency investments. For example, Erik Finman, who invested in Bitcoin as a teenager with just $1,000, became a millionaire by his twenties, proving that early adoption could yield extraordinary returns. Likewise, the Winklevoss twins, known for their legal battle with Mark Zuckerberg over Facebook, strategically invested in Bitcoin during its early days and turned their holdings into billions, eventually founding the Gemini cryptocurrency exchange.

However, not everyone has been as fortunate. Many retail investors who bought at market peaks have suffered heavy losses due to price crashes, often fueled by speculation and hype. A notable example is the Mt. Gox hack, where the exchange lost approximately 850,000 Bitcoins, leaving thousands of investors in financial ruin. Similarly, the collapse of TerraUSD and Luna in 2022 wiped out billions in investor funds as a so-called "stablecoin" turned out to be anything but stable. These cases highlight the high-risk nature of digital asset investments, where fortunes can be made—but also lost in an instant.

Hence, while cryptocurrency and blockchain technology present unprecedented opportunities to reshape wealth distribution, they also come with significant risks. Understanding the evolving landscape of digital finance is crucial for anyone looking to navigate this emerging market successfully.

The Role of Artificial Intelligence in Financial Markets

How AI-Driven Trading Algorithms Dominate Stock Markets

Artificial Intelligence has transformed stock market trading by enabling rapid data analysis, pattern recognition, and real-time decision-making. High-frequency trading (HFT) firms leverage AI-driven algorithms to execute thousands of trades per second, profiting from minuscule price fluctuations that human traders cannot detect. These algorithms analyze vast amounts of market data, including breaking news, earnings reports, macroeconomic indicators, and social media sentiment, to predict price movements with remarkable accuracy.

For example, firms like Renaissance Technologies and Citadel Securities employ AI-based quantitative strategies to manage billions of dollars in assets. Their proprietary algorithms continuously adapt to shifting market conditions, outperforming traditional investment strategies by minimizing human error and capitalizing on millisecond advantages. This AI-driven approach has allowed these firms to consistently generate high returns, cementing their dominance in the financial sector.

However, the rapid rise of AI in trading has raised concerns about market stability. The automation of trades has led to unintended consequences, such as flash crashes—sudden and extreme price swings caused by cascading algorithmic trades. One of the most infamous examples occurred on May 6, 2010, when the Dow Jones Industrial Average plummeted nearly 1,000 points within minutes before quickly rebounding. Investigations attributed this event to algorithmic trading spirals, where AI-driven systems executed sell orders in response to volatile market conditions, exacerbating the crisis.

Additionally, the widespread use of AI in trading has created an uneven playing field. Large financial institutions with access to cutting-edge AI models gain significant advantages over retail investors, who lack the same computational power and data access. This disparity raises ethical concerns about fairness and market manipulation, prompting regulators to consider implementing safeguards to ensure that AI-driven finance benefits a broader range of investors rather than concentrating wealth among elite financial entities.

The Rise of Robo-Advisors and Automated Wealth Management

The emergence of robo-advisors has transformed wealth management by providing automated investment services that require little to no human intervention. Platforms like Betterment, Wealthfront, and Charles Schwab's Intelligent Portfolios use AI-driven algorithms to assess an individual's risk tolerance, financial goals, and market conditions to construct and rebalance investment portfolios automatically. These platforms leverage machine learning models to refine investment strategies continuously, ensuring that portfolios remain optimized based on real-time market shifts.

Robo-advisors offer a low-cost alternative to traditional financial advisors, making wealth management more accessible to the average investor. Their ability to optimize tax-loss harvesting, asset allocation, and risk diversification has led to widespread adoption among retail investors who seek cost-effective ways to manage their wealth. For instance, Wealthfront's tax-loss harvesting feature strategically sells declining assets to offset taxable gains, improving overall portfolio efficiency.

Despite these advantages, critics argue that AI-driven financial management lacks the human intuition necessary to navigate complex, unpredictable market conditions, potentially exposing investors to unforeseen risks. For example, during times of extreme market volatility, robo-advisors may execute trades based on algorithmic predictions without considering broader economic contexts, leading to unintended losses. Additionally, while automation enhances efficiency, it may not account for highly personalized financial needs that a human advisor could address, such as estate planning or major life changes. As robo-advisors continue to evolve, finding the right balance between automation and human oversight remains crucial for long-term financial success.

The Potential for AI to Widen the Gap Between Elite Investors and the General Public

While AI democratizes access to financial insights through robo-advisors and predictive analytics, it simultaneously exacerbates financial disparities by giving elite investors significant advantages. Wealthy hedge funds and institutional investors have exclusive access to advanced AI models that provide them with an unparalleled edge over retail investors. These proprietary algorithms process vast amounts of real-time market data, enabling institutional players to anticipate price fluctuations, execute high-frequency trades, and capitalize on opportunities long before the general public is even aware of them. Consequently, while everyday investors rely on generic AI-driven tools, the most profitable and precise strategies remain reserved for those with the resources to afford cutting-edge AI infrastructure.

Moreover, AI's ability to automate complex financial decision-making threatens to further concentrate wealth and control within a small group of powerful institutions. The financial industry is witnessing a paradigm shift where traditional roles, such as traders, analysts, and fund managers, are increasingly being replaced by AI-driven systems that require minimal human intervention. This transformation consolidates financial power among firms that can afford to integrate these technologies while leaving smaller players and individual investors struggling to compete. Additionally, AI-driven trading has introduced new forms of systemic risks, such as algorithmic market manipulation and increased volatility, which disproportionately impact retail investors who lack the resources to react as swiftly as institutional giants. Ultimately, as AI continues to redefine financial markets, proactive regulation and widespread AI literacy will be crucial in ensuring a more balanced and equitable playing field.

Furthermore, AI's ability to automate job functions within the financial industry threatens traditional employment. Roles once performed by analysts, traders, and portfolio managers are increasingly being replaced by AI-driven systems, consolidating financial power within a small group of tech-savvy institutions that control these cutting-edge technologies.

Case Studies of Hedge Funds and Institutions Leveraging AI for Massive Profits

- **Renaissance Technologies:** This hedge fund, founded by mathematician Jim Simons, employs AI-driven quantitative strategies that have consistently outperformed the market. Its Medallion Fund, which is closed to outside investors, has reportedly generated annual returns exceeding 66% before fees by leveraging advanced machine learning models. The fund's success stems from its ability to identify complex market patterns that human traders would likely overlook. However, its highly secretive nature means that the exact AI methodologies it uses remain undisclosed.

- **BlackRock's Aladdin Platform:** The world's largest asset manager, BlackRock, utilizes its proprietary AI system, Aladdin, to analyze risk, optimize portfolios, and execute trades. Aladdin processes vast amounts of financial data to provide insights that influence trillions of dollars in global assets. Beyond portfolio management, Aladdin is also used for stress-testing financial models, predicting downturns, and automating compliance procedures. Its widespread adoption has made it a critical tool for institutional investors worldwide.

- **Bridgewater Associates:** Ray Dalio's hedge fund has invested heavily in AI research to enhance its trading strategies. The firm employs predictive analytics and machine learning algorithms to identify macroeconomic trends and anticipate market movements. Bridgewater's AI-driven investment strategies help it execute precise trades that align with global economic shifts, allowing the firm to remain profitable even in volatile markets. The company has also experimented with AI-powered decision-making in internal management, reflecting its deep commitment to machine learning applications in finance.

These case studies illustrate how AI is reshaping financial markets, granting institutional players unprecedented advantages. While AI-driven innovations hold the potential to enhance market efficiency and accessibility, they also pose risks of exacerbating wealth inequality, increasing market volatility, and creating ethical concerns regarding transparency and fairness.

Artificial Intelligence is a double-edged sword in financial markets. It empowers both retail investors and institutional players, but its advanced capabilities favor those with the resources to develop and deploy cutting-edge AI models. As technology continues to evolve, regulators and investors alike must remain vigilant to ensure AI-driven finance promotes fairness and market stability rather than further entrenching economic disparities.

Central Bank Digital Currencies (CBDCs) and Financial Control

How Governments Are Pushing for State-Backed Digital Currencies

As the global financial system undergoes rapid digital transformation, governments worldwide are exploring the introduction of Central Bank Digital Currencies (CBDCs). These state-backed digital currencies represent a shift from traditional physical cash to a fully digital monetary system controlled by central banks. Unlike decentralized cryptocurrencies such as Bitcoin and Ethereum, CBDCs operate within a regulated framework, providing governments with direct oversight and control over financial transactions.

Countries like China have already taken significant steps toward implementing CBDCs, with the digital yuan (e-CNY) being tested in major cities and integrated into various payment systems. Similarly, the U.S. Federal Reserve and the European Central Bank are actively researching the potential implementation of digital dollars and digital euros. Governments argue that CBDCs will enhance financial inclusion, improve transaction efficiency, and reduce illicit financial activities by providing a traceable and transparent monetary system.

Beyond these claims, many governments are motivated by the increasing dominance of private digital payment platforms like PayPal, Apple Pay, and Alipay. With more financial transactions shifting away from cash, central banks aim to maintain control over the monetary system and prevent corporate entities from monopolizing financial infrastructure. Additionally, CBDCs could serve as tools for monetary policy, allowing central banks to implement real-time interest rate changes, distribute stimulus payments directly, and respond more swiftly to economic crises.

However, the push for CBDCs raises critical questions about financial privacy, control, and the potential consequences of a centralized digital monetary system.

The Risks of CBDCs: Financial Surveillance, Programmable Money, and Loss of Privacy

One of the most significant concerns surrounding CBDCs is the potential for financial surveillance. Unlike cash transactions, which allow for anonymity, CBDCs provide governments with complete visibility into every transaction made within the digital currency system. This level of oversight enables authorities to monitor spending habits, enforce tax compliance, and track financial activities in real-time. While proponents argue that this could help combat money laundering and tax evasion, critics warn that it also poses a severe threat to financial privacy and personal freedoms.

Additionally, CBDCs introduce the concept of programmable money—where central banks or governments could impose restrictions on how money is spent. This means that funds could be allocated for specific purposes, restricted from certain transactions, or even have expiration dates to encourage spending within designated time frames. For example, in times of economic downturn, governments could program CBDCs to prevent excessive saving and stimulate consumption by making funds expire after a set period. While this could be seen as a tool for economic management, it also raises concerns about individual autonomy and financial independence.

Moreover, CBDCs could make it easier for governments to implement negative interest rates, where account balances decrease over time to discourage hoarding money. Such measures would fundamentally alter the concept of personal savings and wealth preservation, making individuals more dependent on the financial system's imposed structures. Additionally, the potential for social credit integration—where access to financial services is tied to compliance with government policies—has alarmed privacy advocates, who fear that CBDCs could be weaponized for political and economic control.

Case Studies: China's Digital Yuan and Pilot Projects in the U.S. and Europe

China has emerged as the frontrunner in CBDC development with its digital yuan, which has been undergoing large-scale trials in major cities. The People's Bank of China (PBOC) has integrated the e-CNY into popular payment platforms like Alipay and WeChat Pay, ensuring widespread adoption. The Chinese government touts the digital yuan as a means to enhance financial security and reduce reliance on foreign payment systems. However, concerns have been raised about the potential use of the currency for mass financial surveillance and social control, as the government could theoretically monitor and restrict transactions at will.

In the United States, the Federal Reserve has been conducting research on the feasibility of a digital dollar through initiatives like Project Hamilton. While no official decision has been made, policymakers have debated the implications of a CBDC, particularly its impact on the traditional banking system and consumer privacy. Some experts argue that a digital dollar could streamline financial transactions and reduce costs, but others worry that it could erode financial autonomy, especially if linked to government-mandated financial policies.

In Europe, the European Central Bank (ECB) has been working on the digital euro, with pilot programs evaluating its potential role in the financial ecosystem. While the ECB emphasizes privacy protections, critics warn that a digital euro could still be subject to tracking and control mechanisms, especially as governments seek to enforce financial regulations more stringently.

Other nations, including India, Nigeria, and Sweden, have also launched CBDC pilot programs. The eNaira in Nigeria, for instance, was introduced to boost financial inclusion, but adoption has been slow due to public skepticism and concerns over government control. Sweden's e-krona project, on the other hand, has been positioned as a solution to the country's rapidly declining use of cash, but it remains in the testing phase.

These pilot projects indicate a growing global interest in CBDCs, with each country tailoring its approach to suit its economic and political priorities. However, the widespread adoption of CBDCs would mark a fundamental shift in the relationship between citizens and their financial institutions, potentially reducing the role of commercial banks while increasing state control over monetary flows.

How CBDCs Could Replace Cash and Change Everyday Financial Transactions

One of the primary motivations for introducing CBDCs is the declining use of cash in many economies. As digital payments become the norm, central banks see CBDCs as a way to modernize currency while maintaining control over the monetary system. If CBDCs were to replace cash entirely, everyday transactions would be fully digitized, making physical money obsolete.

This transition could have both positive and negative consequences. On one hand, digital currencies could streamline transactions, reduce fraud, and enhance financial security. On the other hand, the elimination of cash would remove an essential tool for financial autonomy, leaving individuals entirely dependent on the state-controlled digital monetary system. In extreme cases, governments could use CBDCs to freeze accounts, restrict purchases, or impose economic policies that directly impact individual spending habits.

Furthermore, the introduction of CBDCs could disrupt traditional banking models. If consumers were to store their money directly with central banks rather than commercial banks, traditional financial institutions could face liquidity challenges, potentially leading to higher interest rates on loans and mortgages. The balance between innovation and financial stability would need to be carefully managed to prevent unintended economic consequences.

Additionally, the potential for financial exclusion remains a major concern. While CBDCs are often promoted as tools for increasing financial inclusion, individuals without access to digital infrastructure—such as smartphones or internet connectivity—could be left behind. This could create a new form of economic disparity, where those without technological resources are unable to participate fully in the financial system.

Central Bank Digital Currencies represent a significant shift in the future of money, offering both potential benefits and serious risks. While they promise increased financial efficiency and security, they also introduce concerns about government overreach, financial surveillance, and the erosion of financial privacy. As countries continue to explore CBDCs, it is essential for individuals to stay informed about these developments and consider the implications for their personal finances and economic freedoms. The transition to a fully digital monetary system could redefine wealth, power, and financial autonomy in ways that society must carefully navigate.

The Rise of Decentralized Finance (DeFi) and Its Risks

How DeFi Aims to Remove Middlemen from Finance

Decentralized Finance, commonly known as DeFi, is a financial movement that seeks to eliminate traditional financial intermediaries such as banks, brokers, and lending institutions. Using blockchain technology and smart contracts, DeFi platforms offer direct peer-to-peer transactions, reducing reliance on centralized authorities.

Unlike traditional banks that require intermediaries to process transactions, DeFi allows users to access financial services directly through decentralized applications (dApps). Platforms like Uniswap, Aave, and Compound enable users to trade assets, borrow funds, and earn interest on their holdings without needing approval from banks or government entities. This democratization of finance provides greater accessibility to financial services, particularly for those in underbanked regions.

For example, in many developing countries, individuals lack access to traditional banking systems due to high fees, strict requirements, and geographic limitations. With DeFi, anyone with an internet connection can engage in financial activities such as lending, borrowing, and investing, leveling the playing field for global economic participation.

DeFi's peer-to-peer nature also removes delays and bureaucratic red tape. In traditional finance, bank transfers and loan approvals can take days or even weeks, while DeFi transactions settle almost instantly. This efficiency is one of DeFi's strongest appeals, offering faster, more accessible financial services worldwide. However, the rapid expansion of DeFi also brings new challenges and risks that investors must carefully navigate.

The Promise of High Returns Through Staking, Lending, and Yield Farming

One of the main attractions of DeFi is the potential for high returns on investments. Unlike traditional savings accounts, which offer minimal interest rates, DeFi platforms provide significantly higher yields through mechanisms such as staking, lending, and yield farming.

- **Staking:** Users lock up their cryptocurrency assets to support blockchain operations and earn rewards in return. For instance, Ethereum 2.0 staking allows users to earn an annual percentage yield (APY) of up to 6-7%, significantly higher than traditional bank savings rates. Some newer projects offer even higher returns, though often with greater risks. Staking also helps secure blockchain networks, incentivizing long-term investment in the ecosystem. However, staked assets are often locked up for extended periods, limiting liquidity and exposing investors to market downturns.

- **Lending:** Platforms like Aave and Compound allow users to lend their crypto assets to others and earn interest. Unlike banks, which often take a large cut of the interest earned on loans, DeFi platforms distribute most of the earnings directly to the lenders. Some platforms offer flexible lending terms, while others have fixed-rate options to attract different types of investors. While lending can provide steady returns, it is also subject to smart contract vulnerabilities and borrower defaults, making risk management crucial.

- **Yield Farming:** This process involves users moving their assets across different DeFi protocols to maximize returns. Some yield farming strategies can offer APYs exceeding 100%, but they come with high risks, including impermanent loss, market volatility, and exposure to unstable platforms that may collapse. For instance, during the 2020 DeFi boom, investors flocked to high-yield farming projects like Yearn Finance, some reaping substantial gains, while others suffered losses when projects failed due to liquidity crises or exploitative coding flaws.

While the prospect of earning high yields is appealing, investors must be aware of the risks associated with DeFi investments, particularly in a largely unregulated market. Scams, liquidity issues, and extreme price swings can quickly turn lucrative opportunities into financial disasters.

The Dark Side: Rug Pulls, Hacks, and Lack of Regulation

Despite the benefits of DeFi, the sector is rife with risks, including fraud, cyberattacks, and regulatory uncertainty. The lack of centralized oversight makes DeFi a prime target for malicious actors looking to exploit vulnerabilities.

- **Rug Pulls:** A common scam in the DeFi space where developers create a seemingly legitimate project, attract investors, and then disappear with the funds. For instance, in 2021, the Squid Game token skyrocketed in value before the creators abruptly withdrew all liquidity, leaving investors with worthless tokens. Rug pulls continue to plague the DeFi market, often targeting inexperienced investors with promises of high returns.

- **Hacks:** Since smart contracts control DeFi platforms, any flaw in their code can be exploited. High-profile attacks, such as the $600 million Poly Network hack in 2021, highlight the risks of vulnerabilities in DeFi protocols. Though some stolen funds were recovered in this case, many other attacks have left investors with irreparable losses. The rise of flash loan attacks, where hackers manipulate the market using borrowed funds, further exposes DeFi's weaknesses.

- **Lack of Regulation:** Traditional financial markets operate under strict regulatory frameworks designed to protect consumers. DeFi, on the other hand, exists in a legal gray area. If users fall victim to scams or hacks, they often have no legal recourse. Governments worldwide are beginning to address DeFi regulation, but the decentralized nature of these platforms makes enforcement difficult. Countries like the U.S. and China have issued warnings or taken regulatory actions against certain DeFi activities, but the global landscape remains fragmented and uncertain.

Notable DeFi Successes and Failures—What Investors Can Learn

While DeFi has experienced notable success stories, it has also seen significant failures that serve as cautionary tales for investors.

Successes:

- **Uniswap:** A decentralized exchange (DEX) that allows users to trade cryptocurrencies without intermediaries. Since its launch, Uniswap has processed billions of dollars in transactions and remains one of the most popular DeFi platforms. It has also inspired numerous competitors, contributing to a more diversified and accessible crypto trading environment. Uniswap's automated market maker (AMM) model has changed the way crypto trading functions, enabling users to provide liquidity and earn fees without needing a centralized order book.

- **Aave:** A decentralized lending protocol that enables users to borrow and lend crypto assets with smart contracts, revolutionizing the lending industry by removing the need for traditional banks. Aave's introduction of flash loans—instant, unsecured loans—has demonstrated the innovative potential of DeFi, despite being exploited by bad actors in some cases. Flash loans, while useful for arbitrage and liquidation processes, have also been misused in market manipulation attacks, leading to significant losses for some platforms.

Failures:

- **Terra/Luna Collapse:** In 2022, the Terra stablecoin ecosystem collapsed due to flaws in its algorithmic stability mechanism, wiping out over $40 billion in investor funds and causing widespread panic in the crypto markets. This event served as a reminder of the risks associated with algorithmic stablecoins and overly complex financial models. The failure of Terra/Luna had a domino effect, triggering liquidity crises in other major crypto platforms such as Celsius and Three Arrows Capital, leading to a broader market downturn.

- **Iron Finance:** A DeFi project that promised high yields but ultimately suffered a bank run, leading to a catastrophic price crash that left many investors with massive losses. The sudden collapse exposed the risks of relying on unsustainable yield farming strategies and insufficient liquidity mechanisms. Investors who had staked their funds saw their assets drop to near-zero value within hours, highlighting the fragility of projects that lack robust financial backing and security measures.

The DeFi movement represents a revolutionary shift in the financial landscape, offering financial autonomy and high-yield opportunities while eliminating middlemen. However, with great rewards come great risks. Investors must navigate the sector with caution, conducting thorough research before engaging with DeFi platforms.

As traditional financial institutions and governments grapple with the rise of decentralized alternatives, the future of finance remains uncertain. Will DeFi continue to expand, or will regulatory intervention curb its growth? Regardless of the outcome, financial education and adaptability remain crucial in navigating this evolving digital economy.

Chapter 13: Smart Money Strategies for Regular People

Building wealth is often perceived as a privilege reserved for the ultra-rich. However, financial success is not limited to those born into wealth—it is accessible to anyone who understands and applies smart money strategies. The key difference between the rich and the average person is not just the size of their income but how they manage, invest, and grow their money over time.

Many regular people fall into common financial traps that prevent them from achieving long-term security. Living paycheck to paycheck, accumulating high-interest debt, and failing to invest are just a few of the mistakes that can keep people from reaching financial freedom. Additionally, a lack of financial education in schools and workplaces leaves many individuals without the necessary knowledge to make informed decisions about their money. Without this understanding, people often make costly mistakes that hinder their ability to build wealth, such as spending impulsively, relying solely on a salary, or failing to leverage financial tools that could work to their advantage.

By adopting wealth-building strategies used by the rich—such as tax optimization, strategic investing, and shifting from an employee mindset to an investor mindset—regular individuals can take control of their financial future. The wealthy do not just earn money; they make their money work for them through intelligent investment choices, minimizing tax burdens, and diversifying income streams. These strategies are not exclusive to billionaires; they can be implemented by anyone willing to learn and take action.

This chapter will explore practical steps to help people maximize their earnings, minimize unnecessary expenses, and make smart investments that lead to financial independence. By incorporating principles such as budgeting effectively, understanding compound interest, and recognizing the power of assets over liabilities, individuals can significantly improve their financial standing. Additionally, learning about alternative income sources—such as passive income, side businesses, and real estate—can help build long-term security.

Understanding and implementing these concepts can be life-changing, providing not just security but also the opportunity to build generational wealth. Taking charge of one's financial future requires education, discipline, and strategic decision-making, but the rewards are well worth the effort. With the right mindset and knowledge, anyone can escape financial struggles and create a prosperous future for themselves and their families.

Legal Tax-Saving Strategies Used by the Rich

How Tax Codes Favor Asset Owners Over Wage Earners

The tax system is structured in a way that provides significant advantages to asset owners over wage earners. Traditional employees are subject to higher tax rates due to progressive income tax brackets, payroll taxes, and limited deductions, whereas asset owners benefit from lower capital gains tax rates, depreciation deductions, and other incentives. For example, long-term capital gains, which apply to assets held for more than a year, are typically taxed at a lower rate than ordinary income, encouraging investment in stocks, real estate, and other appreciating assets. Additionally, businesses and investors can strategically reinvest profits and claim deductions that are not available to salaried workers, further widening the financial gap between wage earners and asset holders.

The Power of Tax Deductions, Write-Offs, and Legal

Loopholes

Wealthy individuals and corporations use a variety of deductions and loopholes to legally minimize their taxable income. Some of the most common methods include:

- **Depreciation:** Real estate investors can deduct depreciation on their properties, allowing them to reduce their taxable income without incurring real financial losses. This paper loss can offset rental income, significantly lowering tax obligations.

- **Business Expenses:** Entrepreneurs can write off a wide range of business expenses, including travel, meals, office space, equipment, and even home office deductions, substantially reducing taxable income while maintaining operational flexibility.

- **Charitable Donations:** Philanthropy is often a strategic move for high-net-worth individuals to reduce their tax liability. By donating appreciated assets like stocks or real estate instead of cash, individuals can avoid capital gains taxes while receiving a deduction for the full market value of the asset.

- **Tax-Loss Harvesting:** Investors can strategically sell underperforming investments at a loss to offset gains in other areas. This practice, commonly used by high-net-worth investors, ensures that capital gains taxes are minimized while allowing for reinvestment in new opportunities.

- **Municipal Bonds:** Investing in municipal bonds provides tax-free interest income, making them an attractive option for high-income earners looking to shelter earnings from federal and sometimes state taxes.

- **Deferred Compensation Plans:** Executives often use deferred compensation plans to push taxable income into future years, ideally when they are in a lower tax bracket, further reducing immediate tax burdens.

Using Real Estate, Business Structures, and Investments to Minimize Tax Liability

The wealthy strategically structure their finances to take advantage of tax-saving opportunities. Some of the most effective strategies include:

- **Real Estate Investments:** By owning rental properties, individuals can deduct mortgage interest, property taxes, and maintenance costs while benefiting from appreciation and passive income. Real estate also offers the advantage of 1031 exchanges, allowing investors to defer capital gains taxes when selling properties and reinvesting in new ones. Additionally, real estate professionals can claim unlimited passive losses to offset other income, significantly reducing their tax burden.

- **Trusts and Foundations:** High-net-worth individuals often use family trusts and charitable foundations to legally shelter wealth from excessive taxation and ensure long-term financial security. These structures allow assets to be passed down through generations with minimal tax consequences. For example, dynasty trusts enable families to preserve wealth across multiple generations while avoiding estate taxes.

- **Retirement Accounts and Tax-Deferred Investments:** Wealthy investors maximize contributions to retirement accounts such as IRAs and 401(k)s while utilizing tax-deferred accounts like Health Savings Accounts (HSAs) to reduce taxable income. Some also take advantage of Roth conversions to minimize tax burdens over time. Additionally, backdoor Roth IRAs provide high-income earners with a legal way to bypass income limits on Roth contributions.

- **Offshore Tax Strategies:** While controversial, offshore accounts and international business structures are used by some wealthy individuals and corporations to take advantage of lower tax jurisdictions, legally reducing tax obligations through proper compliance with international tax laws. Countries like the Cayman Islands and Switzerland are known for favorable tax treatments that attract wealthy individuals and multinational corporations seeking tax efficiency.

Case Studies of How Wealthy Individuals Legally Reduce Their Tax Burden

- **Elon Musk & Stock-Based Compensation:** Instead of taking a traditional salary, many wealthy executives, including Elon Musk, receive stock-based compensation. By borrowing against their shares instead of selling them, they access liquidity without triggering taxable events, allowing them to pay minimal income tax while benefiting from lower capital gains taxes.

- **Donald Trump & Real Estate Depreciation:** Former President Donald Trump has long utilized real estate depreciation to minimize his tax liability. By claiming paper losses on depreciable assets, real estate investors can significantly reduce taxable income while still generating revenue through rental properties.

- **Warren Buffett & Capital Gains Tax Strategies:** Buffett has famously stated that he pays a lower tax rate than his secretary due to the way capital gains are taxed at a lower rate than ordinary income. By primarily earning through long-term capital gains rather than wages, he avoids higher tax rates and benefits from tax-deferred growth.

- **Jeff Bezos & Business Write-Offs:** Amazon founder Jeff Bezos has leveraged business tax strategies such as reinvesting company profits, claiming research and development credits, and utilizing deferred taxation methods to minimize personal and corporate tax burdens. By reinvesting earnings into Amazon's expansion, the company often reported little to no taxable profits despite massive revenues.

- **Peter Thiel & Tax-Free Growth in Roth IRAs:** The co-founder of PayPal, Peter Thiel, reportedly grew his Roth IRA to billions of dollars by strategically placing early-stage investments in the tax-free retirement account. By investing in high-growth startups within his Roth IRA, he ensured that future earnings remained completely untaxed upon withdrawal, highlighting the power of tax-advantaged investing.

By understanding and applying some of these strategies within legal limits, regular people can start implementing wealth-building techniques that reduce tax burdens and promote financial growth.

Investing Like the Wealthy – Focusing on Assets Over Income

The Difference Between Earning a Paycheck and Building Wealth

Many people equate wealth with earning a high salary, but the truly wealthy understand that income alone does not build lasting financial security. The key distinction lies in **active income** versus **passive income**.

- **Active income** is what most people rely on: salaries, hourly wages, and bonuses. This type of income is directly tied to the number of hours worked. Once a person stops working, the income stops as well.

- **Passive income**, on the other hand, comes from investments such as real estate, dividends, and business ownership. These assets continue to generate money even if the owner is not actively working.

To illustrate this distinction, consider two professionals: Sarah, a highly paid doctor, and James, a business owner. Sarah earns a six-figure salary but works long hours, and her financial security depends entirely on her ability to keep working. James, on the other hand, owns multiple rental properties and has invested in dividend-paying stocks. Even if he takes a year off, his assets continue to generate income, allowing him to maintain his lifestyle.

Wealthy individuals prioritize acquiring income-producing assets rather than just working for higher wages. This shift in focus allows them to escape the paycheck-to-paycheck cycle and build long-term financial security.

Why the Rich Prioritize Income-Producing Assets Over Active Income

While many people work hard to earn a paycheck, the wealthy concentrate on **owning assets** that increase in value and generate passive income. These assets include:

1. **Real Estate:** Rental properties, commercial buildings, and real estate investment trusts (REITs) provide ongoing cash flow and appreciation. Wealthy investors often buy properties in prime locations that appreciate in value over time while generating rental income. For example, billionaire Andrew Carnegie built much of his wealth through real estate investments, focusing on prime locations that ensured long-term value growth.
2. **Stocks and Dividends:** Wealthy individuals invest heavily in dividend-paying stocks, which provide them with regular income without having to sell the underlying asset. Warren Buffett, for instance, has made billions by investing in blue-chip dividend stocks such as Coca-Cola and Johnson & Johnson, which provide a steady stream of income while growing in value over time.
3. **Private Equity and Venture Capital:** The rich often invest in startups or private companies, where they can earn substantial returns if the business succeeds. Tech moguls such as Peter Thiel and Elon Musk built fortunes by investing in early-stage companies like Facebook, PayPal, and Tesla, reaping immense rewards as these businesses

skyrocketed in value.

4. **Alternative Investments:** Assets like cryptocurrency, fine art, collectibles, and commodities (gold, silver, oil) provide diversification and potential high returns. Hedge funds and ultra-high-net-worth individuals often invest in rare collectibles and artwork by renowned artists such as Picasso and Van Gogh, seeing them as safe-haven assets during economic downturns.
5. **Businesses and Franchises:** Owning a business or a share in one provides both income and control over financial outcomes. Many wealthy individuals choose to start or invest in businesses, generating wealth through ownership rather than just employment. For example, Jeff Bezos originally started Amazon as an online bookstore, which later evolved into one of the most valuable companies in the world, making him one of the richest individuals globally.

By focusing on these income-generating assets, the wealthy ensure that money works for them instead of the other way around.

Asset Classes the Wealthy Invest In

1. Real Estate

Real estate is one of the most preferred investments among the wealthy because it offers multiple streams of income, long-term appreciation, and tax advantages.

- **Rental Properties:** Monthly rent provides consistent cash flow, while property values appreciate over time. For example, real estate mogul Sam Zell built his fortune by investing in undervalued rental properties and commercial spaces, turning them into lucrative cash-generating assets.

- **Commercial Real Estate:** Office spaces, shopping centers, and industrial properties often yield higher returns than residential properties. Wealthy investors strategically invest in prime commercial locations to benefit from both rental income and long-term value appreciation.

- **Real Estate Syndications and REITs:** Those who don't want to manage properties directly can invest in real estate investment trusts (REITs) or syndications, where they pool money with other investors. This method allows investors to benefit from real estate income without direct property ownership. For instance, major REITs like Realty Income and Simon Property Group have provided significant passive income to their shareholders.

- **House Flipping:** Some wealthy investors buy undervalued properties, renovate them, and sell for a profit. A famous example is Barbara Corcoran, who built a multimillion-dollar empire by flipping real estate in New York City. House flipping can be highly profitable if done strategically, focusing on location, renovation costs, and market timing.

- **Vacation Rentals:** Platforms like Airbnb allow property owners to generate higher returns than traditional rentals by catering to short-term stays. Many investors have turned their properties into highly profitable vacation rentals in tourist hotspots, taking advantage of fluctuating seasonal pricing to maximize revenue.

2. Stocks and Bonds

- **Dividend Stocks:** Stocks of established companies (e.g., Coca-Cola, Procter & Gamble) pay dividends, creating a passive income stream. Wealthy investors like Warren Buffett rely on dividends for consistent, long-term income.

- **Index Funds & ETFs:** These provide diversified exposure to the stock market while minimizing risk. Index funds tracking the S&P 500 have historically provided strong returns with lower volatility.

- **Municipal Bonds:** These are tax-free investment options that provide stable income, making them a popular choice among high-net-worth individuals looking for risk-free, tax-advantaged returns.

- **Growth Stocks:** Wealthy investors look for companies with high growth potential, often in technology and healthcare sectors. Examples include Tesla, Amazon, and Nvidia, which have delivered exponential returns for early investors.

- **Blue-Chip Stocks:** Reliable, established companies that have stood the test of time offer stability and long-term appreciation. These stocks, such as Johnson & Johnson and Microsoft, form the foundation of many high-net-worth investment portfolios.

How Regular People Can Start Investing with Small Amounts

Even those who don't have large amounts of money can adopt the strategies of the wealthy by starting small and being consistent. The key is to develop an investment habit and take advantage of accessible investment options that require minimal capital. Here are some ways to get started:

- **Fractional Shares:** Brokerage platforms now allow investors to buy fractions of a stock, making it possible to own shares of expensive companies like Amazon or Tesla with as little as $5.

- **Index Funds and ETFs:** Instead of picking individual stocks, regular investors can buy low-cost index funds or ETFs that track the overall market, offering instant diversification with minimal risk.

- **Robo-Advisors:** Automated investment platforms like Betterment and Wealthfront help beginners invest without deep financial knowledge, creating tailored portfolios based on risk tolerance and goals.

- **Real Estate Crowdfunding:** Platforms like Fundrise and RealtyMogul allow individuals to invest in properties with small amounts, benefiting from rental income and property appreciation.

- **Employer-Sponsored Retirement Accounts:** Many companies offer 401(k) plans with employer matching, which is essentially free money for employees, growing significantly over time.

- **Side Hustle Income Allocation:** Setting aside earnings from side gigs or freelance work into investments can compound wealth over time, leading to substantial gains through compound interest.

The Mindset Shift: Thinking Like an Investor, Not an Employee

How Financial Education Changes Long-Term Wealth Outcomes

The way people think about money has a profound impact on their financial future. Many individuals grow up learning to work hard, earn a salary, and save what they can. However, the wealthy take a different approach: they focus on **financial education** and **investment strategies** to ensure their money works for them.

Financial literacy plays a crucial role in determining whether someone thrives financially or struggles to stay afloat. Schools rarely teach students about investing, asset accumulation, or passive income. Instead, most people are conditioned to think in terms of earning and spending rather than investing and growing wealth.

For example, consider two friends: John and Lisa. Both earn the same salary of $70,000 per year. John follows the traditional path—he saves a portion of his income in a bank account, occasionally splurges on luxury items, and relies on his paycheck to cover expenses. Lisa, on the other hand, educates herself on investing. She directs a portion of her salary into dividend-paying stocks, real estate, and a side business. Over time, Lisa's assets generate additional income, allowing her to reinvest and compound her wealth. In contrast, John remains dependent on his job.

The key difference? **Lisa understood that wealth isn't built by earning alone—it's built by smart investing and financial education.**

The Importance of Strategic Risk-Taking and Long-Term Planning

One of the most significant mindset shifts that separates the wealthy from the middle class is **strategic risk-taking**. While many people fear financial risk and prefer the safety of a steady paycheck, successful investors understand that taking calculated risks is essential for financial growth.

Wealthy individuals evaluate risks based on **potential returns** rather than just possible losses. They also recognize that **short-term discomfort can lead to long-term gains**. This is why they focus on assets like:

- **Stocks and Bonds:** While the stock market fluctuates, long-term investments in solid companies or index funds have historically provided strong returns. For instance, investing in companies like Apple, Microsoft, and Amazon decades ago has turned modest investments into fortunes. Bonds, on the other hand, offer stability and a fixed income, making them a reliable component of a diversified portfolio.

- **Real Estate Investments:** Property values tend to appreciate over time, generating both rental income and capital gains. For example, real estate mogul Grant Cardone emphasizes multi-family rental properties as a means of building long-term wealth, allowing investors to generate steady cash flow and benefit from asset appreciation.

- **Entrepreneurial Ventures:** While starting a business involves risk, it also offers unlimited income potential compared to a fixed salary. Elon Musk took significant risks by investing his PayPal earnings into Tesla and

SpaceX, despite financial uncertainty. His long-term vision and willingness to take risks paid off, making him one of the wealthiest individuals in history.

The lesson? **Smart risk-taking and long-term vision are essential to breaking free from financial limitations.**

Developing Multiple Streams of Income to Achieve Financial Independence

The average person relies on a single source of income—usually a salary. However, the wealthy understand the power of **diversified income streams**. By having multiple sources of revenue, they create financial security that isn't tied to one job or economic condition.

Here are some common **income streams** wealthy individuals develop:

1. **Earned Income** – Money from a job or business.
2. **Investment Income** – Profits from stocks, bonds, and other investments.
3. **Rental Income** – Earnings from real estate properties.
4. **Passive Business Income** – Royalties, licensing fees, or automated business revenue.
5. **Side Hustles and Online Businesses** – Selling digital products, consulting, or freelancing.

For example, bestselling author Robert Kiyosaki, known for *Rich Dad Poor Dad*, emphasizes the importance of **building multiple income streams** to achieve financial freedom. He invested in real estate, created educational courses, and wrote books—each providing independent revenue sources that continue generating income regardless of economic conditions.

Moreover, consider YouTuber Graham Stephan, who turned his earnings into a diversified empire. Starting as a real estate agent, he reinvested his commissions into rental properties. Then, he expanded his income by launching a successful YouTube channel, selling online courses, and partnering with financial brands. His diversified approach allowed him to build wealth rapidly while maintaining financial security.

The takeaway? **Relying on one income stream is a financial risk—diversifying ensures long-term stability and wealth growth.**

Steps to Shift from a Consumer Mindset to an Investor Mindset

The final step in this mindset shift is moving from being a **consumer** to becoming an **investor**. This requires a change in daily financial habits and long-term thinking.

Here's how to start:

1. **Prioritize Investing Over Spending** – Instead of upgrading to the newest gadgets, designer clothing, or luxury vacations, allocate money toward investments like stocks, real estate, or starting a business. For example, instead of spending $1,000 on the latest smartphone, putting that same amount into an index fund could grow exponentially over time.
2. **Automate Savings & Investments** – Set up automatic transfers to investment accounts so you're consistently growing wealth without needing to think about it. Many successful investors use this strategy to ensure they consistently build assets rather than relying on leftover income at the end of the month.
3. **Think in Terms of Assets, Not Just Income** – Before making a financial decision, ask: *Will this purchase help me generate wealth in the future?* If not, reconsider the

purchase. For instance, buying a rental property that generates cash flow is an asset, while an expensive car that depreciates in value is a liability.

4. **Surround Yourself with Financially-Savvy People** – The people you spend time with influence your financial mindset. Seek mentors, join investing groups, and follow financially successful individuals. For example, Warren Buffett credits much of his success to learning from his mentor Benjamin Graham, whose investment principles shaped Buffett's approach to wealth-building.
5. **Educate Yourself Continuously** – Read books, take courses, and stay updated on market trends. The more knowledge you acquire, the better financial decisions you'll make. Legendary investors like Charlie Munger emphasize lifelong learning, stating that the more you read and expand your knowledge, the more opportunities you'll recognize.

A real-world example of this shift can be seen in athletes. Many professional athletes earn millions but retire broke because they only focused on spending, not investing. On the other hand, NBA legend Shaquille O'Neal invested heavily in businesses, franchises, and real estate, ensuring his wealth lasted far beyond his playing career.

Breaking free from the paycheck-to-paycheck cycle requires a **fundamental shift in thinking**. Wealth isn't about how much you earn—it's about how well you invest and manage money.

By embracing financial education, taking strategic risks, developing multiple income streams, and shifting to an **investor's mindset**, regular people can achieve financial freedom and long-term security.

The journey to financial independence starts with small, consistent steps. Whether it's setting aside a percentage of your income for investments, educating yourself on wealth-building strategies, or developing a business, every step brings you closer to a future where money works for you, rather than you working for money.

Chapter 14: Avoiding Financial Traps & Scams

The financial world is full of risks, but the wealthy know how to safeguard their assets. While the ultra-rich employ financial advisors, diversified investments, and legal strategies to protect their wealth, regular people often find themselves vulnerable to financial pitfalls. These traps range from poor money management habits to outright scams designed to exploit people's lack of financial knowledge.

Financial mistakes are often rooted in psychological biases—fear, greed, and a desire for quick financial success. Scammers and predatory financial institutions prey on these emotions, luring people into high-risk investments, fraudulent schemes, and bad financial decisions. Understanding these traps and how to avoid them is crucial for anyone seeking financial stability and long-term security.

This chapter will explore how the wealthy protect themselves from financial downturns, common financial mistakes the middle class makes, and how to recognize and avoid scams targeting investors. By adopting a more strategic and informed approach to money, individuals can minimize risks and make better financial choices that lead to lasting wealth.

How the Wealthy Protect Themselves from Inflation and Market Crashes

Strategies the Rich Use to Hedge Against Inflation

Inflation erodes the purchasing power of money, making it a silent wealth destroyer for those who rely solely on cash savings. The wealthy understand this and implement strategies to protect and even grow their assets in inflationary periods. Some of the key strategies include:

- **Investing in Gold and Precious Metals**: Historically, gold has been a safe-haven asset that retains value during economic downturns and inflationary periods. Investors like Ray Dalio advocate for gold as a hedge against currency devaluation. Silver, platinum, and other precious metals are also considered effective stores of value.

- **Real Estate as a Tangible Asset**: Property values tend to rise with inflation, and rental income often increases to match the rising cost of living. The rich acquire real estate to generate passive income, build long-term wealth, and benefit from tax advantages such as depreciation and mortgage interest deductions.

- **Diversified Investments in Stocks and Commodities**: Holding a diversified portfolio with investments in stocks, commodities, and alternative assets helps mitigate the risks of inflation. Energy, agricultural products, and raw materials are often inflation-resistant and can serve as effective hedges.

- **Allocating Funds to Inflation-Indexed Bonds**: Treasury Inflation-Protected Securities (TIPS) and other inflation-indexed bonds adjust their value based on inflation, offering protection against decreasing currency value. High-net-worth individuals use these instruments to ensure a stable return on their investments.

- **Holding Foreign Currencies and International Investments**: To reduce exposure to local economic downturns, the wealthy invest in foreign currencies, global markets, and international real estate, ensuring their wealth is spread across multiple economies. By diversifying across regions, they reduce the impact of inflation in any single country.

The Role of Inflation-Resistant Assets

Not all assets perform well during inflationary periods. The wealthy strategically focus on inflation-resistant investments, such as:

- **Commodities and Natural Resources**: Prices of commodities like oil, wheat, copper, and timber tend to rise with inflation. Billionaire investors like Jim Rogers emphasize the importance of owning commodity-based investments to hedge against rising costs.

- **Real Estate and REITs (Real Estate Investment Trusts)**: Real estate has intrinsic value and appreciates over time. REITs allow investors to gain exposure to property markets without directly owning physical real estate. Industrial and commercial properties, in particular, benefit from inflation due to rising rental prices.

- **Dividend-Paying Stocks**: Companies that pay consistent dividends, such as those in consumer staples and utilities, provide income that can outpace inflation. Investors reinvest dividends to benefit from compounding returns, a common strategy among the wealthy.

- **Private Equity and Venture Capital**: The wealthy invest in startups and private businesses that have high growth potential, allowing them to benefit from economic shifts rather than being hurt by them. Investing in disruptive industries like technology, healthcare, and clean energy helps hedge against inflation by targeting sectors with rapid expansion.

- **Cryptocurrencies and Digital Assets**: While highly volatile, some investors view cryptocurrencies like Bitcoin as a hedge against fiat currency devaluation. Digital assets and decentralized finance (DeFi) platforms are increasingly becoming part of sophisticated investment strategies.

How Market Crashes Create Opportunities for the Wealthy

Market crashes often trigger panic selling among average investors, but the wealthy view downturns as opportunities to buy undervalued assets. Some of the tactics they use include:

- **Buying Stocks at a Discount**: When markets crash, quality stocks become significantly undervalued. Investors with cash reserves take advantage of these lower prices, acquiring shares in strong companies at bargain rates, setting themselves up for substantial long-term gains.

- **Acquiring Real Estate During Economic Downturns**: Property values often decline during recessions, allowing wealthy investors to purchase assets at lower prices and benefit from appreciation in the long run. For example, after the 2008 housing crisis, institutional investors bought thousands of foreclosed properties and turned them into profitable rental assets.

- **Investing in Distressed Assets and Businesses**: The rich seek out businesses and assets that are struggling but have long-term potential. By acquiring them at a discount, they can turn them into profitable ventures. Private equity firms often specialize in buying distressed companies, restructuring them, and selling them for significant profits later.

- **Holding Cash to Buy During Dips**: Wealthy individuals and hedge funds maintain liquidity so they can invest during downturns when most people are selling out of fear. By having capital ready, they can make strategic acquisitions at rock-bottom prices.

- **Utilizing Options and Hedging Strategies**: Many high-net-worth investors use derivatives like put options and futures contracts to protect their portfolios from extreme volatility. This ensures that they can limit losses during downturns while positioning themselves for gains as the market recovers.

Case Study: Warren Buffett's Investment Strategy During Market Crashes

Warren Buffett, one of the world's most successful investors, follows the philosophy of "be greedy when others are fearful, and fearful when others are greedy." He has consistently profited by investing during market downturns:

- **During the 2008 Financial Crisis**, Buffett invested heavily in companies like Goldman Sachs and Bank of America when their stock prices were plummeting. He negotiated special preferred stock deals that provided Berkshire Hathaway with strong returns while also stabilizing these institutions. These investments yielded massive profits as the economy recovered.

- **In the COVID-19 Market Crash of 2020**, Berkshire Hathaway increased its stakes in industries poised for long-term growth, taking advantage of temporary stock price declines. While many investors panicked and sold off assets, Buffett focused on acquiring stocks at a discount.

- **Buffett's Holding Strategy**: Instead of selling during downturns, Buffett focuses on strong fundamentals and holds investments for the long term, allowing them to recover and appreciate in value. His patient, disciplined approach contrasts with the short-term panic reactions of average investors.

By adopting these strategies, the wealthy not only protect their assets from inflation and market crashes but also capitalize on economic downturns to grow their wealth exponentially. The key takeaway for regular investors is that financial crises create opportunities for those who are prepared, disciplined, and financially educated. Implementing these principles can help individuals build long-term wealth and safeguard their financial future.

Common Financial Mistakes the Middle Class Makes

Overreliance on a Single Source of Income (Paycheck Dependency)

Many middle-class individuals depend entirely on a single paycheck to cover their expenses. While having a stable job is essential, relying solely on one source of income puts individuals at significant financial risk. If an unexpected job loss occurs, it can lead to immediate financial hardship, forcing individuals to dip into savings, rely on credit cards, or even take out high-interest loans just to stay afloat. Additionally, career stagnation or industry downturns can leave individuals vulnerable to financial instability if they have no alternative income streams.

Example: During the COVID-19 pandemic, millions of people lost their jobs with little to no warning. Those who had additional income streams, such as rental properties, dividend-paying stocks, or side businesses, were able to weather the storm far better than those who relied only on their salaries. Many gig workers or side hustlers, for instance, pivoted to online freelancing, e-commerce, or remote consulting, helping them maintain some level of income despite the widespread layoffs. The key takeaway is that diversifying income sources can provide financial stability and reduce dependence on a single employer.

The Dangers of Lifestyle Inflation

As people earn more, they tend to increase their spending proportionally, a phenomenon known as lifestyle inflation. Instead of using additional income to invest or save, many choose to upgrade their cars, move into larger homes, or spend more on luxury items.

While these purchases may bring short-term satisfaction, they often prevent long-term wealth accumulation and can leave individuals in a precarious financial position if their income unexpectedly decreases.

Example: A professional who receives a raise from $60,000 to $80,000 per year may decide to buy a more expensive car with a higher monthly payment, move into a more luxurious apartment, or dine out more frequently instead of increasing contributions to investments or savings. As a result, despite earning more, they continue living paycheck to paycheck with little to no financial security. In contrast, someone who maintains their current lifestyle and allocates additional income toward assets—such as an investment portfolio, rental property, or retirement savings—will significantly increase their net worth over time. To build wealth, individuals must resist the urge to inflate their lifestyles and instead focus on growing their assets.

Misunderstanding Debt: Good Debt vs. Bad Debt

Debt, when used strategically, can be a powerful tool for wealth creation. However, many middle-class individuals fail to differentiate between good debt and bad debt.

- **Good Debt:** Includes investments that generate income or appreciate in value, such as real estate, student loans for high-earning potential careers, and business loans used for growth. Properly managed, these debts can build long-term wealth and increase financial security.

- **Bad Debt:** Includes high-interest consumer debt, such as credit card balances, payday loans, and unnecessary car loans, which do not contribute to wealth-building and often lead to financial stress.

Example: Consider two individuals: One takes out a $200,000 mortgage on a rental property that generates $1,500 in monthly rent, covering the mortgage and expenses while building long-term equity. Over time, the property appreciates in value, increasing their wealth. The other accumulates $20,000 in credit card debt from vacations, shopping, and dining out, paying over 20% interest. As a result, they struggle to make minimum payments, and their financial future is compromised. The first individual is using debt to build wealth, while the second is using it to fund a lifestyle that leads to financial stress. Understanding how to leverage debt for growth rather than consumption is a crucial step toward financial independence.

Failure to Plan for Financial Downturns

A common mistake among the middle class is failing to prepare for economic downturns or personal financial emergencies. Many people lack an emergency fund, have insufficient insurance coverage, and do not account for market volatility in their investment strategies. Without proper planning, unexpected expenses such as medical bills, home repairs, or job loss can lead to severe financial instability.

Example: An individual with no emergency savings loses their job and is forced to rely on credit cards to cover basic expenses, quickly accumulating high-interest debt. In contrast, someone with six months' worth of expenses saved in a high-yield savings account can navigate the situation with far less financial stress. Additionally, investors who panic-sell their stocks during a market downturn often lock in losses, while those who remain patient and continue investing can benefit from market recoveries. Having an emergency fund, a well-diversified portfolio, and an insurance plan can serve as a safety net in difficult times.

The Importance of Financial Education

Many financial mistakes stem from a lack of financial literacy. Schools rarely teach personal finance, leaving individuals to learn through trial and error. The middle class often misses out on opportunities because they are unaware of effective investment strategies, tax-saving techniques, or ways to leverage debt for wealth creation. Without proper financial education, individuals are more likely to fall for high-interest loans, predatory financial products, and investment scams.

Example: A financially literate individual might invest in tax-advantaged accounts like a 401(k) or Roth IRA, allowing their money to grow tax-free over time. They may also take advantage of employer-matching contributions, compound interest, and diversified investment strategies. Meanwhile, someone without financial education may leave their money in a low-interest savings account, missing out on potential growth or failing to plan for retirement adequately. Additionally, financial literacy helps individuals recognize scams, such as Ponzi schemes, fraudulent investment opportunities, and misleading financial products, preventing them from falling victim to financial fraud.

Avoiding common financial mistakes requires awareness, discipline, and a proactive approach to managing money. By diversifying income sources, controlling lifestyle inflation, understanding debt, preparing for downturns, and investing in financial education, middle-class individuals can break free from financial insecurity and work toward long-term wealth. The key to financial success is not just earning more but making smarter financial decisions with the money you already have. Developing financial literacy, adopting a long-term investment mindset, and cultivating habits that prioritize financial stability over short-term gratification will pave the way for a more secure and prosperous future.

Recognizing and Avoiding Scams Targeting Investors

The Psychology Behind Scams: Why People Fall for "Get Rich Quick" Schemes

Scams often exploit basic human emotions—greed, fear, and the desire for security. Many fraudulent schemes promise quick financial gains with little effort, making them attractive to individuals looking for an easy way to build wealth. Scammers use high-pressure tactics, social proof, and a false sense of urgency to manipulate victims into making impulsive decisions. They often present their schemes as "once-in-a-lifetime" opportunities, using testimonials from supposed success stories to make their offers seem credible. Additionally, scammers prey on those in financial distress, offering solutions that appear to be a quick fix but ultimately lead to significant losses.

One psychological tactic scammers frequently use is the principle of authority—posing as financial experts, successful entrepreneurs, or investment gurus to gain trust. People are more likely to believe in a scheme if they think a credible or wealthy individual is backing it. Scammers also leverage herd mentality, making victims believe that "everyone else" is investing, creating an illusion of safety in numbers.

Example: The FOMO (Fear of Missing Out) effect is commonly used in scams, particularly in cryptocurrency pump-and-dump schemes. Investors see rapid gains and jump in, only to realize too late that they've been manipulated by insiders who sell at the peak, leaving latecomers with losses. For instance, during the 2017 cryptocurrency boom, numerous altcoins experienced artificial price inflation due to coordinated social media hype, only to crash once insiders cashed out, leaving uninformed investors with worthless assets. The key takeaway is that emotional decision-making, rather than rational analysis, often leads to financial losses in fraudulent schemes.

Common Investment Scams

Ponzi and Pyramid Schemes (e.g., Bernie Madoff Scandal)

Ponzi schemes rely on using funds from new investors to pay returns to earlier investors, creating the illusion of profitability. These schemes often claim to generate profits through legitimate investments, but in reality, they use incoming funds from new participants to pay earlier investors. As long as new money flows in, the scheme appears to function, but once recruitment slows or stops, it collapses, leaving the majority of investors with significant losses. Pyramid schemes, on the other hand, require participants to recruit others in order to profit, creating an unsustainable structure that inevitably fails when recruitment slows.

Case Study: Bernie Madoff's Ponzi scheme, one of the largest financial frauds in history, defrauded investors out of an estimated $65 billion. Madoff, a well-respected financier and former chairman of NASDAQ, promised consistent, high returns through what he claimed was a proprietary trading strategy. Investors, including hedge funds, banks, and individual clients, were drawn in by his reputation and the illusion of steady profits. However, his firm was merely redistributing new investor funds to pay off earlier clients, without making legitimate investments. When the 2008 financial crisis led to a surge in withdrawal requests, the scheme unraveled, revealing its fraudulent nature. This case highlights how even highly sophisticated investors can fall victim to well-orchestrated financial fraud when they neglect proper due diligence and rely too heavily on reputation and perceived exclusivity.

High-Yield Investment Programs (HYIPs)

HYIPs promise unrealistically high returns, often claiming to double or triple investments in a short period. These schemes typically involve crypto or forex trading and lure victims with flashy websites, fake testimonials, and deceptive marketing tactics. Scammers use persuasive language, such as "guaranteed returns" and "proven profit systems," to entice unsuspecting investors who are eager for quick financial gains.

Example: Many HYIPs promote their services on social media, leveraging influencer endorsements and paid advertisements to gain credibility. They often offer 10-20% daily returns with "zero risk" claims, making them appear legitimate. Investors deposit funds and may receive small initial payouts, designed to build trust and encourage them to invest larger amounts. However, these payouts are typically funded by new investor deposits rather than actual profits. Eventually, the scheme collapses when recruitment slows, leaving later investors with devastating losses while the orchestrators vanish with the majority of the funds. A notorious example is the case of "Mirror Trading International (MTI)," a South African-based HYIP that promised lucrative bitcoin trading returns but ended up defrauding investors out of over $589 million before shutting down in 2020.

Pump-and-Dump Schemes in Crypto and Penny Stocks

Pump-and-dump schemes involve artificially inflating the price of an asset through misleading promotions, social media hype, or false endorsements. Once the price spikes, insiders sell off their holdings, causing the price to crash and leaving regular investors with worthless assets. These schemes are particularly rampant in cryptocurrency markets and penny stocks, where regulatory oversight is weaker and volatility is high. Unsuspecting investors are drawn in by aggressive marketing tactics, including social media influencers, fraudulent news articles, and coordinated buying efforts that create the illusion of demand.

Case Study: In 2017, several small cryptocurrencies saw massive price spikes due to coordinated social media campaigns. Groups of traders manipulated prices by buying in bulk and promoting false narratives about these digital assets. Influencers and online forums hyped the coins, convincing retail investors that they were the "next big thing." Once the hype peaked, the original traders dumped their holdings at inflated prices, triggering a market collapse. One of the most infamous cases involved the coin "Verge (XVG)," which saw its value increase by over 800% in a short span before crashing dramatically when insiders offloaded their holdings. Many investors who bought at the peak suffered huge losses as the coin lost nearly all its value within weeks. This example illustrates how pump-and-dump schemes thrive in unregulated markets, leaving uninformed investors financially devastated.

Red Flags to Watch For

1. **Promises of "Guaranteed" High Returns with Low Risk**

    ○ No legitimate investment is risk-free. Scammers often advertise unrealistic returns to lure in victims. If an opportunity claims to have high rewards with little to no risk, it is likely fraudulent.

2. **Pressure to Invest Quickly Without Time for Research**

○ Scammers create urgency, claiming opportunities are "limited-time offers" or "exclusive deals" to prevent individuals from conducting proper due diligence. High-pressure tactics are a major red flag.

3. **Lack of Transparency and Unregistered Investment Firms**

○ Legitimate investment opportunities are registered with regulatory bodies. If a company avoids providing details about its team, financials, or business model, it's likely a scam. Always check regulatory databases before investing.

Case Study: The Rise and Fall of BitConnect – One of the Biggest Crypto Scams

BitConnect was a cryptocurrency lending platform that promised investors exceptionally high returns through its so-called "trading bot," which claimed to generate consistent profits by executing automated cryptocurrency trades. The company operated as a classic Ponzi scheme, where funds from new investors were used to pay returns to earlier participants, creating the illusion of profitability.

To fuel its growth, BitConnect engaged in aggressive marketing campaigns, utilizing social media influencers, extravagant promotional events, and promises of financial freedom. The platform encouraged users to reinvest their earnings rather than withdraw, further sustaining the scheme. The company even introduced its own cryptocurrency, BCC, which experienced extreme price volatility driven by artificial hype rather than actual utility.

Despite growing skepticism and regulatory warnings, BitConnect continued to expand until early 2018, when regulators in the U.S. and other countries issued cease-and-desist orders. Soon after, the company abruptly shut down its lending program, causing BCC's value to plummet by over 90% within days. Investors collectively lost over $2 billion, with many left financially devastated. The collapse of BitConnect serves as a stark reminder of the dangers of unregulated investment schemes and the importance of due diligence before trusting any financial opportunity that seems too good to be true.

Avoiding financial scams requires vigilance, skepticism, and proper financial education. By understanding the tactics scammers use and recognizing red flags, individuals can protect themselves from fraud. Due diligence, research, and consulting financial professionals before investing can prevent devastating financial losses. In the digital age, where scams evolve rapidly, staying informed is the best defense against fraudulent schemes.

Interactive Elements: Quizzes, Exercises, and Action Steps for Financial Mastery

The key to truly mastering financial principles is not just reading about them but actively applying them in real-world scenarios. This chapter provides interactive exercises, quizzes, and action steps designed to reinforce the financial strategies covered in this book. Engaging with these elements will help solidify your understanding and enable you to make informed financial decisions confidently.

1. Financial Self-Assessment Quiz

Before implementing any financial strategies, it's crucial to understand your current financial position. Take this short quiz to assess where you stand:

Question 1: How many months' worth of living expenses do you have saved in an emergency fund?

- A) None
- B) Less than 3 months
- C) 3-6 months
- D) More than 6 months

Question 2: What percentage of your income do you invest each month?

- A) 0%
- B) 1-5%
- C) 6-15%
- D) More than 15%

Question 3: How do you primarily handle debt?

- A) I rely on credit cards and struggle to pay them off.
- B) I make minimum payments on loans and credit cards.
- C) I strategically pay off high-interest debt first.
- D) I have no debt or use it solely for wealth-building.

Question 4: What is your primary source of income?

- A) A single job with no additional income sources.

- B) A job with occasional freelance/side income.

- C) A job and multiple income streams (investments, side businesses, etc.).

- D) Passive income sources that provide financial security.

Scoring:

- Mostly A's: You may need to develop a stronger financial foundation.
- Mostly B's: You're making progress but need to build more security.
- Mostly C's: You have good financial habits but can optimize further.
- Mostly D's: You're on track for financial independence!

2. Practical Exercises for Financial Growth

Exercise 1: Expense Tracking and Optimization

1. Write down every expense you make for the next 30 days.
2. Categorize expenses into essential (rent, food, utilities) and non-essential (entertainment, luxury items).
3. Identify at least three areas where you can cut unnecessary spending.
4. Redirect these savings into investments or an emergency fund.

Example:

- If you spend $200 a month on coffee and dining out, consider reducing this to $100 and investing the other $100 into an index fund.

Exercise 2: Building a Passive Income Plan

1. List your skills, interests, and available capital.
2. Research at least three ways you can generate passive income (real estate, dividend stocks, online businesses, etc.).
3. Choose one method and outline a step-by-step plan to start.

Example:

- If you have $500 to invest, research high-yield dividend stocks or REITs (Real Estate Investment Trusts) and allocate your funds accordingly.

3. Action Steps for Financial Independence

Step 1: Set Clear Financial Goals

- Short-term (within a year): Save $5,000 for an emergency fund.
- Medium-term (1-5 years): Pay off high-interest debt and start investing.
- Long-term (10+ years): Achieve financial independence through multiple income streams.

Step 2: Implement the 50/30/20 Budgeting Rule

- 50% of income for necessities (housing, food, transportation).
- 30% for discretionary spending (entertainment, travel, hobbies).
- 20% for savings and investments.

Example:

- If you earn $4,000 per month, allocate:
  - $2,000 for necessities
  - $1,200 for discretionary spending
  - $800 for investments and savings

Step 3: Automate Your Financial Success

- Set up automatic transfers to savings and investment accounts.
- Use financial apps to track spending and manage budgets.

- Schedule periodic financial check-ins to adjust strategies.

Taking Action for Financial Mastery

The journey to financial independence starts with awareness and action. By engaging with these interactive elements, you can turn financial knowledge into practical results. Challenge yourself to complete each quiz, exercise, and action step to gain full control over your financial future. Remember, wealth-building is not about how much you earn but how well you manage, invest, and grow your resources. Start today!

VISHAL SHOW

Knowledge is Power – Using the System to Your Advantage

How to Use This Knowledge to Improve Your Financial Future

Understanding how the financial system operates is the first step toward gaining control over your financial destiny. Throughout this book, we've explored how the wealthy leverage legal tax strategies, invest in income-generating assets, and avoid common financial traps. Now, it's time to put that knowledge into action by implementing practical, informed strategies that align with long-term wealth-building goals.

Financial freedom isn't a privilege reserved for the ultra-rich—it is attainable for anyone willing to educate themselves and make intentional financial choices. The key is to transition from a mindset of paycheck dependency to one that prioritizes asset accumulation, strategic risk-taking, and diversified income streams. Instead of simply earning and spending, financial success requires an approach focused on wealth preservation and growth.

By adopting the principles outlined in this book, you can begin making smarter financial moves that safeguard and expand your wealth over time. Whether it's through smart investing, leveraging tax advantages, or avoiding common financial pitfalls, each step taken brings you closer to financial independence. The most critical takeaway is that knowledge alone isn't enough—action is what turns financial education into tangible results.

Why Financial Education Is the Key to Breaking the Cycle

One of the biggest differentiators between the wealthy and the middle class is financial literacy. Schools primarily focus on teaching students how to earn a living but often neglect to educate them on how to manage, grow, and protect their wealth. This knowledge gap leaves many individuals vulnerable to financial pitfalls, including excessive debt, poor investment choices, and susceptibility to scams. Without a strong foundation in financial literacy, people may unknowingly make decisions that hinder their long-term financial stability.

Financial education empowers individuals to navigate the complexities of the modern economy with confidence. Understanding core financial concepts—such as inflation, market cycles, compound interest, and wealth preservation—enables individuals to make informed decisions rather than reacting emotionally to financial challenges. Instead of panic-selling during market downturns or falling for get-rich-quick schemes, those with financial literacy develop patience and foresight, ensuring stability even in volatile economic conditions.

For example, consider the impact of inflation on savings. Someone without financial education may leave all their money in a regular savings account, unaware that inflation erodes its value over time. In contrast, someone with financial literacy understands the importance of investing in inflation-resistant assets like stocks, real estate, or commodities to preserve their purchasing power.

Continuous learning is essential in an evolving economic landscape where technological advancements, policy changes, and global events can dramatically impact personal finance. Staying informed through books, courses, financial news, and mentorship helps individuals adapt to new opportunities and risks. Ultimately, those who prioritize financial education gain the ability to take control of their financial futures, break free from paycheck-to-paycheck living, and build lasting wealth.

Actionable Steps to Start Applying These Principles Today

To truly benefit from this knowledge, it must be put into practice. Here are some actionable steps to get started:

1. **Build an Emergency Fund**

   ○ Set aside at least three to six months' worth of living expenses.

   ○ Keep these funds in a high-yield savings account or money market fund for accessibility.

   ○ Example: If your monthly expenses are $3,000, aim to save at least $9,000–$18,000 in a liquid account. This financial cushion protects against job loss or unexpected expenses like medical emergencies.

2. **Start Investing, No Matter How Small**

   ○ Focus on assets that generate passive income, such as dividend stocks, real estate, or index funds.

   ○ Automate investments through dollar-cost averaging to mitigate market volatility.

   ○ Example: Investing just $100 a month in an S&P 500 index fund can grow significantly over time due to compound interest. Historically, the S&P 500 has averaged around 8-10% annual returns.

3. **Leverage Tax-Advantaged Accounts**

○ Maximize contributions to retirement accounts like 401(k)s, IRAs, and HSAs.

○ Utilize tax-efficient investment strategies, such as holding long-term capital gains and using tax-loss harvesting.

○ Example: Contributing to a Roth IRA allows you to invest post-tax income and withdraw it tax-free in retirement, maximizing long-term gains.

4. **Diversify Your Income Streams**

○ Look into side businesses, freelancing, or real estate investments.

○ Aim to create multiple streams of passive income to reduce reliance on a single paycheck.

○ Example: A person earning $50,000 annually from a job can supplement their income by earning $1,000 a month through rental property or an online business, creating financial stability.

5. **Avoid High-Interest Debt**

○ Pay off credit card balances in full each month to avoid unnecessary interest charges.

○ Refinance or consolidate loans where possible to secure lower interest rates.

○ Example: A $5,000 credit card balance at a 20% interest rate will cost over $1,000 annually in interest if only minimum payments are made. Paying it off quickly saves money and improves financial health.

6. **Stay Informed About Financial Trends**

○ Keep up with economic news, market trends, and investment opportunities.

○ Read books, listen to financial podcasts, and attend seminars to continue expanding your knowledge.

○ Example: Those who stayed informed about the 2008 financial crisis recognized warning signs and adjusted their investments accordingly, minimizing losses and seizing opportunities during the market recovery.

7. **Conduct Due Diligence Before Any Investment**

○ Research opportunities thoroughly before committing capital.

○ Be skeptical of any investment promising high returns with little to no risk.

○ Example: Scams like BitConnect lured investors with promises of "guaranteed" returns, only to collapse and leave thousands in financial ruin. Researching its business model beforehand would have exposed its fraudulent nature.

Final Takeaways: Breaking Free from the Paycheck-to-Paycheck Cycle

The journey to financial independence starts with a mindset shift. Instead of solely working for money, the goal should be to create systems where money works for you. This involves shifting focus from active income to passive income, leveraging investments, and continuously learning about financial strategies. Wealth-building is not an overnight process—it requires discipline, patience, and a long-term vision. By avoiding common financial pitfalls, making informed investment choices, and staying updated on economic trends, you can gradually break free from the paycheck-to-paycheck cycle and achieve true financial security.

One of the biggest challenges for many people is overcoming financial inertia—the tendency to stick with familiar but ineffective financial habits. Breaking free from financial struggles requires taking proactive steps, such as tracking expenses, building an emergency fund, and ensuring your money is allocated efficiently toward wealth-generating activities. The key is to be intentional with every financial decision and to prioritize financial growth over temporary gratification.

This book has provided the necessary tools and strategies to help you take control of your financial future. However, knowledge alone is not enough—action is what drives results. The next step is yours to take. Begin by implementing small but significant changes in your financial habits, remain committed to lifelong learning, and stay adaptable to evolving financial landscapes. Remember, knowledge is power, but applied knowledge is the foundation of financial freedom.

Thank You...

Thank You, Dear Reader

As this book comes to a close, I want to take a moment to express my deepest gratitude to you. Whether you picked up this book out of curiosity, a desire to break free from financial struggles, or an ambition to build lasting wealth, your journey toward financial empowerment is commendable. Your willingness to seek knowledge, challenge traditional financial narratives, and take control of your future is a powerful step toward a better, more secure life.

Writing this book has been a journey of passion and purpose. I have strived to break down complex financial strategies into practical, actionable steps that anyone can use to improve their financial well-being. But knowledge alone is not enough—what truly matters is the action you take from here. Your success will not be determined by luck, but by the choices you make, the habits you build, and the consistency with which you apply these principles in your life.

I sincerely hope that the insights, strategies, and lessons shared in these pages have provided you with valuable tools to navigate the financial landscape with confidence. More importantly, I hope this book has inspired you to think differently about money, to question the financial traps society sets, and to take bold steps toward your financial independence.

If this book has made a difference in your life—even in a small way—I would love to hear your story. Your feedback, experiences, and insights not only inspire me but also help improve future editions and empower even more people like you.

Lastly, I want to remind you that financial freedom is a continuous journey, not a one-time destination. Stay committed to learning, growing, and adapting to the ever-evolving world of finance. Surround yourself with knowledge, take calculated risks, and never stop striving for the wealth and security you deserve.

Thank you for allowing me to be a part of your financial journey. Your time, trust, and dedication to bettering your future mean more than words can express. Wishing you success, prosperity, and a future filled with abundance.

With gratitude,
Vishal Show

Did you love *How The Rich Stay Rich While You Struggle*? Then you should read *A Con in Couture*[1] by Vishal Show!

[2]

A Con in Couture: Fraud, Fame, and the Illusion of Power

She infiltrated New York's elite, dined at the finest restaurants, lived in luxury hotels, and convinced some of the most powerful people in the city that she was a wealthy European heiress. But it was all a lie.

Anna Sorokin, better known as Anna Delvey, crafted an intricate web of deception that fooled the upper echelons of society and left a trail of financial and emotional devastation in her wake. From lavish trips on borrowed money to audacious business proposals for a fake art foundation, Anna's ability to manipulate and charm those around her seemed limitless—until it all came crashing down.

---

1. https://books2read.com/u/3RkOnp

2. https://books2read.com/u/3RkOnp

This book delves deep into the mind of a modern con artist, exploring the psychological tactics she used, the vulnerabilities of the system that allowed her fraud to flourish, and the shocking unraveling of her carefully constructed facade. Was Anna Delvey merely a fraud, or was she a product of a world obsessed with status and wealth?

Through detailed accounts and gripping storytelling, *A Con in Couture* takes you on a thrilling journey through Anna's rise to notoriety, her dramatic trial, and the lingering impact of her crimes. Step inside the scandal that captivated the world—and uncover the truth behind the illusion.

Read more at https://www.kavisht.com/.

About the Author

Vishal Show is a serial entrepreneur, business strategist, and author who somehow survived an MBA without losing his creativity. With multiple ventures under his belt (some wildly successful, some providing excellent "learning experiences"), he blends real-world business acumen with sharp psychological insights.

As the founder of www.kavisht.com, Vishal has built a platform for the endlessly curious. Whether it's history, science, business, or the mysteries of the universe, Kavisht delivers deep, offbeat insights that keep your brain buzzing. If there's something you've always wondered about, chances are, you'll find the answer here.

When he's not busy building businesses, Vishal writes books on business and psychology—because understanding human behavior is the ultimate cheat code to success. His work simplifies complex ideas with humor, making even the most serious business lessons entertaining.

His biggest achievements? Scaling companies, mentoring aspiring entrepreneurs, and convincing people that reading business books can actually be fun. If you're looking for practical wisdom with a side of wit, Vishal's work is where strategy meets storytelling.

You can contact me here: **vishalshow786@gmail.com**

Read more at https://www.kavisht.com/.

www.ingramcontent.com/pod-product-compliance
Lightning Source LLC
LaVergne TN
LVHW100253210926
848480LV00003B/914